# Welcome to

# zoom Deutsch 2

Corinna Schicker
Chalin Malz

Meet Leo and Sira. Find out more about them in this book and on the *Zoom Deutsch 2* video.

## Symbols and headings you will find in t

A video activity

A listening activity

A speaking activity

A reading activity

A writing activity

Do this with a partner

Work with a group

*Grammatik* → p.000 Grammar information

*Grammatik* Grammar reference

*Vokabular* Glossary

# OXFORD
## UNIVERSITY PRESS

CW01391649

# Inhalt

- Vocabulary: describe your and other people's appearance
- Grammar: use the correct adjective endings
- Skills: use knowledge you already have to work out language rules

**HÖREN 1** 🎧 **Hör zu und lies.**

- Hallo Leo! Wie siehst du aus? Hast du lange braune Haare? Trägst du eine Brille?
- Hallo Sira! Nein, ich habe kurze braune Haare. Ich habe blaue Augen und ich trage keine Brille. Und du, Sira? Wie siehst du aus? Hast du schwarze glatte Haare?
- Nein, ich habe rote lockige Haare. Ich habe auch blaue Augen und ich trage Ohrringe.

**LESEN 2** **Wer ist Leo? Finde das passende Foto.**

**a**

**b**

**c**

Wie siehst du aus?
Wie sieht er/sie aus?
Ich habe/Er hat/Sie hat …
   blaue/braune/grüne Augen.
   blonde/braune/rote/schwarze
    Haare.
   lange/kurze/lockige/glatte
    Haare.
Trägst du/Trägt er/Trägt sie …
   eine Brille/einen Ohrring?
   Ohrringe?
Ich trage/Er trägt/Sie trägt …
   eine/keine Brille.
   einen/keinen Ohrring.
   Ohrringe.

**SPRECHEN 3** 👥 **Beschreibt die anderen Fotos: „Ich habe/trage …" A ↔ B.**

NC 4   *Beispiel:* **A** *Bild a – wie siehst du aus?*
                  **B** *Ich trage einen Ohrring und ich habe …*

**SPRECHEN 4**

**NC 3**

👥 **Ratespiel! Wie ist dein Lieblingsstar? (Musik, Sport, TV, …)**

*Beispiel:* **A** *(mimes 'football') Er ist ein Sportstar. Er hat lange schwarze lockige Haare.*
**B** *Das ist …*

> Er/Sie ist ein Popstar/Sportstar/TV-Star.

---

⚙️ **Grammatik →** p.160

**Adjective endings**
Remember:
Ich habe schwarz**e** Haare.
Er hat lockig**e** Haare.
Sie hat grün**e** Augen.

---

❓ **Think**

Look at the adjectives in the **Grammatik** box. Can you work out a rule to explain what has happened to them?

What other rules for adjective endings do you know? (Tip: Think back to when you learned about clothes!)

---

**SCHREIBEN 5**

**Schreib Sätze mit „Er/Sie hat …"**

*Beispiel:* **a** *Sie hat lange schwarze lockige Haare.*

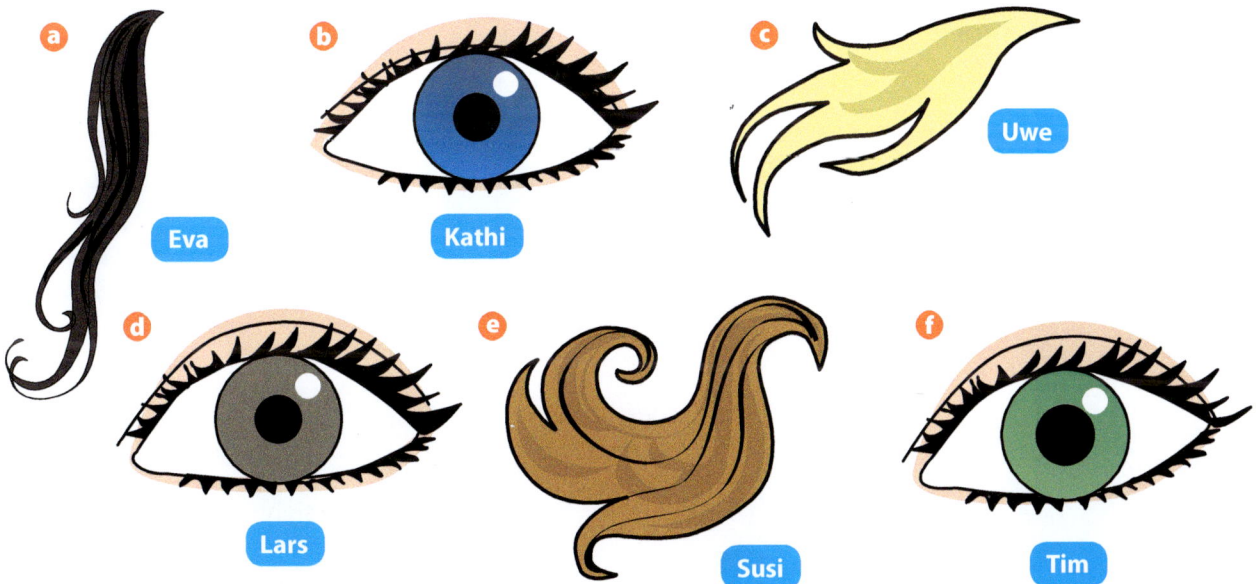

**a**

Eva

**b**

Kathi

**c**

Uwe

**d**

Lars

**e**

Susi

**f**

Tim

---

**SCHREIBEN 6**

**Du bist dran! Füll die Lücken aus.**

Ich heiße _____. Ich bin _____ alt. Ich wohne in _____. Ich habe _____ Augen und ich habe _____ _____ Haare. Ich trage _____ _____.

---

🎯 **Challenge**

Describe three students in your class: appearance, size, etc. Think back to when you learned about clothes and try to describe what they're wearing!

Don't forget to use words like *ziemlich* (quite) and *sehr* (very), and linking words such as *und* (and) and *auch* (also).

*Beispiel: Sarah hat blaue Augen und lange blonde Haare. Sie trägt keine Brille. Sie ist ziemlich klein und sie trägt einen grauen Rock …*

**NC 4**

# 0.2 Wie bist du?

- Vocabulary: describe your and other people's personality
- Grammar: use *weil*
- Skills: work out meaning; build longer more complex sentences, including opinions and reasons

**LESEN 1** **Lies die Adjektive. Wie heißen sie auf Englisch?**

*Beispiel:* arrogant – *arrogant*

arrogant    nett    nervig

gemein    lustig

frech    launisch    schüchtern

freundlich    unfreundlich    sympathisch

**SPRECHEN 2** **Ratespiel!**

*Beispiel:*
- **A** *Ich bin f – r*
- **B** *Frech!*
- **A** *Nein! Ich bin f – r – e – u*
- **C** *Freundlich!*

**HÖREN 3** 🎧 **Hör zu. Lies die Adjektive in Übung 1. Wie ist Leo ✓? Wie ist er nicht ✗?**

*Beispiel:* ✓ *nett, …* ✗ *…*

**SPRECHEN 4** **„Wie bist du …?" A ↔ B.**

*Beispiel:*
- **A** *Wie bist du nie?*
- **B** *Ich bin nie arrogant.*

---

**? Think**

You can often guess the meaning of unknown German words because they look similar to English.

- How many adjectives can you guess in activity 1? Use the Glossary to find any you can't work out.
- Which of the adjectives are positive (+)? Which are negative (–)? Which are both (+ –)? Write them down like this:

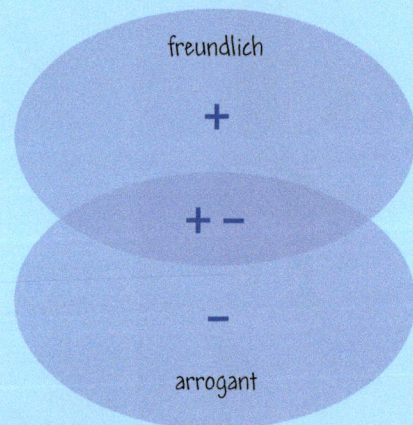

freundlich

**+**

**+ –**

**–**

arrogant

---

**? Think**

Be more specific! Match up the German with the English:

nicht
selten
manchmal
nie
oft
immer

rarely, seldom
often
not
sometimes
always
never

**HÖREN 5** 🎧 **Hör zu und lies.**

Ich mag Justin Bieber, weil er sehr nett ist. Ich mag ihn auch, weil er nicht gemein ist.

Aisha

Ich mag Lena, weil sie nicht arrogant ist. Und ich mag sie, weil sie lustig ist.

Lukas

**? Think**

Look at the second part of each sentence in activity 5. Do you notice anything unusual about the word order? What has happened to the verbs?

| Ich mag … (nicht), weil er/sie … | | |
|---|---|---|
| immer | arrogant | ist. |
| nicht | frech | |
| sehr | freundlich | |
| ziemlich | gemein | |
| … | nett | |
| | … | |

**? Think**

- What other linking words do you know that **don't** change the word order?
- Why do you think using linking words improves your spoken and written German? Discuss with a partner.

⚙️ **Grammatik →** p.167

**weil**

Some linking words like *weil* change the word order. They send the verb to the end:

Ich mag Tom. Er **ist** nett. → Ich mag Tom, **weil** er nett **ist**.

**SCHREIBEN 6** **Schreib neue Sätze mit *weil*.**

NC 3

*Beispiel:* **a** *Ich mag Lukas, weil er nett ist.*
**b** *Ich mag Sira, weil sie nicht unfreundlich ist.*

**a** Lukas: ✓ nett
**b** Sira: ✗ unfreundlich
**c** Felix: ✓ sympathisch
**d** Mila: ✗ frech
**e** Leo: ✓ freundlich
**f** David: ✗ arrogant
**g** Aisha: ✓ schüchtern
**h** Meike: ✗ gemein

**SCHREIBEN 7** **Wie ist dein Freund/deine Freundin? Schreib sechs Sätze mit *weil*, *und*, *aber*, *oder* und *denn*.**

NC 4

*Beispiel:* *Verena ist sehr … und sie ist immer … Sie ist ziemlich …, aber sie ist selten … Ich mag Verena, weil sie nie … ist. Ich mag sie auch, weil sie … ist.*

🎯 **Challenge**

Make a list of all the adjectives you know to describe:
- appearance
- personality
- colours
- opinions

Write a sentence for each adjective, using *weil* as often as possible.

*Beispiel: Ich mag Monika, weil sie lustig ist.*

NC 3

- Vocabulary: talk about family relationships and helping at home
- Grammar: use the present tense
- Skills: work out meaning

**HÖREN 1** 🎧 **Hör zu und lies.**

**Sira**

Meine Eltern sind **modern** – das finde ich super! Wir verstehen uns gut, weil sie sehr **tolerant** sind.

**Leo**

Also, mein Vater ist zu **streng**. Und meine Mutter ist sehr **altmodisch**. Wir verstehen uns nicht so gut.

**Aisha**

Wir verstehen uns ziemlich gut, weil meine Eltern **lieb** sind. Aber mein Vater ist oft **ungeduldig** – das finde ich nicht so gut.

**LESEN 2 Lies die Sätze (a–c). Finde die passenden Namen in Übung 1 (Sira, Leo oder Aisha).**

Who says …?

a We get on quite well but my father is often impatient.
b I don't get on with my parents – they're neither tolerant nor modern.
c My parents are modern and we get on very well.

**❓ Think**

- What do the **adjectives** in activity 1 mean? Which ones are positive? Which ones are negative?
- What do you think *Wir verstehen uns gut* means?

**SPRECHEN 3** 👥 **Wie sind deine Eltern? Macht Dialoge.**
A ↔ B.

NC 4

Beispiel: **A** *Wie ist deine Mutter?*
**B** *Sie ist sehr nett, aber sie ist manchmal altmodisch. Mein Vater ist …*

**SCHREIBEN 4 Beschreib deine Eltern für einen Elternblog.**

NC 4

Beispiel: *Mein Vater ist oft …, aber er ist auch …*
*Wir verstehen uns nicht so gut, weil er … ist.*
*Das finde ich …*

| Meine Eltern sind Mein Vater ist Meine Mutter ist | immer oft sehr ziemlich | lieb. modern. streng. tolerant. altmodisch. ungeduldig. |
|---|---|---|
| Wir verstehen uns (nicht) gut, weil/aber … Das finde ich (nicht) gut/schlecht/gemein. | | |

**LESEN 5** Lies die Sätze (a–g) und finde die passenden Bilder (1–7).

*Beispiel: a 2*

a  Ich decke den Tisch.
b  Ich wasche ab.
c  Ich putze das Badezimmer.
d  Ich füttere die Katze.
e  Ich sauge Staub.
f  Ich kaufe im Supermarkt ein.
g  Ich räume mein Zimmer auf.

**HÖREN 6** 🎧 Ist alles richtig? Hör zu.

**LESEN 7** Lies Leos Text. Beantworte die Fragen auf Englisch.

What chores does Leo do …
a  always?       e  once a week?
b  every day?    f  rarely?
c  often?        g  never?
d  sometimes?

Ich helfe zu Hause im Haushalt – na klar! Ich füttere jeden Tag die Katze. Ich sauge auch einmal pro Woche Staub. Ich decke oft den Tisch, aber ich wasche nie ab – das macht mein Vater. Ich putze auch immer das Badezimmer. Ich kaufe manchmal im Supermarkt ein. Aber ich räume selten mein Zimmer auf …

**SPRECHEN 8** 👥 Was machst du zu Hause und wie oft? Macht Dialoge. A ↔ B.

*Beispiel:* A Ich decke jeden Tag den Tisch. Und du?
B Ich …

Wie oft machst du das?
einmal pro Woche
jeden Tag, immer, oft, nie, …

▶ **Die Video-Aufgabe**

**VIDEO 9** Sieh dir das Video an. Finde die passenden Adjektive für Leo (L), Sira (S) und Siras Vater (V).

a  arrogant      d  ungeduldig    f  sympathisch
b  freundlich    e  nervig        g  lustig
c  launisch

**VIDEO 10** Lies a–d. Richtig (R) oder falsch (F)?

a  Leo muss zu Hause sein Zimmer aufräumen.
b  Sira muss nicht den Tisch decken.
c  Sira muss putzen und Staub saugen.
d  Leo muss den Hund füttern.

**VIDEO 11** 👥 Who do you think won the cake competition?

**Challenge** Describe your ideal (or the worst!) home and parents. Say how often you help at home. Include your opinions!

NC 4

**? Think**
- Look at a–d in activity 10. What do you think *muss* means? How many verbs do these sentences have?
- Do you know any other verbs like *muss*?

- Vocabulary: talk about what you've done recently
- Grammar: use the perfect tense with *haben* and *sein*
- Skills: think about language patterns; use your knowledge of language to adapt sentences and texts

**HÖREN 1** 🎧 „Warum bist du in Köln, Leo?" Hör zu. Was passt zusammen?

*Beispiel:* **a 4**

1

2 *Fahrkarte* ... von Zürich–Köln nach ...

3 ZÜRICH

4 Praktikum bei Radio Zoom

5

6 Leo Dürlewanger, du kannst am 18. Mai dein Praktikum bei Radio Zoom beginnen!

**SPRECHEN 2** 👥 **A zeigt auf ein Bild. B antwortet. A ↔ B.**

*Beispiel:* **A** Bild 6!
**B** Ich habe das Praktikum bekommen!

a Ich habe eine Anzeige im Internet gelesen.
b Ich habe eine E-Mail geschrieben.
c Ich habe einen Telefon-Test gemacht.
d Ich habe das Praktikum bekommen!
e Ich bin nach Zürich gefahren.
f Ich habe ein Ticket nach Köln gekauft.

## ⚙️ Grammatik → p.164–5

**The perfect tense**

- Most verbs form their perfect tense with *haben* and the past participle of the main verb, which starts with *ge-* and ends with *-t*:

  Ich **habe** ein Ticket **gekauft**.
  Du **hast**/Er **hat**/Sie **hat** einen Test **gemacht**.

- Some verbs have past participles that don't follow this pattern:

  Ich **habe** eine E-Mail **geschrieben**.
  Du **hast** das Praktikum **bekommen**.
  Er/Sie **hat** eine Anzeige **gelesen**.

- Some verbs form their perfect tense with *sein* instead of *haben*:

  Ich **bin** nach Köln **gefahren**.
  Du **bist** in die Stadt **gefahren**.
  Er/Sie **ist** ins Kino **gegangen**.

## ❓ Think

- What tense is used in activity 1?
- What do you notice about the words at the end of the sentences (the past participles)?
- Which verbs do you think use *sein* instead of *haben*?

**SPRECHEN 3**

NC 3

👥 „Was hast du gestern gemacht?" Macht Dialoge. **A ⟷ B**.

*Beispiel:* **A** *Was hast du gestern gemacht?*
**B** *Ich habe Pizza gemacht.*

> Ich habe/Du hast/Er hat/Sie hat …
>   Pizza/einen Test gemacht.
>   ein Ticket/eine CD gekauft.
>   in der Disco getanzt.
>   eine Anzeige/ein Buch gelesen.
>   eine E-Mail/einen Brief
>     geschrieben.
>   das Praktikum bekommen.
> Ich bin/Du bist/Er ist/Sie ist …
>   nach Köln gefahren.
>   in die Stadt gegangen.

**a**
Pizza

**b**
ein Buch

**c**
eine CD

**d**
mit dem Bus nach Berlin

**e**
einen Brief

**f**
in den Park

**? Think**

> You can use your knowledge of how the perfect tense is formed to create new sentences:
> You know that *Ich habe Pizza gemacht* means 'I made pizza'.
> So how would you say 'He made a picnic'?

**SCHREIBEN 4**

NC 4

**Schreib neue Sätze im Perfekt mit den Verben aus Übung 3.**

*Beispiel:* *Ich habe Abendessen gemacht. Ich bin …*

**LESEN 5**

**Lies Annes Blog und füll die Lücken aus.**

> Ich _____ am Samstagmorgen Tennis gespielt. Danach habe ich mit Sira Mittagessen _____ – Spaghetti Bolognese.
> Sira _____ am Nachmittag neue Sportschuhe _____. Ich _____ dann mit dem Fahrrad in den Park gefahren. Ich _____ abends in die Disco _____ und habe bis zehn Uhr _____!
> Ich habe am Sonntagmorgen ein Buch für die Schule _____. Und am Nachmittag habe ich meinen Blog _____!

> gelesen   habe   gemacht   bin   gekauft   geschrieben
>       hat   getanzt   bin   gegangen

**Challenge**

> What did **you** do last weekend?
> Write a blog like Anne's (activity 5).

NC 5

**HÖREN 6**

🎧 **Ist alles richtig? Hör zu.**

# 0.5 Familienleben

**HÖREN 1** 🎧 **Hör Leo zu und wähle die passenden Antworten.**

*Beispiel:* **1** *a*

**1** Leos Vater
  **a** ist nicht klein.
  **b** hat blonde Haare und blaue Augen.

**2** Seine Eltern sind sympathisch, aber auch
  **a** sportlich.
  **b** streng.

**3** Seine Mutter ist ziemlich
  **a** gemein.
  **b** ungeduldig.

**4** Monika ist sehr
  **a** laut.
  **b** fleißig.

**5** Monika hat
  **a** ein Praktikum gemacht.
  **b** Ferien in Frankreich gemacht.

**6** Eva ist Leos
  **a** große Schwester.
  **b** kleine Schwester.

**7** Leo findet Eva
  **a** ziemlich nett.
  **b** nicht so nett.

**8** Eva hat
  **a** kein eigenes Zimmer.
  **b** keinen Computer.

Gestern – also am Sonntag – habe ich total viel **gemacht**! Ich habe den Tisch für das Frühstück **gedeckt** – wie jeden Sonntag. Und dann habe ich mein Zimmer **aufgeräumt**, und ich habe auch Staub **gesaugt**. Das ist anstrengend!

Nach dem Mittagessen haben Susi und ich **abgewaschen**, und wir haben dabei Musik auf dem Computer **gehört**. Am Nachmittag habe ich meinem Vater in der Küche **geholfen** – wir haben einen Salat für das Abendessen **gemacht**. Ich habe auch mein Fahrrad **geputzt** und ich habe unseren Hund **gefüttert**.

Vor dem Abendessen haben wir meine Oma **besucht** – wir sind mit dem Fahrrad **gefahren**. Und nach dem Abendessen habe ich für die Schule **gelernt**.

### LESEN 2

**Lies Siras E-Mail. Finde alle Verben im Perfekt und schreib drei Listen:**

- past participles with *haben* + ge-...-t
- past participles with *haben* + other pattern
- past participles with *sein* + ge-...-en

## Grammatik → p.164–5

**The perfect tense**

| | |
|---|---|
| Ich **habe** <br> Wir **haben** | Pizza **gemacht**. (**haben + ge-...-t**) <br> einen Brief **gelesen/geschrieben/bekommen**. (**haben +** *other pattern*) |
| Ich **bin** <br> Wir **sind** | nach Zürich **gefahren**. (**sein + ge-...-en**) <br> ins Kino **gegangen**. |

### SCHREIBEN 3

**Du bist Sira – was machst du am Sonntag alles? Schreib eine E-Mail im Präsens.**

Imagine you are Sira – what do you do on Sunday? Copy out her email, but replace the perfect tense (in bold) with the present tense.

*Beispiel: Ich mache heute total viel! Ich …*

### ? Think

You already know *ich habe, du hast* and *er/sie hat* + past participle, and *ich bin, du bist, er/sie ist* + past participle.

Which other form of *haben* can you find in Sira's email? And which other form of *sein*? Are they singular or plural?

### Challenge

Imagine you are an undercover inspector at a horrible hotel and you have spent the day cleaning and cooking. Write an account of your day in the perfect tense. Remember to use linking words to make longer sentences. Use the present tense too to improve your work!

*Beispiel: Das Hotel ist sehr altmodisch! Ich habe den ganzen Tag die Zimmer geputzt und ich habe …*  NC 5

## The linking word *weil*, the perfect tense with *haben* and *sein*

### weil

You can link sentences together with words like *und, oder, aber* and *denn* without changing the word order:

Ich mag Leo **und** ich finde Lukas nett.
Tom ist frech, **aber** er ist nicht gemein.

But some linking words like *weil* (because) change the word order. They send the verb to the end:

Ich mag Sira. Sie **ist** lustig. → Ich mag Sira, **weil** sie lustig **ist**.

**1 Unscramble the word order in these sentences.**

*Beispiel:* **a** *Ich mag Leo, weil er lieb ist.*

Ich mag Leo, …

**a** weil lieb / ist / er / .
**b** und David / mag / ich / .
**c** weil ist / arrogant / er / nicht / .
**d** aber nicht / Susi / ich / mag / .
**e** weil ist / cool / er / .
**f** weil total / er / nett / ist / .

**2 Write new sentences using *Ich mag …, weil er/sie …***

*Beispiel:* **a** *Ich mag Tanja, weil sie nicht arrogant ist.*

**a** Tanja ist nicht arrogant.
**b** Lars ist freundlich.
**c** Mila ist nie unfreundlich.
**d** Phillip ist sympathisch.
**e** Heike ist nicht ungeduldig.
**f** Leo ist schüchtern.

**3 Fill in the missing past participles. Use the words from the box.**

*Beispiel:* **a** *Ich habe Ohrringe gekauft.*

**a** Ich habe Ohrringe _____ .
**b** Maja hat eine E-Mail _____ .
**c** Du hast im Jugendzentrum _____ .
**d** Leo hat ein Praktikum _____ .
**e** Ich habe Computerspiele _____ .
**f** Hast du den Fragebogen _____ ?

> geschrieben   gespielt   gekauft
> getanzt   gemacht   gelesen

### The perfect tense with *haben*

- The perfect tense of regular verbs is formed with *haben* and the past participle of the main verb. The past participle is formed by adding *ge-* and *-t* to the beginning and end of the main verb:

  **ge + mach + t** → Ich **habe** einen Test **gemacht**.
  **ge + kauf + t** → Du **hast** eine CD **gekauft**.
  Er/Sie **hat** ein Ticket **gekauft**.

- A small number of verbs have past participles that don't follow this *ge-* … *-t* pattern:

  Ich **habe** ein Buch **gelesen**.
  Du **hast** das Praktikum **bekommen**!
  Er/Sie **hat** einen Brief **geschrieben**.

**4** Fill in each gap with the correct form of *haben* or *sein*.

*Beispiel:* **a** *Ich* _habe_ *in der Disco getanzt.*

**a** Ich ___ in der Disco getanzt.
**b** Du ___ nach Spanien gefahren.
**c** Susi ___ ein Picknick gemacht.
**d** Ich ___ in den Park gegangen.
**e** Tom ___ ein Eis gekauft.
**f** Ich ___ das Praktikum bekommen!

**5** Write a sentence in the perfect tense for a–f. Start each sentence with *Ich bin …*

*Beispiel:* **a** *Ich bin nach Berlin gefahren.*

### The perfect tense with *sein*

A few verbs use *sein* instead of *haben* to form the perfect tense. These are mostly verbs describing movement (where you went/travelled to). Their past participles are also different: most of them still start with *ge-* but end with *-en*:

Ich **bin** in die Disco **ge**gang**en**.
Du **bist** nach Frankreich **ge**fahr**en**.

Remember the other forms of *sein*:

er/sie/es ist   wir sind   ihr seid   Sie/sie sind

| **a** | **b** | **c** | **d** | **e** | **f** |
|---|---|---|---|---|---|
| Berlin | ins Kino | nach Spanien | in die Schule | in den Park | nach Zürich |
| nach Berlin | | | | | |

## Learning new words

- Write down all new words in a notebook.
- Write down the gender (**masculine**, **feminine**, **neuter**) and plural of all nouns.
- Close your notebook and write out the new words on a piece of paper. Check you got them right. Correct any you got wrong.
- Record the new words on your MP3 player or mobile. Listen and repeat them regularly, for example on the way to school.

- Ask someone to test you.
- Learn new words little and often – five minutes a day is best!
- Focus on words you find difficult. Write them on sticky labels with English translations and stick them where you can see them, for example on your bedroom door or the wall by your desk.

**6** Try these strategies to learn the new words from this unit. Which ones worked best for you? Compare with a partner.

## Pronunciation of *ch*, *sch* and the word endings *-isch* and *-ich/-ig*

**7** Listen carefully (1–8). Do you hear the sound *ch* or *sch*?

**8** Now listen for the word endings (1–9). Do you hear *-isch* or *-ich/-ig*?

- Vocabulary: describe appearance and personality; talk about helping at home
- Grammar: use adjectives; use the perfect tense
- Skills: read for gist and detail

**SCHREIBEN 1**

**Lies die Adjektive. Positiv (+) oder negativ (–)? Schreib zwei Listen.**
Which of these adjectives are positive (+)?
Which are negative (–)? Make two lists.
Which adjective could go in either list?

*Beispiel:* + lustig, …   – …

arrogant   gemein   nett   ungeduldig
frech   launisch   lustig
freundlich   schüchtern
lieb   unfreundlich   sympathisch

**LESEN 2**

**Finde die passenden Bilder (1–6) für die Sätze (a–f).**
Match each picture (1–6) to a sentence (a–f).

*Beispiel:* a 6

a Ich habe blaue Augen und glatte blonde Haare.
b Ich habe kurze rote Haare und grüne Augen.
c Ich habe braune Augen und lange schwarze Haare.
d Ich habe kurze schwarze Haare und blaue Augen.
e Ich habe lange braune Haare und grüne Augen.
f Ich habe lockige blonde Haare. Ich trage eine Brille.

**LESEN 3** NC 3

**Finde die Paare.**
Match the sentence halves.

*Beispiel:* a 3

a Ich habe E-Mails
b Wir haben Pizza
c Sandra hat Musik
d Ich bin ins Kino
e Ich habe eine CD
f Wir haben Fußball

1 gegangen.   4 gespielt.
2 gekauft.   5 gehört.
3 gelesen.   6 gemacht.

**SCHREIBEN 4** NC 3

**Schreib die Sätze richtig auf.**
Write out these sentences using the correct word order.

*Beispiel:* a Ich decke den Tisch.

a den / Ich / decke / Tisch / .
b mein / auf / Zimmer / räume / Ich / .
c das / Ich / Badezimmer / putze / .
d Ich / Hund / den / füttere / .
e Staub / Ich / sauge / .
f ein / im / kaufe / Supermarkt / Ich / .

- Vocabulary: describe appearance and personality; talk about what you have done
- Grammar: use adjectives and express opinions; use the perfect tense
- Skills: use knowledge of grammar to understand detail in texts

**SCHREIBEN 1**

**„Wie siehst du aus?" Schreib Sätze.**

*Beispiel:* **a** *Ich habe blaue Augen.*

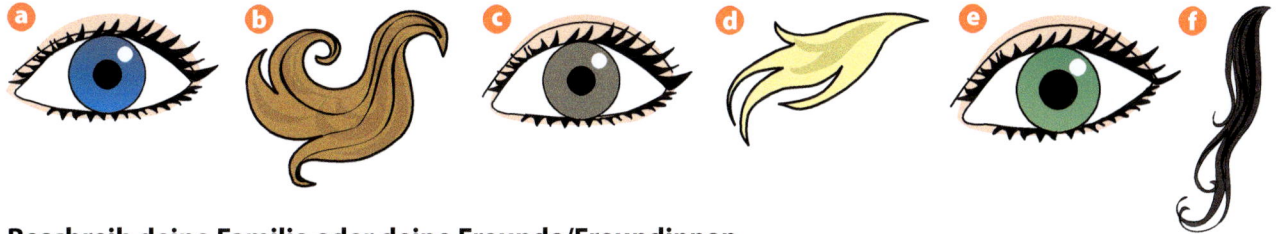

**a** **b** **c** **d** **e** **f**

**SCHREIBEN 2**

**Beschreib deine Familie oder deine Freunde/Freundinnen. Schreib sechs Sätze mit den Wörtern aus a–c.**

*Beispiel:* **1** *Mein Bruder ist oft frech – das finde ich nicht gut.*

**a** arrogant  lustig  frech  nett  freundlich  schüchtern  gemein  sympathisch  launisch  unfreundlich  lieb  ungeduldig

**b** immer  oft  manchmal  nie

**c** super  gut  nicht gut  schlecht

**LESEN 3**

NC 5

**Lies Davids E-Mail. Richtig oder falsch?**

*Beispiel:* **a** *falsch*

- **a** Tanja is very friendly.
- **b** David has to do all the chores at home.
- **c** He made lunch and dinner yesterday.
- **d** He has to go shopping today.
- **e** It rained yesterday.
- **f** Tanja is spending today on the computer and phoning her friends.

> Meine Schwester Tanja ist total faul! Ich wasche jeden Tag ab, ich decke den Tisch, ich sauge Staub … und sie sagt: „Ich habe keine Zeit!"
>
> Ich habe gestern Mittagessen und Abendessen gemacht und ich bin zum Supermarkt gegangen – ich habe für die Woche eingekauft. Ich bin zu Fuß gegangen und es hat geregnet. Und was hat Tanja gemacht? Sie hat ihren Blog geschrieben, und sie hat telefoniert!

**SCHREIBEN 4**

NC 3

**„Was hast du gestern gemacht?" Füll die Lücken aus.**

*Beispiel:* **a** *Wir haben Pizza gemacht.*

- **a** Wir haben _____ .
- **b** Ich habe _____ .
- **c** Wir sind _____ .
- **d** Ich habe _____ .
- **e** Wir haben _____ .
- **f** Ich habe _____ .

**a** **b** **c** **d** **e** **f**

**HÖREN 1**

**NC 5**

**Listen and answer the questions.** (See pages 10–11).

*Beispiel:* **a** *into town – by bus*

**a** Where did Katja go – and how?
**b** What did she buy – and why?
**c** What did she do next – and why?

**d** What did Ulla do – and what did Katja do?
**e** What did Katja do first at home?
**f** What did she do afterwards?

**LESEN 2**

**NC 5**

**Read Svenja's letter and answer the questions below in English.**
**(See pages 4–11).**

*Beispiel:* **a** *She's very shy.*

**a** What does Svenja say about herself?
**b** Who is Putzi and what does Svenja say about him?
**c** What does she say about her parents?
**d** What does she say about the other girls?
**e** What does Svenja have to do at home?
**f** What does she say about her brother?

Liebe Clara,

ich habe ein Problem: ich bin sehr schüchtern. Mein bester Freund ist mein Hund Putzi. Er ist groß und er hat braune Augen. Putzi ist sehr lieb. Aber ich mag meine Eltern nicht, weil sie zu streng sind – wir verstehen uns nicht, weil sie so altmodisch sind …

Die Mädchen in meiner Klasse gehen zum Beispiel am Wochenende in die Disco oder ins Kino. Aber ich nicht, weil ich immer zu Hause helfe: ich wasche ab und ich decke den Tisch – aber mein Bruder sieht fern! Ich mag meinen Bruder nicht, weil er frech und gemein ist. Er hat gestern meine E-Mails gelesen – das ist furchtbar!

Deine Svenja

**SPRECHEN 3**

**NC 3–4**

**Give a mini-presentation about yourself and your family and friends.** (See pages 4–9.)

Talk about:

- appearance: *Ich habe … Er/Sie hat … Augen/Haare. Ich trage … Er/Sie trägt …*
- character: *Ich bin … Er/Sie ist … immer/oft/ selten/manchmal/nie …*
- whether you get on with the members of your family – and why (not): *Wir verstehen uns (nicht) gut, weil …*
- what you do to help at home – and your opinion of it: *Ich wasche jeden Tag ab – das ist sehr langweilig …*

**SCHREIBEN 4**

**NC 4–5**

**Write a paragraph of at least five sentences about a recent event or activity.** (See pages 10–11.)

Include:

- where you went
- how you got there
- what you did
- your opinion

# Vokabular

## Wie siehst du aus? — What do you look like?

|  |  |
|---|---|
| Wie sieht er/sie aus? | What does he/she look like? |
| Ich habe/Er hat/Sie hat … | I have/He has/She has … |
| blaue/braune/grüne Augen. | blue/brown/green eyes. |
| blonde/braune/rote/schwarze Haare. | blonde/brown/red/black hair. |
| lange/kurze/lockige/glatte Haare. | long/short/curly/straight hair. |
| Trägst du …? Trägt er/sie …? | Do you wear …? Does he/she wear …? |
| Ich trage/Er trägt/Sie trägt … | I wear/He wears/She wears … |
| eine Brille/einen Ohrring. | glasses/an earring. |
| Ohrringe. | earrings. |
| Ich trage keine Brille/keinen Ohrring. | I don't wear glasses/an earring. |

## Wie bist du? — What's your character like?

|  |  |
|---|---|
| Ich bin/Er ist/Sie ist … | I am/He is/She is … |
| arrogant | arrogant |
| frech | naughty |
| freundlich | friendly |
| gemein | mean |
| launisch | moody |
| lustig | funny |
| nervig | irritating |
| nett | nice |
| schüchtern | shy |
| sympathisch | nice |
| unfreundlich | unfriendly |
| immer | always |
| manchmal | sometimes |
| nicht | not |
| nie | never |
| oft | often |
| sehr | very |
| selten | rarely, seldom |
| ziemlich | quite |
| Ich mag …, weil er/sie (nicht) … ist. | I like … because he/she is (isn't) … |

## Zu Hause — At home

|  |  |
|---|---|
| Meine Eltern sind … | My parents are … |
| Mein(e) Vater/Mutter ist … | My father/mother is … |
| altmodisch | old-fashioned |
| lieb | gentle, sweet, lovely |
| modern | modern |
| streng | strict |
| tolerant | tolerant |
| ungeduldig | impatient |

|  |  |
|---|---|
| Wir verstehen uns (nicht) gut. | We (don't) get on well. |
| Das finde ich (nicht) … | I (don't) think that's … |
| gut/schlecht/gemein. | good/bad/mean. |

## Was machst du zu Hause? — How do you help at home?

|  |  |
|---|---|
| Ich decke den Tisch. | I set the table. |
| Ich wasche ab. | I do the washing-up. |
| Ich putze das Badezimmer. | I clean the bathroom. |
| Ich füttere die Katze. | I feed the cat. |
| Ich sauge Staub. | I do the vacuuming. |
| Ich kaufe im Supermarkt ein. | I go shopping in the supermarket. |
| Ich räume mein Zimmer auf. | I tidy my room. |
| Wie oft machst du das? | How often do you do that? |
| jeden Tag | every day |
| einmal pro Woche | once a week |

## Warum bist du in Köln? — Why are you in Cologne?

|  |  |
|---|---|
| Was hast du gemacht? | What did you do? |
| Ich habe/Du hast/Er hat/Sie hat … | I/You/He/She … |
| Pizza/einen Test gemacht. | made pizza/did a test. |
| ein Ticket/eine CD gekauft. | bought a ticket/CD. |
| in der Disco getanzt. | danced in the disco. |
| eine Anzeige/Buch gelesen. | read an advert/book. |
| eine E-Mail/einen Brief geschrieben. | wrote an email/a letter. |
| das Praktikum bekommen. | got the work experience placement. |
| Ich bin/Du bist/Er ist/Sie ist … | I/You/He/She … |
| nach Zürich gefahren. | went to Zurich. |
| in die Stadt/in den Park gegangen. | went into town/to the park. |

### I can...

- say what I look like and what other people look like
- describe my own and other people's personality
- say whether I get on with people and why (not)
- say what I do to help at home
- talk about what I've done recently
- use the correct adjective endings
- use the linking word *weil*
- use the perfect tense
- use different strategies to learn new words
- pronounce *ch*, *sch* and the endings *-isch*, *-ich/-ig*

- Vocabulary: talk about your daily routine and ask others about theirs
- Grammar: use separable verbs and reflexive verbs
- Skills: tell the time

## HÖREN 1

🎧 **Hör zu (1–10) und finde die passenden Bilder (a–j).**

*Beispiel:* **1 d**

**a** **b** **c** **d** **e**

**f** **g** **h** **i** **j**

| | |
|---|---|
| **1** Ich wache auf. | **6** Ich frühstücke. |
| **2** Ich stehe auf. | **7** Ich fahre zur Arbeit. |
| **3** Ich wasche mich. | **8** Ich fahre nach Hause. |
| **4** Ich putze meine Zähne. | **9** Ich ziehe mich aus. |
| **5** Ich ziehe mich an. | **10** Ich gehe ins Bett. |

## SPRECHEN 2

👥 **Ist alles richtig? Macht Dialoge. A ↔ B.**

*Beispiel:* **A** *Was machst du zuerst?*
**B** *Bild d – ich wache auf. Und dann?*
**A** *Bild … – ich …*

### ? Think

Can you work out what the words in **purple** and **orange** mean?

Ich stehe **auf**.
Ich wasche **mich**.
Ich ziehe **mich an**.

### ⚙ Grammatik → p.163–4

**Separable and reflexive verbs**

- The infinitives of some German verbs need to be split into two parts when you use them. These are called **separable verbs** (*trennbare Verben*):

  **auf**wachen → Ich wache **auf**.

- With other German verbs – called **reflexive verbs** (*Reflexivverben*) – you need to use an extra **pronoun**. The pronoun that goes with *ich* (I) is *mich* (myself):

  Ich setze **mich** auf den Stuhl.

- A few verbs are both **separable** and **reflexive**:

  Ich ziehe **mich aus**.

**Wie spät ist es?**
Es ist Viertel vor acht.
Es ist acht Uhr.
Es ist Viertel nach acht.
Es ist halb neun.

**? Think**

Do you remember how to say the time in German?
- Look at the phrases beside the clock. Where do they go on the clock?
- How would you say 'It is four o'clock', 'It is half past six', 'It is quarter past ten'? Can you work out the rules?

**SPRECHEN 3** **Uhrzeiten-Quiz! A ↔ B.**
Challenge your partner to a time quiz!

*Beispiel:* **A** (points to 7.45 on the clock) Wie spät ist es?
**B** Es ist …

**LESEN 4** **NC 4** **Was macht Sira wann? Lies den Text und schreib die Uhrzeiten auf.**

*Beispiel: 6:45 Uhr: Ich stehe auf.*

____ Uhr: Ich stehe auf.
____ Uhr: Ich trinke Kaffee.
____ Uhr: Ich gehe in die Schule.
____ Uhr: Ich esse Mittagessen.
____ Uhr: Ich höre Musik.
____ Uhr: Ich esse Abendessen.
____ Uhr: Ich sehe fern.
____ Uhr: Ich gehe ins Bett.

Ich stehe um Viertel vor sieben auf. Dann wasche ich mich und ziehe mich an. Ich trinke um Viertel nach sieben Kaffee. Ich esse kein Frühstück, weil ich dafür keine Zeit habe.

Danach checke ich schnell meine E-Mails und gehe um Viertel vor acht in die Schule. Nach der Schule – also um halb zwei – esse ich zu Hause Mittagessen und dann mache ich meine Hausaufgaben – leider …

Am Nachmittag, so um vier Uhr, höre ich Musik. Abends um halb sieben gibt es Abendessen und um acht Uhr sehe ich fern – oder ich sehe DVDs auf meinem Computer. Ich gehe um zehn Uhr ins Bett.

**SPRECHEN 5** **NC 3–4** **„Was machst du wann?" Macht Dialoge (a–g). A ↔ B.**

*Beispiel:* **A** Wann stehst du auf?
**B** Ich stehe um Viertel nach sieben auf.

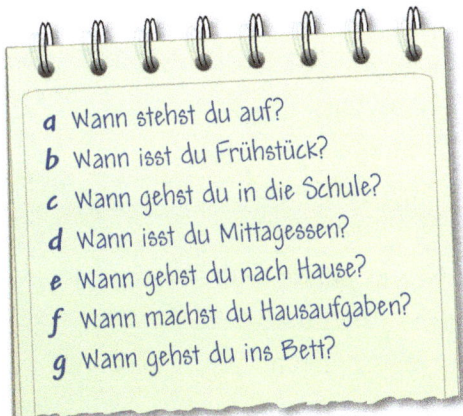

a Wann stehst du auf?
b Wann isst du Frühstück?
c Wann gehst du in die Schule?
d Wann isst du Mittagessen?
e Wann gehst du nach Hause?
f Wann machst du Hausaufgaben?
g Wann gehst du ins Bett?

**Challenge**
You are a school student with a very hectic schedule! Describe your daily routine in 8–10 sentences. Remember to link your sentences together and use correct word order.

*Beispiel: Mein Alltag ist so hektisch! Ich stehe um halb sieben auf und …* **NC 4**

- Vocabulary: talk about what you did yesterday
- Grammar: use the perfect tense with *haben* and *sein*
- Skills: identify word families

**HÖREN 1**

**NC 5**

🎧 **Hör zu und lies. Finde im Dialog die passenden Sätze für die Bilder.**

*Beispiel:* **a** *Ich habe nach dem Abendessen in meinem Zimmer Musik gehört.*

**David:** Was hast du gestern gemacht, Sira?

**Sira:** Ich habe viel gemacht! Ich bin nach der Schule in die Stadt gefahren.

**David:** Mit dem Bus?

**Sira:** Nein, mit dem Fahrrad. Ich habe ein Wörterbuch gekauft. Ich habe auch ein Eis gegessen – lecker! Und du, David – was hast du gemacht?

**David:** Ich bin mit Lars in den Park gegangen. Wir haben dort Fußball gespielt.

**Sira:** Und was hast du abends gemacht?

**David:** Nicht viel: ich habe nach dem Abendessen in meinem Zimmer Musik gehört. Und du?

**Sira:** Ich habe mit Aisha telefoniert – bis halb zehn! Danach bin ich ins Bett gegangen.

**? Think**

- When you've done activity 1, find all the other perfect tense sentences in the dialogue.
- How do you make the perfect tense? Which two parts do you need? What do you know about the past participle? Explain the rules to a partner.

**⚙ Grammatik →** p.164–5

**The perfect tense with *haben***

- Regular verbs:

  **haben + ge-…-t (past participle)**
  Ich **habe** CDs **gekauft**.
  Wir **haben** Salat **gemacht**.

- Irregular verbs don't follow the *ge-…-t* pattern:

  Ich **habe** mit Lisa **telefoniert**.
  Wir **haben** Pizza **gegessen**.

**The perfect tense with *sein***

**sein + ge-…-en (past participle)**
Ich **bin** nach Köln **gefahren**.
Wir **sind** ins Kino **gegangen**.

See pages 163 and 165 for all the forms of *haben* and *sein* and a list of irregular past participles.

**? Think**

**Word families**

- Word families have the same stem (main part) from which lots of different words are derived.
- Can you spot two words in the dialogue on page 22 that belong to the same word family as *fahren*?

die Fahrt (*journey*)

das Fahrrad (*bicycle*)

**fahren** (*to travel, drive, go*)

mitfahren (*to travel with someone*)

die Autofahrt (*car journey*)

gefahren (*travelled*)

abfahren (*to leave*)

---

**SPRECHEN 2** 👥 **Macht Dialoge. A ↔ B.**

*Beispiel:* **A** *Was hast du gestern gemacht?*
**B** *Ich habe Kaffee gekocht.*

| Ich habe | … gespielt/gemacht/ gekauft/… |
| | … gegessen. |
| | … gelesen. |
| | … geschrieben. |
| | … telefoniert. |
| Ich bin | … gegangen. |
| | … gefahren. |

**a**
**Kaffee kochen**

**b**
**Hausaufgaben machen**

**c**
**Pizza essen**

**d**
**in die Stadt fahren**

**e**
**Tennis spielen**

**f**
**ins Kino gehen**

**g**
**E-Mails schreiben**

**h**
**ein Buch lesen**

---

**SCHREIBEN 3** **Schreib Sätze im Perfekt.**

*Beispiel:* **a** *Ich habe den Tisch gedeckt.*

**a** den Tisch decken
**b** E-Mails checken
**c** frühstücken
**d** Zähne putzen
**e** die Katze füttern
**f** Staub saugen

**SCHREIBEN 4** **Du bist dran: „Was hast du gestern gemacht?" Schreib 8–10 Sätze.**

NC 5

*Beispiel:* *Ich bin gestern in den Park gegangen. Ich habe …*

**Challenge**

You're the busy assistant of a famous person! Write a blog describing everything you had to do for him or her yesterday. Give the times too.

*Beispiel: Ich bin um sieben Uhr in die Stadt gefahren und habe Schokolade gekauft. Ich habe um acht Uhr …*

NC 5

# 1A.3 Und gestern Abend …?

- Vocabulary: talk about what you did yesterday evening
- Grammar: use separable verbs in the perfect tense
- Skills: use the 24-hour clock

**LESEN 1** „Wie spät ist es?" Finde die passenden Bilder für die Sätze.

*Beispiel:* **a 3**

Es ist …

**a** neunzehn Uhr fünfunddreißig.
**b** siebzehn Uhr zwanzig.
**c** dreizehn Uhr fünfundfünfzig.
**d** achtzehn Uhr zehn.
**e** zwanzig Uhr fünf.

**①** 17:20  **②** 20:05  **③** 19:35
**④** 18:10  **⑤** 13:55

**HÖREN 2** 🎧 Ist alles richtig? Hör zu.

**SPRECHEN 3** 👥 „Wie spät ist es?" Macht Dialoge. Benutzt 1–5 in Übung 1. A ↔ B.

*Beispiel:* **A** *Bild 3! Wie spät ist es?*
**B** *Es ist neunzehn Uhr fünfunddreißig.*

**HÖREN 4** 🎧 „Was machst du heute Abend?" Was sagt Sira? Hör zu und schreib die Uhrzeiten auf.

*Beispiel:* **a** *17 Uhr 10*

**a** Ich sehe um ▭ Uhr ▭ fern.
**b** Ich spiele um ▭ Uhr ▭ am Computer.
**c** Ich mache um ▭ Uhr ▭ Hausaufgaben.
**d** Ich esse um ▭ Uhr ▭ Abendessen.
**e** Ich höre um ▭ Uhr ▭ Radio Zoom.
**f** Ich lese um ▭ Uhr ▭ im Bett.

**SCHREIBEN 5** Was machst du wann? Schreib sechs Sätze.

*Beispiel:* Ich mache um siebzehn Uhr dreißig Hausaufgaben. Ich …

**HÖREN 6** 🎧 Hör zu (a–f). Was hat Leo gestern Abend gemacht? Finde die richtigen Reihenfolge.

**NC 3**

*Beispiel:* **c** , …

**a** Ich habe nach dem Abendessen abgewaschen.
**b** Ich bin ins Bett gegangen.
**c** Ich habe mit meinen Eltern telefoniert.
**d** Ich habe in meinem Zimmer ferngesehen.
**e** Ich habe meine Tasche für das Praktikum aufgeräumt.
**f** Ich bin Skateboard gefahren.

**? Think**

What do you notice about some of the past participles in activity 6?

**⚙ Grammatik → p.165**

**Separable verbs in the perfect tense**

Ich wasche **ab**. →
Ich habe **ab**gewaschen.

Ich sehe **fern**. →
Ich habe **fern**gesehen.

**SPRECHEN 7**
NC 4–5

👥 **Wann hat Leo a–f aus Übung 6 gemacht? Macht Dialoge. Benutzt die Uhrzeiten rechts. A ↔ B.**

| | | |
|---|---|---|
| 17:50 | 18:05 | 19:10 |
| 20:45 | 21:30 | 22:20 |

*Beispiel:* **A** *Leo, was hast du um achtzehn Uhr fünf gemacht?*
**B** *Ich bin um achtzehn Uhr fünf Skateboard gefahren.*

**LESEN 8**
NC 5

**Lies Kaja Ks Nachricht. Sind die Sätze a–e richtig (R) oder falsch (F)?**

**a** Kaja K ist am Nachmittag aufgewacht.
**b** Sie hat am Computer gearbeitet.
**c** Sie ist zu Fuß zur Konzerthalle gegangen.
**d** Das Konzert hat um zehn vor acht begonnen.
**e** Sie ist sehr früh ins Bett gegangen.

**SCHREIBEN 9**
NC 4–5

**Du bist dran! „Was hast du gestern Abend gemacht? Und wann?" Schreib 6–8 Sätze.**

*Beispiel: Ich habe um 18 Uhr Hausaufgaben gemacht …*

🎯 **Challenge**
Imagine you are a famous star (TV, sports, music, …). Write a detailed description of your evening routine yesterday, including your opinions!
*Beispiel: Hallo! Ich heiße … Um neunzehn Uhr fünfzehn habe ich …*
NC 5

„Was habe ich gestern Abend gemacht?"
Also, ich bin auf Tournee – ich wohne also im Hotel. Gestern habe ich nachmittags geschlafen und ich bin um fünfzehn Uhr dreißig aufgestanden. Dann habe ich meinen Blog geschrieben und mit meinen Fans auf meiner Webseite gechattet.

Danach habe ich mich angezogen und ich bin mit dem Taxi zum Konzert gefahren. Das Konzert hat um zwanzig Uhr zehn begonnen.

Danach habe ich meine Fans getroffen. Um dreiundzwanzig Uhr bin ich zurück ins Hotel gefahren. Ich bin dann sofort ins Bett gegangen.

Kaja K

▶ **Die Video-Aufgabe**

**VIDEO 10** **Sieh dir das Video an. Was macht Leo wann? Wer kommt wann?**

**Der Arbeitsplan:**

**a** _____ Uhr: Leo steht auf.
**b** _____ Uhr: Er frühstückt.
**c** _____ Uhr: Er ist im Büro.
**d** _____ Uhr: Die Kollegen kommen.

**Und im Büro:**

**e** _____ Uhr: Leos Boss kommt.
**f** _____ Uhr: Sie machen ein Interview.

**VIDEO 11** 👥 **What do you think? Which outfit is best? Why?**

# 1A.4 Es war super!

- Vocabulary: give your opinion about your day
- Grammar: use the imperfect tense
- Skills: express more complex opinions

**HÖREN 1**

**NC 5**

🎧 **Hör zu und lies den Dialog unten. Finde die richtige Reihenfolge für die Bilder.**

*Beispiel:* **d**, …

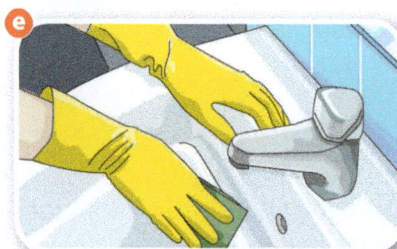

**Maja**: Na Leo, wie war deine erste Woche in Köln?

**Leo**: Es war interessant, Maja! Ich habe alle Kollegen bei Radio Zoom kennengelernt und sie haben mir sehr geholfen.

**Maja**: Und wie war dein Boss?

**Leo**: Er war auch total nett!

**Maja**: Und wie war Köln?

**Leo**: Toll! Aber Köln ist so groß – und die Fahrt zu Radio Zoom war zu lang! Die U-Bahn war immer total voll – das war ziemlich stressig.

**Maja**: Und wie war das Konzert gestern Abend?

**Leo**: Das Konzert war toll, weil die Band super war!

**Maja**: Und was war diese Woche nicht so gut?

**Leo**: Na ja, also, ich habe am Dienstag zu Hause geholfen: ich habe den Tisch gedeckt und ich habe das Badezimmer geputzt. Das war sehr anstrengend – und auch langweilig! Und am Mittwoch habe ich nicht gefrühstückt – das war schlimm!

## ? Think

What new verb form is used in the dialogue? What tense is it in – present, past or future?

## ⚙ Grammatik → p.165

**The imperfect tense**

There is another past tense in German – the **imperfect**. A small number of common verbs usually use the imperfect tense instead of the perfect tense – *sein* is one of them:

Es **ist** super. → Es **war** super.

Das Konzert **ist** langweilig. → Das Konzert **war** langweilig.

**HÖREN 2**

**NC 5**

🎧 **Hör zu. Was haben Tanja, Sven und Hannah gemacht? Beantworte die Fragen auf Deutsch.**

*Beispiel:*

|  | **Was hast du gemacht?** | **Wie war es?** |
|---|---|---|
| Tanja | *ich habe meine Oma besucht, ich habe …* | *die Arbeit war …* |

| | | toll/super. |
|---|---|---|
| Es | | interessant. |
| Das Konzert | war | gut/nett. anstrengend. |
| Die Arbeit | | langweilig. laut/schlecht. |
| Die Woche | | schlimm. schwer. stressig. |

**SPRECHEN 3**

**NC 5**

👥 **Du bist Tanja, Sven oder Hannah (Übung 2). Macht Dialoge. A ⟷ B.**

*Beispiel:* **A** *Tanja, was hast du gemacht?*
**B** *Ich habe …*
**A** *Wie war die Arbeit?*

**SCHREIBEN 4**

👥 **Schreibt ein Adjektiv-ABC (positiv und negativ).**

*Beispiel:* **A** *altmodisch* **B** *blöd* **C** *cool* **D** *…*

**SPRECHEN 5**

**NC 5**

👥 **Umfrage: „Was hast du gestern gemacht? Wie war es?"**

*Beispiel:* **A** *Was hast du gestern gemacht? Wie war es?*
**B** *Ich habe Hausaufgaben gemacht. Das war langweilig!*
**C** *Ich habe …*

**SCHREIBEN 6**

**NC 5**

**Du bist dran! Schreib Sätze für die Bilder. Was hast du gemacht? Wie war es?**

*Beispiel:* **a** *Ich habe … Das war …*

**?** **Think**

**Giving opinions**

- You can use the perfect tense to say what you liked or disliked:
  *… hat mir (nicht) gefallen.*
  *Ich habe …. (nicht) gemocht.*
- Try to vary the adjectives you use. Don't always say *super* – say *interessant* instead!
- Add in some extra words for emphasis: *sehr* (very), *ziemlich* (quite), *zu* (too), *gar nicht* (not at all), *nicht so* (not so).
- Don't forget to use *weil* sometimes:
  *Das Praktikum war super, weil die Kollegen nett waren.*

**Challenge**

○ Imagine you are writing an article for the Radio Zoom website about a recent day out. Describe what you did, the friends you were with, etc. Give your opinion about everything!

*Beispiel: Letzten Samstag bin ich mit meinen Freunden in die Stadt gefahren. Das war total toll! Wir sind mit dem Zug gefahren – das hat mir gefallen, weil …*

**NC 5**

# 1A.5 Letztes Wochenende

- Vocabulary: talk about what you did last weekend
- Grammar: use the perfect tense
- Skills: build answers from questions

## HÖREN 1
**NC 5**

🎧 **Hör zu. Was hat Leo letztes Wochenende gemacht? Finde die richtige Reihenfolge für die Bilder.**

*Beispiel:* **e, …**

## HÖREN 2
**NC 5**

🎧 **Hör noch einmal zu und wähle die passenden Antworten.**

*Beispiel:* **1 b**

1  Urs hat Fotos
   a  in Köln gemacht.
   b  vom Wochenende geschickt.

2  Leo ist am Samstag
   a  nach Zürich gefahren.
   b  ins Kino gegangen.

3  Leo ist auch
   a  in den Supermarkt gegangen.
   b  ins Schwimmbad gegangen.

4  Sie haben bei Urs
   a  Spaghetti gegessen.
   b  Pizza gemacht.

5  Am Sonntag hat Leo
   a  mit seiner Cousine telefoniert.
   b  an seiner Webseite gearbeitet.

6  Danach hat er
   a  ein Konzert besucht.
   b  seine Oma besucht.

> Ich habe …
> … gehört/gekauft.
> … gespielt.
> … getroffen.
> … besucht.
> getanzt/gechattet.
> mich entspannt.
>
> Ich bin …
> gegangen/gefahren.
> geschwommen.

## SPRECHEN 3

👥 **Macht Dialoge: „Was hast du am Wochenende gemacht?" Benutzt a–d (rechts). A ↔ B.**

*Beispiel:* **A** *Was hast du am Wochenende gemacht?*
**B** *Ich habe Fußball gespielt.*

## SCHREIBEN 4
**NC 4–5**

**Und du – was hast du am Wochenende gemacht? Schreib sechs Sätze.**

*Beispiel:* *Ich bin in die Stadt gefahren. Ich habe …*

**LESEN 5**
NC 5

**Lies Annes Nachricht. Dann lies die Sätze (a–f). Richtig (R), falsch (F) oder nicht im Text (NiT)?**

*Beispiel:* **a** *R*

a   Anne und ihre Freundin sind nach Berlin geflogen.
b   Das Hotel war nicht so gut.
c   Sie haben eine Stadtrundfahrt mit dem Bus gemacht.
d   Das Konzert war ziemlich laut.
e   Sie haben ein Jessie-J-T-Shirt gekauft.
f   Am Sonntag sind sie wieder nach Hause geflogen.

> Das letzte Wochenende war super! Ich habe bei Radio Zoom eine Reise nach Berlin gewonnen – für mich und meine Freundin. Wir sind am Freitagabend von Augsburg nach Berlin geflogen. Wir haben dort in einem Hotel gewohnt – das Hotel war modern und sehr schön. Unser Zimmer war sehr groß!
>
> Am Samstagmorgen haben wir zu Fuß die Sehenswürdigkeiten besichtigt. Am Nachmittag haben wir Souvenirs gekauft.
>
> Und am Abend sind wir zu einem Konzert von Jessie J gegangen! Das Konzert war toll – und danach haben wir eine CD und Autogrammkarten gekauft.
>
> Am Sonntagmorgen sind wir erst um 10 Uhr aufgestanden. Und später um 15 Uhr war die Reise in Augsburg zu Ende – leider …

**SPRECHEN 6**
NC 5

**Macht einen Dialog (a–f).**

*Beispiel:*   **A** *Wohin bist du letztes Wochenende gefahren?*
               **B** *Ich bin …*

a   Wohin bist du letztes Wochenende gefahren?   **Zürich**
b   Wo hast du gewohnt?
c   Was hast du am Samstag gemacht?
d   Was hast du gegessen und getrunken?   Cola
e   Wann bist du am Sonntag aufgestanden?   9:30
f   Was hast du am Sonntag gemacht?   **Zürich**

**? Think**

In activities 6 and 7, you can use the questions to help you build your answers. Remember to change the *du* form of the verb to the *ich* form:

– Wohin <u>bist du</u> letztes Wochenende <u>gefahren</u>?
→ <u>Ich bin</u> mit dem Zug nach Zürich <u>gefahren</u>.

**Challenge**

You're a very busy person! Describe in your blog everything you did last weekend, and when. Don't forget to give your opinions too.

*Beispiel: Ich habe um fünf Uhr Frühstück gegessen – Müsli mit Milch. Das war lecker!*   NC 5

**SPRECHEN 7**

**Macht andere Dialoge wie in Übung 6. A ←→ B.**

**SCHREIBEN 8**
NC 5

**Dein Traumwochenende – was hast du gemacht? Wie war es? Schreib 8–10 Sätze.**

## Separable verbs, reflexive verbs, the perfect tense

### Separable and reflexive verbs

- The infinitives of some German verbs need to be split into two parts when you use them. They are called **separable verbs** and the first part of their infinitive (the **prefix**) goes to the end of the sentence:

  **auf**stehen → Ich stehe **auf**. *I get up/I stand up.*

- With some German verbs (called **reflexive verbs**), you need to use an extra **pronoun**. The pronoun that goes with *ich* is *mich* (myself):

  Ich wasche **mich**. *I have a wash. (I wash myself.)*

- With a few verbs, you need to use both a **prefix** and an extra **pronoun**:

  Ich ziehe **mich aus**. *I get undressed.*
  (*I undress myself.*)

**1** Write down the six sentences in the word snake.

*Beispiel: Ich wache …*

ichwacheaufichziehemichanichräumemeinzimmeraufichwaschemichichsteheaufichwascheab

### The perfect tense

- The perfect tense of regular verbs is formed with *haben* and the past participle of the main verb:

  **haben + ge-...-t (past participle)**

  Ich **habe** CDs **gekauft**. Wir **haben** Pizza **gemacht**.

- A small number of verbs have past participles that don't follow the *ge-...-t* pattern:

  Ich **habe** E-Mails **geschrieben**. Wir **haben telefoniert**.

- Some verbs form their perfect tense with *sein* instead of *haben*:

  **sein + ge-...-en (past participle)**

  Ich **bin** nach Köln **gefahren**. Wir **sind** ins Kino **gegangen**.

- For separable verbs (*abwaschen, fernsehen*), the prefix (the small part of the verb) is always placed in front of the past participle:

  Ich wasche **ab**. → Ich habe **ab**gewaschen.
  Ich sehe **fern**. → Ich habe **fern**gesehen.

- See pages 163 and 165 for all the forms of *haben* and *sein* and a list of irregular past participles.

**2** Fill in the gaps using the words from the box.

*Beispiel: Wir haben gestern ein Picknick <u>gemacht</u>.*

Wir haben gestern ein Picknick _____. Jan und Susi haben im Supermarkt Brötchen und Salat _____. Dann sind wir mit dem Fahrrad zum Park _____, aber Susi ist zu Fuß _____. Ich habe mit Jan Fußball _____. Abends habe ich mit Tanja in der Disco _____. Am Sonntag habe ich Musik _____ und mit meiner Tante in Spanien _____.

| | | |
|---|---|---|
| getanzt | gekauft | gegangen |
| gehört | gemacht | telefoniert |
| | gefahren | gespielt |

**3** Fill in each gap using the correct form of *haben* or *sein*.

*Beispiel:* **a** hat

**a** Maja _____ eine CD gekauft.
**b** _____ du in den Park gegangen?
**c** Jan und Eva _____ Pizza gegessen.
**d** Wir _____ Musik gehört.
**e** Sven _____ in die Stadt gefahren.
**f** _____ ihr ferngesehen?

**4** Rewrite the sentences in the perfect tense.

*Beispiel:* **a** *Wir haben unsere Freunde getroffen.*

**a** Wir treffen unsere Freunde.
**b** Ich fliege nach Hamburg.
**c** David kauft im Supermarkt ein.
**d** Ihr geht in die Stadt.
**e** Paul und Tim kochen Kaffee.
**f** Ich räume mein Zimmer auf.

## Word families, using a bilingual dictionary

### Word families

Word families are made up of words that all have the same main part. They can be nouns, verbs, past participles or adjectives, and they help you to expand your vocabulary.

### Using a bilingual dictionary

A bilingual dictionary (German–English, English–German) is a very important tool for learning German – but you also need to know how to use it properly!

For example, is the word you're looking for a verb, noun or adjective? Make sure you understand the grammatical information that the dictionary gives you for each word.

**5** Write a word family for each of the following words. Use a dictionary to help you.

**spielen**  **Schule**  **Tag**

♪ **aufstehen** *verb* ✧ (*imperfect* **stand auf**, *perfect* **ist aufgestanden**)

♪ **gehen** *verb* ✧ (*imperfect* **ging**, *perfect* **ist gegangen**)

♪ **waschen** *verb* ✧ (*present* **wäscht**, *imperfect* **wusch**, *perfect* **hat gewaschen**)
1 **to wash**
2 **sich waschen** to have a wash
**sich die Hände waschen** to wash your hands

♪ **der Zahn** (*plural* **die Zähne**)

♪ indicates key words
✧ irregular verb

**6** Look at these extracts from a German dictionary.

- If it's a noun: what shows you its gender? And its plural?
- If it's a verb: how can you tell if it's reflexive or separable?
- What other grammatical information do you notice?

## The *ß/ss* and *s* sounds, the *au* sound

**7** 🎧 Listen (1–12). Do you hear *ß* or *ss* (sharp *s*) or *s* (soft *s*)?

*Beispiel:* **1** *ss*

**8** 🎧 The *au* sound: listen and repeat.

**9** Read the poem aloud!

*Die Maus aus Augsburg steht auf –*
*und räumt laut in der Pause das Haus auf!*
*Sie saugt auch Staub…*

- Vocabulary: describe your daily routine and what you did recently
- Grammar: practise reflexive verbs, separable verbs and the perfect tense
- Skills: read for gist and detail

**LESEN 1**

**Finde die passenden Bilder (1–6) für die Sätze (a–f).**
Match each picture (1–6) to a sentence (a–f).

*Beispiel:* **a 6**

a Ich ziehe mich aus.
b Ich wache auf.
c Ich gehe ins Bett.
d Ich wasche mich.
e Ich putze meine Zähne.
f Ich ziehe mich an.

**SCHREIBEN 2**

**Was ist die richtige Reihenfolge für a–f in Übung 1?**
Write out sentences a–f in activity 1 in the correct order.

*Beispiel: Ich wache auf. Ich …*

**LESEN 3**

**NC 2**

**Finde die Paare.**
Match the clocks to the times.

*Beispiel:* **a 6**

a Es ist fünfzehn Uhr fünfundfünfzig.
b Es ist Viertel nach sechs.
c Es ist neunzehn Uhr fünfundzwanzig.
d Es ist vierzehn Uhr zehn.
e Es ist halb sechs.
f Es ist Viertel vor fünf.

**LESEN 4**

**NC 5**

**Beantworte die Fragen auf Englisch.**
Answer the questions in English.

a Where did Tom go yesterday?
b When did he get up?
c What does he say about the journey?
d Whom did he meet in Cologne?
e What did he do after lunch?
f What does he say about the cinema?

Ich heiße Tom und ich bin gestern nach Köln gefahren. Ich bin um acht Uhr aufgestanden und ich bin mit dem Bus gefahren. Die Fahrt war lang – und langweilig …
Ich habe in Köln meine Cousine getroffen und wir haben CDs gekauft. Zum Mittagessen haben wir Pizza gegessen. Wir sind danach in den Park gefahren und haben dort Frisbee gespielt. Dann sind wir ins Kino gegangen – das war super!

- Vocabulary: describe your daily routine and what you did recently
- Grammar: use reflexive verbs, separable verbs and the perfect tense
- Skills: read for gist and detail

**SCHREIBEN 1**

NC 3

**Was machst du? Und wann? Schreib Sätze für a–f.**

*Beispiel:* **a** *Ich stehe um sieben Uhr fünfundzwanzig auf.*

**a** 07:25  **b** 07:30  **c** 07:40  **d**  **e**  **f** 23:20

**SCHREIBEN 2**

NC 4

**Du bist dran! Beschreib deinen Alltag. Was machst du und wann?**

*Beispiel:* *Ich wache um sieben Uhr auf …*

**SCHREIBEN 3**

**„Was hast du gestern Abend gemacht?" Schreib Sätze.**

*Beispiel:* **a** *Ich habe Pizza gemacht.*

**a**  **b** TINA  **c**  **d**

**e**  **f**

**LESEN 4**

NC 5

**Beantworte die Fragen auf Englisch.**

- **a** Where did Mila go at the weekend?
- **b** What does she say about the journey?
- **c** What does she say about her hotel?
- **d** What did she do after lunch?
- **e** What does she say about the museum?
- **f** When did they return home?

Ich heiße Mila, und ich bin am Wochenende mit meiner Freundin nach Berlin gefahren. Es war super! Aber die Fahrt war ziemlich lang und langweilig. Wir haben in einem Hotel gewohnt. Das Hotel war schön und modern. Zum Mittagessen haben wir Currywurst gegessen. Wir sind danach in den Park gefahren und haben dort Frisbee gespielt. Dann sind wir ins Museum gegangen. Das war nicht so gut, weil es ziemlich langweilig war. Am Nachmittag habe ich Postkarten geschrieben und Souvenirs gekauft. Am Sonntag sind wir um siebzehn Uhr nach Hause gefahren.

**HÖREN 1**

NC 4

🎧 **Lukas describes his weekend. Listen and answer the questions in English. Note down the times too. (See pages 20–25.)**

*Beispiel:* **a** *He gets up at …, he makes … and he works …*

**a** What does Lukas do on Saturday morning?
**b** What does he do in the afternoon?
**c** What does he do in the evening?

**d** What does he do on Sunday morning?
**e** What does he do on Sunday afternoon?
**f** What does he do on Sunday evening?

**LESEN 2**

NC 5

**Read Aisha's blog and answer the questions in English. (See pages 20–25.)**

*Beispiel:* **a** *She got up at … and then …*

**a** What did Aisha do this morning?
**b** What does she say about lunch?
**c** What is she doing now?

**d** What is she doing this afternoon?
**e** What is she doing after that?
**f** What is she doing last?

> Ich habe heute so viel zu tun! Ich bin um sechs Uhr fünfundfünfzig aufgestanden und um halb acht habe ich Hausaufgaben gemacht. Danach habe ich E-Mails geschrieben.
>
> Zum Mittagessen habe ich an meinem Schreibtisch Salat mit Brot gegessen. Jetzt koche ich Kaffee.
>
> Danach, also am Nachmittag, telefoniere ich mit meiner Freundin. Um fünfzehn Uhr fünfundvierzig höre ich Radio Zoom im Internet. Und um sechzehn Uhr dreißig arbeite ich an meiner Webseite.

**SPRECHEN 3**

NC 5

**Give a mini-presentation about your daily routine during the week. (See pages 20–25.)**

*Beispiel:* *Ich stehe um halb sieben auf, ich wasche mich und …*

Include the following and give a time for each activity:

- what you do in the morning
- what you do at lunchtime
- what you do in the afternoon
- what you do in the evening
- what you did yesterday

**SCHREIBEN 4**

NC 5

**Write at least five sentences about your usual weekend activities and what you did last weekend. (See pages 20–27.)**

*Beispiel:* *Ich fahre am Wochenende mit meinen Freunden in die Stadt und … Aber letztes Wochenende …*

Include:
- what you normally do at the weekend
- where you went last weekend and with whom
- what you did and your opinion of it

| Mein Alltag | My daily routine |
|---|---|
| Ich wache auf. | I wake up. |
| Ich stehe auf. | I get up. |
| Ich wasche mich. | I have a wash. |
| Ich putze meine Zähne. | I brush my teeth. |
| Ich ziehe mich an. | I get dressed. |
| Ich frühstücke. | I have breakfast. |
| Ich fahre zur Arbeit. | I go to work. |
| Ich fahre nach Hause. | I go home. |
| Ich ziehe mich aus. | I get undressed. |
| Ich gehe ins Bett. | I go to bed. |

| Wie spät ist es? | What time is it? |
|---|---|
| Es ist Viertel vor acht. | It's quarter to eight. |
| Es ist acht Uhr. | It's eight o'clock. |
| Es ist Viertel nach acht. | It's quarter past eight. |
| Es ist halb neun. | It's half past eight. |

| Was hast du gemacht? | What did you do? |
|---|---|
| Was hast du gestern gemacht? | What did you do yesterday? |
| Ich habe … | I … |
| CDs gekauft. | bought CDs. |
| E-Mails gelesen. | read emails. |
| Fußball gespielt. | played football. |
| Hausaufgaben gemacht. | did homework. |
| Kaffee gekocht. | made coffee. |
| Musik gehört. | listened to music. |
| eine Nachricht geschrieben. | wrote a message. |
| Pizza gegessen. | ate pizza. |
| getanzt. | danced. |
| telefoniert. | talked on the phone. |
| Ich bin … | I … |
| ins Kino gegangen. | went to the cinema. |
| in die Stadt gefahren. | went into town. |

| Und gestern Abend …? | And yesterday evening …? |
|---|---|
| Es ist …/Um … | It is …/At … |
| neunzehn Uhr fünfunddreißig | 19.35 |
| siebzehn Uhr zwanzig | 17.20 |
| achtzehn Uhr zehn | 18.10 |
| zwanzig Uhr fünf | 20.05 |
| dreizehn Uhr fünfundfünfzig | 13.55 |
| Ich habe … | I … |
| aufgeräumt. | tidied up. |
| abgewaschen. | did the washing-up. |
| ferngesehen. | watched TV. |

| Es war super! | It was great! |
|---|---|
| Es/Das Konzert war … | It/The concert was … |
| Die Arbeit/Die Woche war … | Work/The week was … |
| anstrengend | tiring, exhausting |
| gut | good |
| interessant | interesting |
| langweilig | boring |
| laut | loud, noisy |
| nett | nice |
| schlecht | bad |
| schlimm | awful |
| schwer | difficult, hard |
| stressig | stressful |
| super | super, great |
| toll | great |

| Letztes Wochenende | Last weekend |
|---|---|
| Ich habe … | I … |
| Fotos geschickt. | sent photos. |
| Freunde getroffen/besucht. | met/visited friends. |
| ein Konzert besucht. | went to a concert. |
| gearbeitet. | worked. |
| gechattet. | chatted. |
| gegessen/getrunken. | ate/drank … |
| gewohnt. | stayed/lived … |
| mich entspannt. | relaxed. |
| Ich bin geschwommen. | I swam. |

## I can …

- describe my daily routine
- tell the time
- describe what I've done recently and give my opinion of it
- use reflexive verbs and separable verbs
- use the perfect tense with *haben* and *sein*
- use the imperfect tense (*Es war …*)
- identify word families
- express my opinions
- use a bilingual dictionary
- pronounce the *ß/ss, s* and *au* sounds

- Vocabulary: talk about national holidays and festivals
- Grammar: use the correct endings for dates
- Skills: work out grammar patterns

**LESEN 1**

## Was passt zusammen?

*Beispiel:* **1 b**

1 Silvester
2 Weihnachten
3 Ostern
4 Rhein in Flammen
5 Fasching
6 Tag der Deutschen Einheit
7 Heiligabend
8 Neujahr

a Christmas
b New Year's Eve
c Day of German Unity
d Easter
e Christmas Eve
f Rhine in Flames
g Carnival
h New Year's Day

**HÖREN 2**

🎧 **Hör zu (1–6). Was passt zusammen?**

*Beispiel:* **1 b**

| a | b | c | d | e | f |
|---|---|---|---|---|---|
| **3.** Oktober | **11.** Februar | **9.** April | **31.** Dezember | **24.** Dezember | **1.** Januar |

### ? Think

For dates in German, you add endings to the numbers. Look at the list of numbers and use the colour-coding to help you work out the rules:

- Add ▬▬▬ to most numbers from 1 to 19.
- The four exceptions are: ▬▬▬, ▬▬▬, ▬▬▬ and ▬▬▬.
- Add ▬▬▬ to number 20 and above.

1. **ersten**
2. zwei**ten**
3. **dritten**
4. vier**ten**
5. fünf**ten**
6. sechs**ten**
7. **siebten**
8. **achten**
9. neun**ten**
10. zehn**ten**
11. elf**ten**
12. zwölf**ten**
13. dreizehn**ten**
20. zwanzig**sten**
30. dreißig**sten**
40. vierzig**sten**

**HÖREN 3**

🎧 **Hör zu und lies.**

**A:** Wann feiert man <u>Heiligabend</u>?

**B:** Man feiert am <u>vierundzwanzigsten Dezember</u> <u>Heiligabend</u>.

**A:** Wie findest du <u>Heiligabend</u>?

**B:** Ich finde <u>Heiligabend klasse</u>!

Wann feiert man …?
Man feiert am (+ *date*) …
Wie findest du …?
Ich finde …
cool/klasse/stark/supergut/…

**SPRECHEN 4**

👥 **Macht Dialoge wie in Übung 3. Benutzt die Informationen aus Übung 1 und 2. A ↔ B.**

**HÖREN 5**

NC 4

🎧 **Hör zu und lies den Text. Beantworte die Fragen auf Englisch.**

a What does Leo want to do today?
b Why does Sira not want to go?
c Leo is confused. Why?
d What kind of day is *der Tag der Deutschen Einheit*?
e What do people celebrate in Switzerland on 3rd October?

**Leo**: Oh! Es ist schon elf Uhr. Ich stehe besser auf. Heute möchte ich mit Sira einkaufen gehen.

**Leo**: Hey Sira! Du musst aufstehen. Wir wollen einkaufen.

**Sira**: Ach Leo! Nicht heute. Heute ist der 3. Oktober. Da sind die Geschäfte geschlossen.

**Leo**: Was? Warum? Heute ist Montag! Ein Wochentag! Die Geschäfte sind geöffnet.

**Sira**: Der 3. Oktober ist der Tag der Deutschen Einheit – seit 1990 ein Feiertag.

**Leo**: Das verstehe ich nicht. Das gibt es in der Schweiz nicht. Und warum sind die Geschäfte geschlossen?

**Sira**: Na, weil heute ein Feiertag ist. In Deutschland arbeitet man dann nicht und die Geschäfte sind geschlossen.

**Leo**: Okay, du hast recht.

**? Think**

What other festivals or national holidays do you know?

How would you say their dates?

**SPRECHEN 6**

NC 3

👥 **Macht eine Klassenumfrage: „Wie findest du …?"**

Agree on three festivals that people in your class celebrate. Copy them into a grid like the one below and do a survey to find the most popular.

Beispiel: **A** *Wie findest du Silvester?*
**B** *Ich finde Silvester supergut!*
**A** *Und wie findest du …*

| Silvester | Diwali | Ostern |
|---|---|---|
| supergut | … | … |

**SCHREIBEN 7**

NC 3

**Was feierst du? Wann? Wie findest du das? (Wähle drei Feste.)**

Beispiel: *Man feiert am einunddreißigsten Dezember Silvester. Ich finde Silvester …*

**Challenge**

Choose one of your festivals from activity 7. Explain why you like it (using *weil*) and say what you did last year.

*Beispiel: Man feiert am einunddreißigsten Dezember Silvester. Ich finde Silvester …, weil … Letztes Jahr war es … Wir haben … gegessen/ getrunken und …* NC 5

- Vocabulary: talk about organising a party
- Grammar: use the modal verbs *können* and *müssen*
- Skills: work out grammar patterns

**LESEN 1** **Leo macht eine Party! Finde die Paare.**

*Beispiel:* **a 4**

a  Ich muss Einladungen schreiben.
b  Ich muss Essen kaufen.
c  Ich muss ein Outfit kaufen.
d  Ich muss das Zimmer dekorieren.
e  Ich muss Musik auswählen.
f  Ich muss einen Kuchen backen.

**HÖREN 2** **Ist alles richtig? Hör zu.**

**SPRECHEN 3** **Was muss Leo machen? A wählt ein Bild und B antwortet. A ↔ B.**

*Beispiel:* **A** *Bild 5!*
**B** *Ich muss ein Outfit kaufen.*

**? Think**

- Did you notice that in activities 1–3 there are two verbs in each sentence? Fill in the gaps on the right using the words below:

  muss   modal   -n   infinitive   -en   second

- In activity 4, you will use another modal verb *Man kann …* What does it mean?

The first verb is _____. It is the _____ idea in the sentence and is called a _____ verb. The second verb is at the end and is called the _____. It always ends in _____ or _____.

**SPRECHEN 4** **Hier ist Leos Einkaufsliste! Wo kann man das kaufen? Macht Dialoge. A ↔ B.**

*Beispiel:*  **A** *Wo kann man Cola kaufen?*
**B** *Man kann Cola im Supermarkt kaufen.*

im Musikgeschäft     im Modegeschäft
im Supermarkt        in der Bäckerei

einen Kuchen
Cola
CDs
ein Outfit
Essen

**SCHREIBEN 5**

**Füll die Lücken mit den passenden Verbformen aus. Wie sagt man das auf Englisch?**

*Beispiel:* **a** *muss (I must organise a lot for the party.)*

**a** Ich _____ viel für die Party organisieren. (müssen)
**b** Wir _____ Essen im Supermarkt kaufen. (müssen)
**c** Sie (She) _____ CDs im Musikgeschäft kaufen. (können)
**d** Die Musik _____ immer laut sein. (müssen)
**e** Auf einer Party _____ ihr viel tanzen. (können)
**f** Auf Partys _____ Sie auch Karaoke singen. (können)

**SPRECHEN 6**

NC 3

**Das Party-Spiel! A ↔ B.**

- **A** chooses a number and a letter.
- **B** finds the square and says a sentence using the correct form of *können* or *müssen*.
- Write ✓ or ✗ to show if **B**'s sentence is correct.
- Then it's **B**'s turn to choose a number and letter for **A**.
- Whoever gets four ticks first is the winner!

*Beispiel:* **A** *Vier, b!*
**B** *Wir müssen Einladungen schreiben.*
**A** *Ja, richtig!* (B gets a ✓)

| | |
|---|---|
| Ich kann | tanzen. |
| Du kannst | Karaoke singen. |
| Er/Sie/Man kann | Pizza essen. |
| Wir können | Spaß haben. |
| … | mit Freunden reden. |
| Ich muss | das Zimmer dekorieren. |
| Du musst | einen Kuchen backen. |
| Er/Sie/Man muss | Einladungen schreiben. |
| Wir müssen | Essen/ein Outfit kaufen. |
| … | Musik auswählen. |
| | aufräumen. |

**Challenge**

You are organising your own party. Make a list of:
- what you have to do to prepare for it
- what people can do at your party

Include lots of detail to improve your work.

*Beispiel:*
*Ich muss … kaufen und ich muss … dekorieren.*
*Ich muss …*
*Auf meiner Party kann man … Meine Gäste können …*

NC 4

**Grammatik → p.164**

| | können <br> *can, to be able to* | müssen <br> *must, to have to* |
|---|---|---|
| ich | kann | muss |
| du | kannst | musst |
| er/sie/man | kann | muss |
| wir | können | müssen |
| ihr | könnt | müsst |
| sie/Sie | können | müssen |

| | a | b |
|---|---|---|
| **1** ich | | |
| **2** du | | |
| **3** er, sie, man | | |
| **4** wir | | |
| **5** ihr | | |
| **6** sie, Sie | | |

# 1B.3 Nichts als Ausreden

- Vocabulary: accept or decline an invitation
- Grammar: use the modal verbs *sollen* and *dürfen*
- Skills: adapt sentences and texts

## ▶ Die Video-Aufgabe

**VIDEO 1** Sieh dir das Video an. Beantworte die Fragen auf Englisch.

a Who do we see at the beginning of this video clip?
b What are they doing?
c What does Leo think of parties?
d Who won the fancy-dress competition last year?
e Leo makes up an excuse to avoid going to the party. What is it?

**VIDEO 2** Füll die Tabelle mit a–j aus.

a einen Wettbewerb gemacht
b Samstag, den 25.
c Musik gehört
d Essen machen
e getanzt
f gesungen
g die Wohnung dekorieren
h Kostüme kaufen
i Einladungen schreiben
j Getränke kaufen

| Karnevalsparty bei Sira und Familie | |
|---|---|
| Wann? | |
| Letztes Jahr? | a, , , |
| Wer organisiert was? | Mutter: , <br> Vater: , <br> Sira und Leo: |

**VIDEO 3** What do you think? Which costume is the best? Why?

## ⚙ Grammatik → p.164

| | dürfen <br> *may, to be allowed to* | sollen <br> *should, to be supposed to* |
|---|---|---|
| ich | darf | soll |
| du | darfst | sollst |
| er/sie/man | darf | soll |
| wir | dürfen | sollen |
| ihr | dürft | sollt |
| sie/Sie | dürfen | sollen |

## ⚙ Grammatik → p.164

You met two modal verbs on pages 38–39: *müssen* and *können*. Here are two more: *sollen* and *dürfen*.

- Use *dürfen* to say what you are allowed to do:
  Ich **darf** auf die Party gehen.
  *I'm allowed to go to the party.*

- Use *sollen* to say what you should do:
  Ich **soll** zu Hause helfen. *I should help at home.*

**LESEN 4** **Was passt zusammen? Finde die passenden Bilder (1–5) für die Sätze (a–e).**

*Beispiel:* **a 4**

**a** Ich soll im Garten arbeiten.
**b** Ich soll mein Zimmer aufräumen.
**c** Ich soll Hausaufgaben machen.

**d** Ich soll zu Hause helfen.
**e** Ich soll auf meine Geschwister aufpassen.

**HÖREN 5** 🎧 **Ist alles richtig? Hör zu.**

**HÖREN 6**
**NC 3**
🎧 **Hör zu und lies. Beantworte die Fragen auf Englisch.**

For each conversation (1 and 2), answer these questions:

**a** What type of party is it?
**b** When and where is the party?
**c** Can the person come or not? If not, why not?

**1**
**A:** Ich mache am Samstag eine Strandparty im Freibad! Kommst du?

**B:** Nein, ich darf leider nicht kommen. Ich soll im Garten arbeiten und zu Hause helfen.

**2**
**A:** Ich mache am Freitagabend eine Karnevalsparty zu Hause! Kommst du?

**B:** Ja, gern. Vielen Dank für die Einladung!

**SPRECHEN 7**
**NC 3**
👥 **Du machst eine Party!**

You're having a party! Invite five people.

*Beispiel:*

**A** Ich mache am Freitag eine Geburtstagsparty. Kommst du?
**B** Ja, gern. Vielen Dank für die Einladung.
**C** Nein, ich darf leider nicht kommen. Ich soll auf meine Geschwister aufpassen.

**? Think**

You can adapt the sentences in activity 4 to make new excuses. Keep the sentence framework but change the details:

Ich soll <u>Hausaufgaben</u> machen.
Ich soll <u>Abendessen</u> machen.

Ich mache am Freitagabend/Samstag/…

… eine Strandparty/Karnevalsparty/ Geburtstagsparty/…

… im Freibad/im Garten/zu Hause.

Kommst du?
✓ Ja, gern. Vielen Dank für die Einladung.
✗ Nein, ich darf leider nicht kommen.

**Challenge**

Write a dialogue between two celebrities, **A** and **B**. **A** invites **B** to a party but **B** doesn't want to come! **A** says:

- what type of party it is
- who is invited: *Viele coole Stars kommen …*
- when and where it is
- what activities are planned: *Wir spielen Computerspiele/essen Chips …*
- *Kommst du?*

**B** gives at least **three** excuses why he/she can't come!

**NC 4**

# 1B.4 Die Party war spitze!

- Vocabulary: describe a party you've organised or been to
- Grammar: use the imperfect tense and the perfect tense
- Skills: evaluate and prepare for language tasks

## HÖREN 1

NC 5

🎧 **Die Party war spitze! Hör zu und lies. Was ist die richtige Reihenfolge (a–e)?**

*Beispiel:* **c**, …

Hallo! Die Party am Samstagabend war spitze – der totale Hammer! Die Organisation war ziemlich anstrengend, aber es hat auch viel Spaß gemacht. Ich habe Einladungen geschrieben, Essen gekauft, Pizza gemacht und Kuchen gebacken, Musik ausgewählt und das Zimmer dekoriert.

Am Samstagmorgen war ich sehr nervös, weil ich eine tolle Party wollte. Ich habe mich immer wieder gefragt: „Leo, hast du alles gut geplant und wird die Party spitze?"

Ja, die Party war spitze! Ich hatte hundert Gäste. Die Gäste haben gefeiert, gegessen, getrunken, getanzt und sich hervorragend amüsiert. Es gab eine Karaoke-Anlage und wir haben gesungen. Und es gab leckeres Essen!

Möchtest du vielleicht auch eine Party organisieren? Es ist wirklich nicht schwer. Du musst sie nur gut planen.

## LESEN 2

NC 5

**Beantworte die Fragen auf Englisch.**

a How was the party?
b How did Leo feel about organising the party?
c What did he do to prepare for the party?
d Why was he worried?
e How many guests were there?
f What did the guests do at the party?
g What advice does Leo give for a successful party?

### Grammatik → p.165

You already know how to use *sein* in the imperfect tense:

| Present tense | Imperfect tense |
|---|---|
| es ist (*it is*) → | es war (*it was*) |

Other useful verbs often used in the imperfect tense include:

| Present tense | Imperfect tense |
|---|---|
| es gibt (*there is/are*) → | es gab (*there was/were*) |
| ich habe (*I have*) → | ich hatte (*I had*) |
| ich will (*I want*) → | ich wollte (*I wanted*) |

How many of these can you spot in Leo's text?

**SCHREIBEN 3**

**Füll die Lücken aus.**

*Beispiel:* **a** *wollte*

> getanzt   war   gab   war   wollte   hatte   hat   haben

**a** Ich _____ letztes Jahr eine große Geburtstagsparty.
**b** Die Party _____ der totale Hammer!
**c** Es _____ eine Karaoke-Anlage und wir _____ gesungen.
**d** Die meisten Gäste haben _____.
**e** Meine Mutter _____ Kuchen gebacken und das Essen _____ lecker.
**f** Ich _____ super viel Spaß!

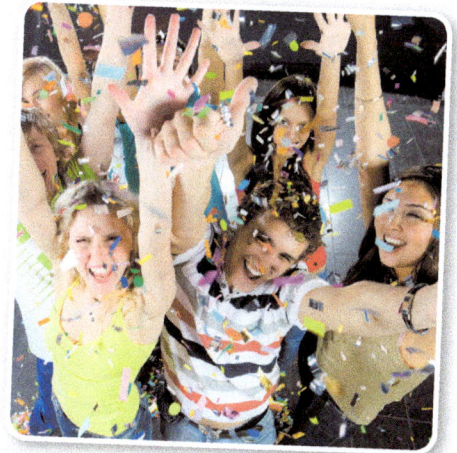

**HÖREN 4**

NC 5

🎧 **Wie war die Party? Hör zu, lies und wähle die passenden Antworten.**

**A:** Was war deine letzte Party?

**B:** Meine letzte Party war **1a** eine Strandparty
  **1b** meine Geburtstagsparty **1c** eine Karnevalsparty.

**A:** Wann war die Party?

**B:** Sie war am **2a** dritten Februar **2b** elften Mai
  **2c** einunddreißigsten Dezember.

**A:** Und wo war die Party?

**B:** Die Party war **3a** im Freibad **3b** zu Hause **3c** in einem Hotel.

**A:** Wie viele Gäste hattest du?

**B:** Ich hatte **4a** keine **4b** hundert **4c** tausend Gäste.

**A:** Was haben die Gäste gemacht?

**B:** Sie haben **5a** getanzt **5b** Computerspiele gespielt
  **5c** Kuchen gegessen **5d** Cola getrunken
  **5e** das Zimmer aufgeräumt **5f** gesungen. (*choose three*)

**A:** Wie war die Party?

**B:** Die Party war **6a** spitze **6b** ziemlich gut **6c** langweilig, weil
  **6d** die Musik sehr laut war **6e** ich viele Gäste hatte
  **6f** mein Geburtstagskuchen fantastisch war.
  (*choose an opinion and a reason*)

**SPRECHEN 5**

NC 5

👥 **Macht ein Interview wie in Übung 4 für das Schulradio!**
**A ↔ B.**

**SCHREIBEN 6**

NC 5

**Schreib dein Interview (Übung 5) auf.**

**? Think**

Before you start the **Challenge** task, look at the level of Leo's text in activity 1.

List the key points that make it level 5 and try to use them in your own writing.

**Challenge**

You've just had a birthday party and it was <u>the</u> party of the year!

Write a description:
- type of party?
- when and where?
- how many guests?
- activities?
- your opinion?

NC 5

- Vocabulary: talk about German festivals
- Grammar: use question words
- Skills: build answers from questions

**HÖREN 1** 🎧 **Hör zu und lies (a–d). Finde die passenden Bilder.**

**1** **2** **3** **4** **5** **6**

**a**

## Rhein in Flammen

*Jedes Jahr feiert man in der Rheinregion „Rhein in Flammen". Viele Touristen besuchen dieses Fest. An fünf Tagen zwischen Mai und September feiert man in vielen Städten wunderschöne Feuerwerke. Man kann die Feuerwerke vom Land oder von einem Boot aus sehen.*

**b**

## Tag der Deutschen Einheit

Der dritte Oktober ist seit dem Jahr 1990 ein Feiertag in Deutschland: „Tag der Deutschen Einheit". Die Deutschen feiern, weil Deutschland ein Land ist. In vielen Städten feiert man große Feste mit Konzerten, Feuerwerken und Paraden. In Berlin feiert man eine große Party am Brandenburger Tor.

**c**

## Der Nikolaus kommt

Am 6. Dezember feiert man in Deutschland den Nikolaustag. Am 5. Dezember putzen die Kinder abends ihre Stiefel und Schuhe. Die Stiefel und Schuhe kommen vor die Tür. Der Nikolaus kommt und füllt sie mit Süßigkeiten und Geschenken.

**d**

## Weihnachten

Weihnachten beginnt in Deutschland mit Heiligabend am 24. Dezember. Dann gibt es die Geschenke! Vom 24. Dezember bis zum 6. Januar haben viele Familien einen Weihnachtsbaum im Wohnzimmer. Das traditionelle Weihnachtsessen ist Gans oder Kartoffelsalat mit Würstchen.

**LESEN 2** **Lies noch einmal und beantworte die Fragen auf Deutsch.**

**NC 4**
a Wo kann man eine Bootsfahrt machen und Feuerwerke sehen?
b Wann feiert man den Tag der Deutschen Einheit?
c Wer kommt am 6. Dezember?
d Was finden die Kinder am Nikolaustag in ihren Schuhen?
e Wann beginnt Weihnachten in Deutschland?
f Was isst man zu Weihnachten in Deutschland?

**Grammatik → p.168**

| Wer? | Who? |
| Wo? | Where? |
| Was? | What? |
| Wann? | When? |
| Wie? | How? |
| Wie viele? | How many? |

**LESEN 3**

**NC 4**

**Lies den Dialog und finde die passenden Fragewörter: *Wann? Wo? Was? Wie viele? Wer?***

*Beispiel: Was, …*

**Sira**: Hey Leo, schau mal! Hier ist ein Artikel über „Rhein in Flammen"!

**Leo**: _____ ist „Rhein in Flammen"?

**Sira**: „Rhein in Flammen" ist ein Feuerwerksfest.

**Leo**: _____ feiert man das?

**Sira**: Das feiert man in der Rheinregion.

**Leo**: _____ feiert man „Rhein in Flammen"?

**Sira**: „Rhein in Flammen" feiert man jedes Jahr von Mai bis September.

**Leo**: _____ kann man machen?

**Sira**: Man kann mit einem Boot auf dem Rhein fahren und tolle Feuerwerke sehen.

**Leo**: _____ besucht das Fest?

**Sira**: Familien, Kinder und Jugendliche besuchen das Fest.

**Leo**: _____ Touristen kommen?

**Sira**: Dreihunderttausend Touristen kommen!

**Leo**: Prima! Ich möchte auch das Fest „Rhein in Flammen" besuchen!

**HÖREN 4** 🎧 **Ist alles richtig? Hör zu.**

**? Think**

When answering a question, try to use words and phrases from the question to help you build your answer. Sometimes you can start your answer by repeating the last part of the question:

- Was ist der Tag der Deutschen Einheit?
- → Der Tag der Deutschen Einheit ist ein Feiertag.
- Wann feiert man den Nikolaustag?
- → Den Nikolaustag feiert man am 6. Dezember.

Remember: the verb is the second idea in the sentence.

**SPRECHEN 5** 👥 **Macht Dialoge über die drei anderen Feste (Seite 44).**
A ↔ B.

Use as many question words as you can!

**SCHREIBEN 6**

**NC 4**

**Wähle ein Fest. Schreib ein Interview für dein Schulmagazin (wie in Übung 3).**

**Challenge**

Write an email to your German penfriend describing how you and your family celebrate a festival that is very important in your culture.

**NC 4**

# 1B.6 Sprachlabor

## Modal verbs, the imperfect tense

### Modal verbs

Use modal verbs to say what you **can**, **are allowed to**, **have to**, **want to** or **should do**. A modal verb is always the second idea in the sentence. It is usually followed by an infinitive at the end of the sentence.

Wir **können** nicht **kommen**. *We can't come.*
Ich **darf** nicht auf Partys **gehen**. *I am not allowed to go to parties.*
Er **muss** Hausaufgaben **machen**. *He has to do homework.*
Wir **wollen** eine große Party **machen**. *We want to have a big party.*
Man **soll** immer zu Hause **helfen**. *One should always help at home.*

You can also use *wollen* without an infinitive:

Ich **will** Schokoladenkuchen! *I want chocolate cake!*

| | **können** can, to be able to | **dürfen** may, to be allowed to | **müssen** must, to have to | **wollen** to want (to) | **sollen** should, to be supposed to |
|---|---|---|---|---|---|
| ich | kann | darf | muss | will | soll |
| du | kannst | darfst | musst | willst | sollst |
| er/sie/es | kann | darf | muss | will | soll |
| wir | können | dürfen | müssen | wollen | sollen |
| ihr | könnt | dürft | müsst | wollt | sollt |
| sie/Sie | können | dürfen | müssen | wollen | sollen |

**1** Write new sentences using the modal verbs.

*Beispiel:* **a** *Ich darf nicht auf die Party gehen.*

**a** Ich gehe nicht auf die Party. (dürfen)
**b** Mein Bruder und ich helfen zu Hause. (müssen)
**c** Meine Familie isst gesund. (sollen)
**d** Am Wochenende gehen wir länger aus. (können)
**e** In den Ferien fliegen Paul und ich nach Neuseeland. (wollen)
**f** Ich sehe keine Horrorfilme. (dürfen)
**g** Er singt Karaoke. (wollen)

### The imperfect tense

In German, the perfect tense is used for describing events in the past, particularly when <u>talking</u> about what you have done and referring to the <u>recent</u> past.

The imperfect tense is used for descriptions in the past (as in French). It is also used for writing about events in the past in a more formal way, for example in novels and newspapers.

Two of the most commonly used verbs are *sein* and *haben*. You have also met *es gab* (there was/were) and *ich wollte* (I wanted).

| | **sein** to be | **haben** to have |
|---|---|---|
| ich | war (was) | hatte (had) |
| du | warst (were) | hattest (had) |
| er/sie/es | war (was) | hatte (had) |
| wir | waren (were) | hatten (had) |
| ihr | wart (were) | hattet (had) |
| sie/Sie | waren (were) | hatten (had) |

**2** Fill in the correct form of *haben* or *sein* in the imperfect tense.

*Beispiel:* **a** Weihnachten <u>war</u> ich in Australien.

**a** Weihnachten ﹍﹍﹍ ich in Australien.
**b** Meine Familie und ich ﹍﹍﹍ viel Spaß.
**c** Das Wetter ﹍﹍﹍ sehr heiß.
**d** Das Hotel ﹍﹍﹍ ein Schwimmbad.
**e** Der Urlaub ﹍﹍﹍ klasse.
**f** Und du – wo ﹍﹍﹍ du?

**3** Rewrite the sentences in the imperfect tense.

*Beispiel:* **a** *Das Essen war lecker.*

**a** Das Essen ist lecker.
**b** Ich will eine tolle Party feiern.
**c** In meiner Stadt gibt es ein Freibad.
**d** Ich will das neue Karaoke-Spiel.
**e** In den Ferien haben wir viel Freizeit.
**f** Es gibt viele Gäste auf der Party.

## Improve your listening skills

Use these strategies to help you with listening:

- Before listening, look at any pictures or headings. They might give you a clue to some of the answers.
- Read the questions carefully. They will tell you what to do and what to listen for.
- Try to predict what you might hear.
- When listening, try to get the gist of it first, then focus on identifying the key information you need.
- Listen to people's tone of voice. This can help you to work out their opinion or how they feel about something, even when you don't understand their actual words.

**4** Listen and answer the questions in German. Use the strategies above to help you.

**a** Was für eine Party?
**b** Wo?
**c** Wie war die Party letztes Jahr?
**d** Was haben sie gemacht? (4)

## Pronunciation of *a*, *ä* and *u*, *ü*

**5** Listen and repeat these words.

**a** ich fahre
**b** er fährt
**c** warm
**d** März
**e** müssen
**f** Hamburg
**g** für
**h** zur

- The *ä* sound is like *ai* in 'air' or 'fair'.
- To pronounce *ü*: say 'ee', then with your tongue still in that position, round your lips and try to say 'oo'.

- Vocabulary: identify dates and festivals; talk about parties
- Grammar: practise the perfect tense
- Skills: adapt a text

## LESEN 1

**Finde die Feste und Daten.**
Find the festivals and dates.

*Beispiel: Ostern, …*

osternneujahrtagderdeutscheneinheitweihnachten

samstagdeneinundzwanzigstenjulinikolaustag

## LESEN 2 / NC 4

**Wie findet Antje Allesdoof Partys?**

What does Antje Allesdoof think of parties? Which activities (a–g) does she give <u>her</u> opinion on? What does she say about each activity?

*Beispiel: f boring*

Ich heiße Antje Allesdoof! Ich finde Partys richtig doof. Meine Freundin Anna Allestoll findet, Partys machen viel Spaß. Sie tanzt gern und singt gern Karaoke.

Warum soll man Partys machen? Man muss zu viel organisieren. Man muss Einladungen schreiben. Das ist langweilig! Man muss auch einen Kuchen backen – sehr teuer! Und man muss das Partyzimmer dekorieren. Das ist anstrengend und man muss aufräumen! Alles doof! Die Gäste auf einer Party sind zu laut und die Musik ist oft altmodisch.

a
b
c
d
e
f
g

## SCHREIBEN 3 / NC 4

**Beschreib eine Party. Benutze Ilkas Text.**
Describe a party. Copy out Ilka's text and replace the <u>underlined</u> words with your own details.

*Hallo! Ich heiße <u>Ilka</u>, ich bin <u>fünfzehn</u> Jahre alt und ich habe <u>letzten Samstag</u> eine fantastische <u>Kostümparty</u> gemacht. <u>Meine Eltern</u> haben beim Organisieren geholfen. Sie haben <u>Einladungen geschrieben</u>, <u>gebacken</u> und <u>Partyspiele organisiert</u>. Das war sehr <u>nett</u>.*

*Ich hatte viel Spaß auf der Party, denn ich <u>habe gesungen und viel gegessen</u>. Die Party war <u>toll</u>.*

# 1B.7 Extra Plus

- Vocabulary: talk about parties
- Grammar: use the correct endings for dates; use modal verbs, the perfect tense and the imperfect
- Skills: use ideas from a text in your own writing

## SCHREIBEN 1

**Schreib die Daten auf Deutsch.**

Beispiel: **a** Freitag, den zweiten Dezember

**a** Friday 2.12.       **c** Wednesday 30.11.   **e** Saturday 3.4.   **g** Thursday 1.1.
**b** Monday 14.9.      **d** Tuesday 10.8.      **f** Sunday 25.5.    **h** Friday 7.2.

## SCHREIBEN 2

**Schreib Sätze für die Bilder. Benutze Modalverben.**

Write a sentence for each picture. Use a modal verb (*sollen, dürfen, müssen, können*) in each sentence.

> kaufen   machen   arbeiten
> backen   essen

Beispiel: **a** Ich soll/darf/muss …

## LESEN 3

**Wie findet Peter Partymuffel Partys? Finde a–e im Text.**

**NC 4**

Beispiel: **a** überbewertet

> **a** overrated   **b** lukewarm   **c** embarrassing   **d** to discuss   **e** championship

Das ist Peter Partymuffel. Peter mag keine Partys. Er findet, sie sind total überbewertet, denn die Musik ist immer zu laut, das Essen kalt, die Getränke lauwarm, Karaoke peinlich und die Gäste diskutieren über „das Wetter" und „Politik". Total langweilig, meint Peter.

Am Samstagabend spielt Peter lieber Computerspiele – sein Lieblingshobby. Er hat viele Spiele und trainiert für eine internationale Meisterschaft im nächsten Jahr.

## LESEN 4

**Lies den Text noch einmal. Beantworte die Fragen auf Englisch.**

**NC 4**

**a** What does Peter think of parties? Mention five things.
**b** Give three details about his favourite hobby.

## SCHREIBEN 5

**Peter hat seine ideale Party organisiert! Wie war die Party?**

**NC 5**

Beispiel: Peters Party war eine Computerspiele-Party …

**HÖREN 1** NC 5

🎧 **Listen to Sira. What did she do to organise the party and what did Leo do? (See pages 42–43.)**

*Beispiel:* Sira (4 things): wrote invitations, …
Leo (3 things): …

**LESEN 2** NC 5

**Read Sira's description of her party. Answer the questions in English. (See pages 42–43).**

a   When was Sira's party?
b   How many stars celebrate the Oscars every year?
c   What was Sira's party like?
d   What did Sira do to organise the party?
e   What did the guests do at the party?
f   What does Sira want to do next year?

Gestern Abend habe ich eine Oscar-Party gefeiert. Mehr als Tausend Stars feiern jedes Jahr die besten Filme des Jahres. Ich habe die Oscars mit meinen Freunden im Fernsehen gesehen! Die Party war spitze und hat viel Spaß gemacht.
Man muss eine Party gut planen! Ich habe Einladungen geschrieben, Kuchen gebacken, Cola gekauft und das Haus dekoriert. Am Freitagabend haben meine Gäste gefeiert, gegessen und getrunken und dann haben wir die Oscars im Fernsehen gesehen. Es war total klasse.
Nächstes Jahr möchte ich wieder eine Oscar-Party organisieren!

**SPRECHEN 3** NC 5

👥 **You have received an invitation to this year's Oscars party. After the party, you discuss the event. (See pages 38–39, 42–43.)**

a   Wann war die Oscar-Party? *Die Oscar-Party war am …*
b   Was muss man für die Oscar-Party organisieren? *Man muss …*
c   Wie war die Party? *Die Party war …*
d   Was haben die Partygäste gemacht? *Die Gäste/Wir haben …*

**SCHREIBEN 4** NC 5

**Write an email to your Swiss friend describing a party that you have every year. (See pages 36–43.)**

Mention:
- type of party: *eine Weihnachtsparty/Geburtstagsparty …*
- when and where: *am … Dezember im/in/…*
- the guests: *viele Freunde/meine Familie/…*
- activities: *Wir essen/trinken/… Man kann …*
- what you did last year and what it was like: *Letztes Jahr haben wir … Es war … Es gab …*
- why your friend must come to this year's party! *Du musst kommen, weil …*

## Feiertage und Feste — National holidays and festivals

| | |
|---|---|
| Fasching | Carnival |
| Heiligabend | Christmas Eve |
| Neujahr | New Year |
| Ostern | Easter |
| Rhein in Flammen | Rhine in Flames |
| Silvester | New Year's Eve |
| Tag der Deutschen Einheit | Day of German Unity |
| Weihnachten | Christmas |

| | |
|---|---|
| Wann feiert man …? | When do you celebrate …? |
| Man feiert am (+ date) … | We celebrate … on the (+ date). |
| Wie findest du …? | What do you think of …? |
| Ich finde … klasse. | I think … is great. |
| stark | great, really cool, wicked |
| supergut | fantastic, excellent |

## Party machen — Organising a party

| | |
|---|---|
| Ich muss … | I must … |
|   Einladungen schreiben. | write invitations. |
|   Kuchen/einen Kuchen backen. | bake cakes/a cake. |
|   Musik auswählen. | choose some music. |
|   ein Outfit kaufen. | buy an outfit. |
|   das Zimmer dekorieren. | decorate the room. |
|   Essen kaufen. | buy food. |
|   aufräumen. | tidy up. |
| Man kann … im Supermarkt kaufen. | You can buy … in the supermarket. |
| in der Bäckerei | at the baker's |
| im Modegeschäft/ Musikgeschäft | at the clothes shop/music shop |

| | |
|---|---|
| Man kann … | You can … |
|   Karaoke singen. | sing karaoke. |
|   Spaß haben. | have fun. |
|   mit Freunden reden. | chat with friends. |
|   tanzen. | dance. |
|   essen/trinken. | eat/drink. |

## Nichts als Ausreden — Excuses, excuses …

| | |
|---|---|
| Ich mache eine Strandparty. | I'm having a beach party. |
| Kommst du? | Will you come? |
| Ja, gern. Vielen Dank für die Einladung. | Yes, I'd love to. Thanks very much for the invitation. |
| Nein, ich darf leider nicht kommen. | No, unfortunately I'm not allowed to come. |

| | |
|---|---|
| Ich soll … | I'm supposed to … |
|   Hausaufgaben machen. | do my homework. |
|   mein Zimmer aufräumen. | tidy my room. |
|   zu Hause helfen. | help at home. |
|   im Garten arbeiten. | work in the garden. |
|   auf meine Geschwister aufpassen. | look after my brothers and sisters. |

## Die Party war spitze! — The party was great!

| | |
|---|---|
| langweilig | boring |
| spitze/toll | great |
| der totale Hammer | totally cool, awesome |

| | |
|---|---|
| Ich hatte hundert Gäste. | I had a hundred guests. |
| Es gab … | There was/were … |
|   eine Karaoke-Anlage. | a karaoke machine. |
|   leckeres Essen. | delicious food. |
|   nette Gäste. | nice guests. |
|   tolle Musik. | great music. |

| | |
|---|---|
| Ich habe … | I … |
|   Einladungen geschrieben. | wrote invitations. |
|   Musik ausgewählt. | chose some music. |
|   das Studio dekoriert. | decorated the studio. |
|   Essen gekauft. | bought food. |
|   gebacken. | baked. |
| Wir/Die Gäste haben … | We/The guests … |
|   Musik gehört. | listened to music. |
|   gesungen/getanzt. | sang/danced. |
|   gefeiert/gegessen/ getrunken. | celebrated/ate/drank …. |

### ⦿ I can …

- ⦿ talk about national holidays and festivals
- ⦿ talk about organising a party and describe a party I've been to
- ⦿ accept or decline an invitation, and give excuses
- ⦿ use the correct endings for dates
- ⦿ use modal verbs
- ⦿ use the imperfect tense and the perfect tense
- ⦿ use different strategies to help with listening
- ⦿ pronounce the *a*, *ä*, *u* and *ü* sounds

# 2A.1 Im Fernsehen

- Vocabulary: talk about TV programmes and how often you watch TV; express opinions about TV programmes
- Grammar: use possessive adjectives
- Skills: use what you already know to build new expressions and work out meaning

**HÖREN 1** **Hör zu. Finde die passenden Bilder für a–i.**

*Beispiel:* **a 6**

1

2

3

4

5

6

7

8

9

| | |
|---|---|
| a | eine Realityshow |
| b | eine Musiksendung |
| c | die Nachrichten |
| d | eine Quizsendung |
| e | eine Sportsendung |
| f | eine Seifenoper |
| g | eine Castingshow |
| h | eine Dokumentarserie |
| i | eine Zeichentrickserie |

**? Think**

How would you say how often you watch TV?

*every day* = jeden ___
*in the morning* = am ___
*in the afternoon* = ___ ___
*in the evening* = ___ ___
*at the weekend* = ___ ___

**SPRECHEN 2** **„Was siehst du gern? Und was ist das?" A ↔ B.**

**A** names a programme and **B** says what type of programme it is.

*Beispiel:* ***A*** *Ich sehe gern „Britain's Got Talent".*
***B*** *Das ist eine Castingshow! Und ich sehe gern …*

Was siehst du gern im Fernsehen?
Wann/Wie oft siehst du …?
Ich sehe … (nicht) gern, weil …
… sie interessant/super/lustig/cool/langweilig/doof/furchtbar/blöd sind.
… Spaß machen.

**HÖREN 3** NC 3–4 **Schreib die Tabelle ab. Hör zu und beantworte die Fragen für Klara, Hasan, Jessica, Lars und Vera.**

*Beispiel:*

| | Sieht gern? | Warum? | Wann? | Sieht nicht gern? | Warum nicht? |
|---|---|---|---|---|---|
| Klara | *Seifenopern* | *super* | *jeden Abend* | *Dokumentarserien* | *nicht interessant* |

**LESEN 4** · NC 4

## Lies Siras Nachricht. Sind die Sätze richtig (R), falsch (F) oder nicht im Text (NiT)?

*Beispiel:* **a** *R*

> Ich liebe Fernsehen – ich sehe jeden Tag fern. Meine Lieblingssendung ist „Die Farm" – das ist eine Realityshow aus Deutschland. Ich sehe auch jeden Nachmittag Seifenopern, und am Abend sehe ich gern Musiksendungen. Aber ich sehe nicht gern Dokumentarserien, weil sie langweilig sind.
>
> Mein Freund Tim ist sehr sportlich. Seine Lieblingssendung ist die „Sportschau". Meine Freundin Aisha sieht am liebsten Castingshows – ihre Lieblingsshow ist „Deutschland sucht den Superstar". Aber ich finde Castingshows blöd. Ich finde Quizsendungen interessant – da kann man viel lernen!
>
> Und du – was ist deine Lieblingssendung?

**? Think**

You know that *meine* means 'my'.

Can you work out what *seine*, *ihre* and *deine* mean in Sira's message?

**a** Ihre Lieblingssendung ist eine Realityshow.
**b** Sie sieht gern Seifenopern aus Deutschland.
**c** Sie findet Dokumentarserien nicht interessant.
**d** Ihr Freund mag keine Sportsendungen.
**e** Ihre Freundin findet Castingshows nicht gut.
**f** Sira mag auch Musik- und Quizsendungen.

**SCHREIBEN 5**

## Finde die passenden Wörter.

*Beispiel:* **a** *Was sind* <u>seine</u> *Lieblingssendungen?*

**a** Was sind seine / ihre Lieblingssendungen? (*his*)
**b** Ist das ihr / dein Computer? (*your*)
**c** Ihre / Deine Lieblingssendung ist „GZSZ". (*her*)
**d** Das ist mein / sein Fernseher. (*my*)
**e** So heißt seine / ihre Schwester. (*his*)

**⚙ Grammatik → p.161**

### Possessive adjectives

The German words for 'my', 'your', 'his' and 'her' have different endings for masculine, feminine, neuter and plural:

| | |
|---|---|
| my | **mein** Freund |
| your | **deine** Freundin |
| his | **sein** Buch |
| her | **ihre** CDs |

**SPRECHEN 6** · NC 4

## Macht eine Klassenumfrage.

*Beispiel:*

| | 1 | 2 |
|---|---|---|
| Was siehst du gern? | Quizsendungen | |
| Warum? | lustig | |
| Wie oft? | jeden Abend | |
| Was siehst du nicht gern? | Nachrichten | |
| Warum nicht? | langweilig | |

**Challenge**

Write a blog about what you like and don't like on TV:

- Answer the five questions from activity 6.
- Describe your favourite programme: say when you watch it and why you like it.

NC 4

**SCHREIBEN 7** · NC 4

## Was sieht dein Freund oder deine Freundin gern/nicht gern? Schreib eine Nachricht wie Sira (Übung 4).

*Beispiel: Meine Freundin sieht gern …*

- Vocabulary: talk about which forms of media you use; compare old and new media
- Grammar: use the present tense and the imperfect tense
- Skills: work out the meaning of new words and recognise 'false friends'

**HÖREN 1**
**NC 4**

🎧 **Hör zu. Welche Medien nutzen sie? Schreib die Tabelle ab und beantworte die Fragen für Aisha, Leo, Sira, David und Ines.**

*Beispiel:*

| | Welche Medien? | Wie? Wo? | Wann? Wie oft? | Warum? |
|---|---|---|---|---|
| Aisha | *ich lese* | *im Internet* | *sehr viel, jeden Tag* | *weil das schnell geht* |

**SPRECHEN 2**

👥 **Macht Dialoge für Aisha, Leo, Sira, David und Ines. A ↔ B.**

*Beispiel:* **A** *Welche Medien nutzt du, Aisha?*
**B** *Ich lese sehr viel im Internet …*

**SPRECHEN 3**
**NC 4**

👥 **Macht eine Klassenumfrage. Schreibt die Resultate auf (wie in Übung 1).**

- Welche Medien nutzt du?
- Wie oft?
- Wann?
- Warum?

**SCHREIBEN 4**
**NC 4**

**Und du? Beantworte die Fragen aus Übung 3. (Schreib 8–10 Sätze.)**

---

**Welche Medien nutzt du?**

Ich höre Radio/Musik auf meinem MP3-Player.

Ich lese am Computer/im Internet.

Ich chatte mit Freunden im Internet.

Ich lade Videoclips aus dem Internet herunter.

**Wann/Wie oft machst du das?**

morgens, mittags, nachmittags, abends

jeden Tag/Abend, jede Woche

oft, manchmal, selten, nie

**Warum machst du das?**

…, weil das schnell geht.

…, weil das Spaß macht.

…, weil es bequem/billig ist.

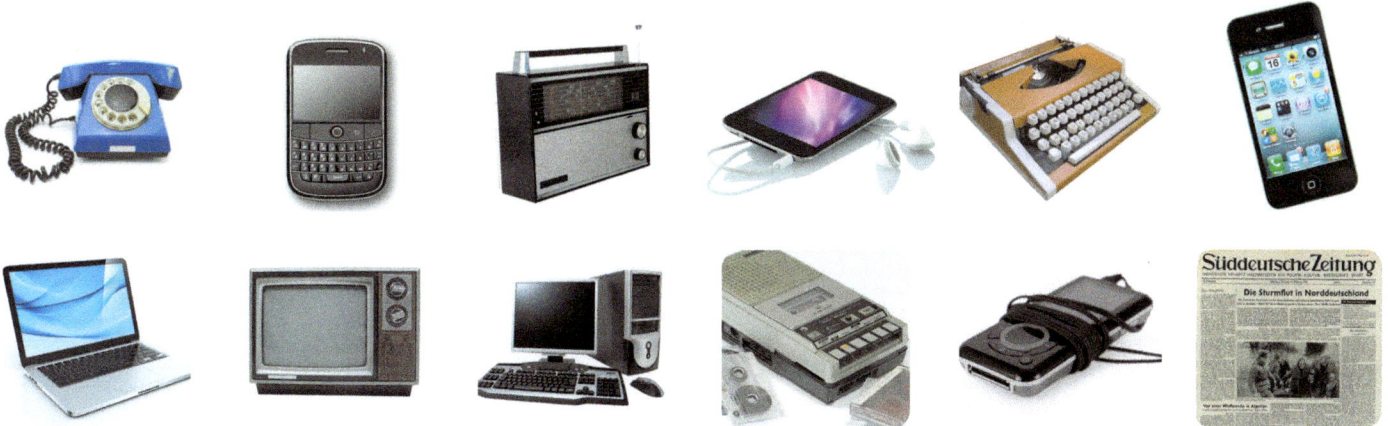

**LESEN 5**

**Lies die Wörter. Was gab es 1972? Und was gibt es heute?**

*Beispiel: 1972: b, … Heute: …*

a  Online-Nachrichten
b  ein Telefon für die ganze Familie
c  Notepads und Laptops
d  das Internet
e  einen Fernseher mit drei Kanälen
f  Computer
g  die Tageszeitung

h  Handys
i  Kassettenrekorder
j  Webseiten
k  Chatten auf Skype
l  Schreibmaschinen
m  MP3- und MP4-Player
n  ein Radio im Wohnzimmer

**HÖREN 6**

🎧 **Ist alles richtig? Hör zu.**

**HÖREN 7**

🎧 **„Neue Medien, alte Medien" – was sagen sie? Hör zu (1–6) und schreib die Antworten auf Deutsch auf.**

*Beispiel:*

|   | alte Medien | Meinung? | neue Medien | Meinung? |
|---|-------------|----------|-------------|----------|
| 1 | *Schreibmaschine* | *langsam* | … | … |

**SCHREIBEN 8**

NC 4–5

**Wie findest du die alten Medien? Wähle zwei Medien aus Übung 5 (1 x positiv und 1 x negativ) und schreib deine Meinung auf.**

*Beispiel: Ein Telefon für die ganze Familie war bestimmt unpraktisch. Aber … war gut!*

**SCHREIBEN 9**

NC 4

**Und wie findest du die neuen Medien? Wähle drei Medien (Übung 5) und schreib deine Meinung auf. (Schreib auch Sätze mit weil!)**

*Beispiel: Online-Nachrichten sind super, weil sie nichts kosten.*

**? Think**

Beware of 'false friends' – German words that look English but have a different meaning!

Look at the words below: what <u>don't</u> they mean in English – and what do you think they <u>do</u> mean?

- das Handy
- der Kanal (*pl.* Kanäle)

Ich finde …

… ist/sind/war/waren …
  (nicht) billig/gut/schlecht.
  bequem/einfach/kompliziert/
  langsam/langweilig/praktisch/
  schnell/teuer/unbequem/
  unpraktisch.
… kostet/kosten viel/nichts.

**Challenge**

Imagine you are a complete technophobe! Describe:

- your opinion of some different forms of old media (using the imperfect tense of *sein*)
- which modern media you don't use, and why not
- what you use instead

NC 5

# 2A.3 Techno ist toll!

- Vocabulary: talk about your favourite music, singers and bands
- Grammar: use *dieser/diese/dieses* and *welcher?/welche?/welches?*
- Skills: explain your opinions

**LESEN 1** **Finde die passende Musik für die Fotos.**

*Beispiel:* **a** Folk

Folk   Electronica   House   Disco   Indie-Rock   Dubstep

**Laura Marling**

**Mark Ronson**

**Skream**

**Bruno Mars**

**Daft Punk**

**f**
**Yeah Yeah Yeahs**

**HÖREN 2** 🎧 **Hör zu und lies die Meinung von Sven, Lola und Paul. Finde a–f im Text.**

| | | |
|---|---|---|
| **a** singer | **b** songs | **c** group |
| **d** style of music | **e** quiet | **f** drummer |

**? Think**

Look at the texts and a–f in activity 3: can you figure out what *diese/dieser* and *welche* mean?

Ich höre am liebsten Hip-Hop und Rap aus Deutschland. Diese Musik ist super, weil sie wie amerikanischer Hip-Hop ist – aber man singt auf Deutsch. Am besten gefällt mir der Rapper Sido – dieser Sänger schreibt tolle Lieder. Welche Musik finde ich nicht gut? Klassische Musik, weil sie altmodisch ist.

**Sven (15)**

Welche Musik höre ich am liebsten? Ich höre am liebsten Lieder und Popmusik aus Amerika – vor allem die Gruppe Black Eyed Peas. Diese Musik gefällt mir gut, weil man gut dazu tanzen kann. Und welche Musik gefällt mir gar nicht? Jazz – dieser Musikstil ist furchtbar, weil es oft keine Sänger gibt!

**Lola (16)**

Welche Musik gefällt mir am besten? Heavy Metal, weil diese Musik schön schnell ist – und gar nicht leise! Ich bin ein Fan von der Band Metallica, weil der Schlagzeuger super ist. Ich mag aber auch Techno, denn dieser Musikstil ist auch ziemlich schnell! Reggae finde ich nicht so gut – diese Musik ist langweilig.

**Paul (14)**

**LESEN 3** **Lies den Text noch einmal. Lies die Sätze a–f. Welche Musik ist das?**

**NC 4** *Beispiel:* **a** Heavy Metal

- **a** Diese Musik ist laut und gar nicht langsam.
- **b** Diese Musik hört man oft in Discos.
- **c** Dieser Musikstil ist nicht interessant.
- **d** Dieser Musikstil kommt aus Amerika – aber mit deutschen Texten.
- **e** Diese Musik ist nicht modern.
- **f** Diese Musik ist oft instrumental.

**SPRECHEN 4** — NC 3

„Welche Musik hörst du am liebsten/nicht gern? Warum?" Macht Dialoge für Sven, Lola und Paul. **A ↔ B.**

*Beispiel:*  **A** *Sven, welche Musik hörst du am liebsten?*
**B** *Ich höre am liebsten Hip-Hop und …*

**SCHREIBEN 5**

**Du bist dran! Schreib Sätze.**

*Beispiel: Ich höre am liebsten …, weil …*

**SCHREIBEN 6**

**Wähle die richtigen Wörter.**

a  Dieses / Diese CD ist super!
b  Dieses / Dieser Karaoke-Spiel macht Spaß.
c  Welche / Welcher Musiksendung kommt aus Deutschland?
d  Welches / Welcher MP3-Player ist billiger?
e  Welche / Welches Lied gefällt dir?

**Challenge**

• Imagine that you are interviewing your favourite band (or singer). Write down your questions and the answers they might give.
• Describe the last concert you saw. Use the perfect tense and the imperfect.

NC 5

---

Welche Musik hörst du am liebsten?
Ich höre am liebsten …

Welcher/Welche/Welches … gefällt dir?
… gefällt mir gut/gar nicht.

weil er/sie … ist.
weil man gut dazu tanzen kann.

altmodisch, furchtbar, langweilig, laut, leise, modern, toll, schnell

---

## Grammatik → p.160

**dieser/diese/dieses (*this/that*)
welcher/welche/welches? (*which?*)**

| | |
|---|---|
| m. | dies**er**/welch**er** Sänger |
| f. | dies**e**/welch**e** Musik |
| n. | dies**es**/welch**es** Lied |
| pl. | dies**e**/welch**e** Filme |

---

## ▶ Die Video-Aufgabe

**VIDEO 7**

**Sieh dir das Video an. Leo und Sira interviewen Oli, den Gitarristen der Band I, Nero. Wähle die passenden Antworten.**

a  Oli hört am liebsten
  1  Rockmusik.
  2  klassische Musik.

b  Er sieht am liebsten
  1  Action- und Abenteuerfilme.
  2  Filme ohne gute Geschichte.

c  Er liest am liebsten
  1  klassische Romane.
  2  Krimis.

d  Er sieht
  1  jeden Tag fern.
  2  nie fern.

e  Er singt am liebsten auf
  1  Deutsch.
  2  Englisch.

f  Die Band hat
  1  letztes Jahr angefangen.
  2  in der Schule angefangen.

**VIDEO 8**

**What do you think? Whose interview was better? Leo's or Sira's?**

- Vocabulary: talk about films; describe the plot of a film
- Grammar: use the perfect tense and the imperfect tense
- Skills: work out the meaning of new words; adapt a text

**LESEN 1** Lies die Texte (1–3). Welcher Film ist das (a–c)?

**a** Sommer

**2** Mein Lieblingsfilm? Das ist _____, eine **Komödie** aus Deutschland. Der Film ist super, weil er **unterhaltsam** ist. Die Dialoge sind total lustig!

**c** Wickie und die starken Männer

**1** Mein Lieblingsfilm ist ein Actionfilm: _____. Die **Schauspieler** und **Schauspielerinnen** sind fast alles Jugendliche – das hat mir sehr gut gefallen. Und die Geschichte ist sehr **spannend**, also sehr interessant.

**b** Spy Kids 4

**3** Mein Lieblingsfilm ist _____. Das ist ein **Liebesfilm**. Dieser Film gefällt mir, weil der Schauspieler Jimi Blue Ochsenknecht so cool ist – und weil die **Geschichte** so schön romantisch ist.

**HÖREN 2** 🎧 Ist alles richtig? Hör zu.

**HÖREN 3** 🎧 Hör zu und lies den Dialog.

| |
|---|
| Welchen Film hast du gesehen? |
| Ich habe „Rio" gesehen. |
| Was für ein Film war das? |
| Das war ein Zeichentrickfilm. |
| Und wie hat dir der Film gefallen? |
| Er hat mir super gefallen, weil er sehr lustig war! |

**? Think**

- How do you work out the meaning of new words? What strategies can you remember? Discuss them with your partner.
- Then look at the **highlighted** words in the texts above. Can you work out their meaning by applying your strategies?

**HÖREN 4** **NC 3** 🎧 Hör zu (1–3). Schreib die Tabelle ab und beantworte die Fragen auf Englisch.

*Beispiel:*

| | Film | Was für ein Film? | Meinung? |
|---|---|---|---|
| 1 | Rock It! | | |
| 2 | Deutschland. Ein Sommermärchen | | |
| 3 | Das Haus Anubis | | |

Welchen Film hast du gesehen?  →  Ich habe … gesehen.

Was für ein Film ist/war das?  →  Das ist/war …

ein Actionfilm/Dokumentarfilm/Fantasyfilm/Liebesfilm/
Science-Fiction-Film/Zeichentrickfilm, eine Komödie, ein Musical

Wie hat dir der Film gefallen?  →  { Dieser Film hat mir … gefallen, weil …
                                    { Dieser Film gefällt mir …, weil …

… er/der Schauspieler/die Schauspielerin/die Geschichte … war/ist.

… die Dialoge/Schauspieler/Schauspielerinnen/Spezialeffekte … waren/sind.

cool, interessant, lustig, romantisch, spannend, super, toll, unterhaltsam

**SPRECHEN 5** **Macht Dialoge wie in Übung 3 und 4. A ↔ B.** NC 3–4

**LESEN 6** **Lies Jans Filmkritik und beantworte die Fragen auf Englisch.**

NC 5

a  What kind of film is it?
b  What are the names of the actors?
c  What is the story about?
d  Why is the film good?
e  What was Jan's favourite film as a child?
f  Why did he like that film?

Mein Lieblingsfilm ist „Tron". Das ist ein Science-Fiction-Film mit Garrett Hedlund, Jeff Bridges und Olivia Wilde.

Der Film spielt in einer digitalen Computerwelt. Er erzählt die Geschichte von Sam Flynn. Sam ist ein Computerspezialist und er sucht seinen Vater – der ist auch ein Computerspezialist und wohnt in einer virtuellen Welt.

Der Film gefällt mir, weil er spannend und unterhaltsam ist. Die Schauspieler und Schauspielerinnen sind super. Die Spezialeffekte gefallen mir auch, weil sie toll sind.

Als Kind war mein Lieblingsfilm „Das fliegende Klassenzimmer". Das war ein lustiger Kinderfilm. Er hat mir gefallen, weil die Dialoge unterhaltsam waren.

**SCHREIBEN 7** **Schreib eine Filmkritik wie in Übung 6.**

NC 5

**? Think**

- Use key phrases from Jan's text, e.g.
  Der Film spielt in … (*The film takes place in …*)
  Er erzählt die Geschichte von … (*It tells the story of …*)
- Change the description and other details.

**Challenge** Write a review of another film you've seen recently for the Radio Zoom Kino-Ecke. Find ten more adjectives in a dictionary and use them to describe:
- the actors
- the story
- the dialogue or special effects

NC 5

# 2A.5 Ich bin eine Leseratte!

- Vocabulary: talk about your reading habits
- Grammar: use the present tense, frequency expressions and *weil*
- Skills: use frequency expressions

**HÖREN 1**

🎧 **Hör zu und finde die passenden Bilder für Sira, David und Aisha.**

*Beispiel: Sira: d 6, …*

a das Jugendbuch
b der Krimi
c die Mädchenzeitschrift
d der Roman
e das Sachbuch
f das Sportmagazin

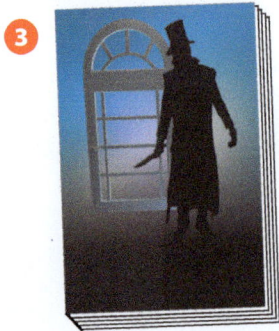

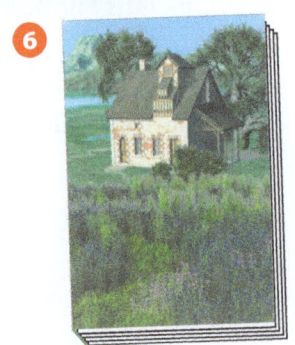

**① DEUTSCHE GESCHICHTE**

②

③

④

⑤

⑥

**HÖREN 2**

**NC 4**

🎧 **Hör noch einmal zu und beantworte die Fragen auf Englisch.**

a How often does Sira read?
b What kind of books does she like to read?
c What does David not like to read? Why not?
d What kind of magazines does he like to read?
e What does Aisha say about reading books?
f What else does she read?

**? Think**

What words and phrases can you use to say how often you read books and magazines? Make a list, then compare it with a partner. Who has the longest list?

**SPRECHEN 3**

**NC 4**

👥 **Macht eine Klassenumfrage. Schreibt die Resultate auf.**

- Welche Bücher liest du gern? Warum?
- Wie oft liest du Bücher?
- Welche Bücher liest du nicht?
- Welche Zeitschriften/Magazine liest du?
- Wie oft liest du Zeitschriften/Magazine?

Ich lese (nicht) gern/am liebsten …

Bücher, Jugendbücher, Sachbücher
Krimis, Romane
Sportmagazine
Mädchenzeitschriften

Mein Lieblingsautor
Meine Lieblingsautorin } ist …

**SCHREIBEN 4**

**NC 4**

**Und du? Beantworte die Fragen aus Übung 3 und schreib einen kurzen Bericht (60 Wörter).**

Write a short report (about 60 words) about your reading habits.

*Beispiel: Ich lese am liebsten Sachbücher, weil …*

Ich heiße Sarah See und ich bin Moderatorin bei Radio Zoom. Radio Zoom ist ein Radiosender speziell für Kinder. Eine Moderatorin oder ein Moderator stellt die verschiedenen Sendungen vor.

Es gibt bei Radio Zoom natürlich verschiedene Programme, so wie im Fernsehen, aber nur zum Hören! Unsere Programme beginnen nach der Schule.
Um vierzehn Uhr dreißig gibt es die Rätselecke. Dort können Kinder ein Quiz machen oder Rätsel lösen und sie können Preise gewinnen. Um fünfzehn Uhr zehn gibt es die Charts-Show. Das ist eine Musiksendung. Und um sechzehn Uhr gibt es jeden Tag ein Hörspiel, also eine Geschichte. Und jeden Tag um sechzehn Uhr fünfundzwanzig gibt es „Radio-Zoom-Magazin". Dort gibt es aktuelle Berichte, Spiele und Interviews.

Es gibt auch Nachrichten bei Radio Zoom: um siebzehn Uhr fünf gibt es „Klaro". Um siebzehn Uhr fünfzehn kommt dann die „Zoom-Reportage". Das ist ein Bericht über ein interessantes Thema für Kinder. Und zum Schluss, um achtzehn Uhr, kommt einmal pro Woche die „Talkshow". Dort diskutieren Kinder und Erwachsene über aktuelle Themen. Das Thema heute ist „Schule in Deutschland".

**LESEN 5**

**NC 4**

**Lies den Radio Zoom-Artikel und füll den Programmplan aus.**

*Beispiel: 14:30 Uhr: Rätselecke*

| ___ Uhr: ▬▬▬ | ___ Uhr: ▬▬▬ |
| ___ Uhr: ▬▬▬ | ___ Uhr: ▬▬▬ |
| ___ Uhr: ▬▬▬ | ___ Uhr: ▬▬▬ |

**LESEN 6**

**NC 4**

**Lies den Artikel noch einmal. Wähle die passenden Antworten.**

*Beispiel:* **a 1**

**a** Was macht Radio Zoom?
  1 Programme für junge Hörer
  2 Kinderfernsehen

**b** Was für eine Arbeit macht eine Moderatorin?
  1 sie hört Sendungen
  2 sie präsentiert Sendungen

**c** Was ist ein Hörspiel?
  1 ein Rätselspiel
  2 eine Geschichte zum Vorlesen

**d** Was gibt es im „Radio-Zoom-Magazin"?
  1 Jugendzeitschriften zum Vorlesen
  2 neue Berichte und Spiele

**e** Was ist die „Zoom-Reportage"?
  1 ein interessanter Bericht
  2 eine Serie

**f** Was macht man in einer Talkshow?
  1 man spricht über aktuelle Themen
  2 man lernt für die Schule

**SCHREIBEN 7**

**NC 4**

**Schreib einen Programmplan (wie in Übung 5) für deinen idealen Radiosender. Beschreib die Sendungen.**

*Beispiel:*

> 14 Uhr: Die Super-Musik-Ecke
>
> Das ist eine Musiksendung für Jugendliche – von Jugendlichen! Die Moderatoren und Moderatorinnen sind alle Jugendliche ...

**Challenge**

You're a big fan of e-books and magazines. Why? Give your opinion in a short article for a website. Use words, phrases and structures from all of Unit 2A.

*Beispiel: Ich lese oft E-Bücher und elektronische Zeitschriften, weil ...*

**NC 4**

Possessive adjectives, demonstrative adjectives, *welcher/welche/welches?*

## Possessive adjectives

The words for 'my', 'your', 'his' and 'her' are called possessive adjectives. They show who or what something belongs to (<u>my</u> book, <u>your</u> sister, <u>his</u> CD).

They come before the noun they describe in place of *der/die/das* or *ein/eine/ein*. Like all adjectives, they have different endings for masculine, feminine, neuter and plural:

|  | masculine | feminine | neuter | plural |
|---|---|---|---|---|
| my | mein | meine | mein | meine |
| your | dein | deine | dein | deine |
| his | sein | seine | sein | seine |
| her | ihr | ihre | ihr | ihre |

**1** Translate the English possessive adjectives into German and fill in the gaps.

*Beispiel:* **a** *seine*

**a** Das ist      Lieblingsband. (*his*)
**b**      Vater ist Sänger. (*her*)
**c**      Lieblingsfilm gefällt mir gut. (*your*)
**d** Wo ist      Computer? (*my*)
**e**      Sendung beginnt um 19 Uhr. (*her*)
**f** Ist das      Lied? (*his*)

**2** Fill in the gaps.

*Beispiel:* **a** *Diese*

**a**      CD ist super! (*feminine*)
**b**      Karaoke-Spiel macht Spaß. (*neuter*)
**c**      Musik kommt aus Deutschland. (*feminine*)
**d**      MP3-Player ist sehr teuer. (*masculine*)
**e**      Gitarre ist sehr alt. (*feminine*)
**f**      Lied ist auf Deutsch. (*neuter*)

**3** Write questions with *Welcher/Welche/Welches …?* for the sentences in activity 2.

*Beispiel:* **a** *Welche CD ist super?*

## Demonstrative adjectives

If you want to say 'this', 'that', 'these' or 'those', use *dieser/diese/dieses/diese* in place of *der/die/das/die*:

masculine: Dies**er** Film ist toll.
feminine: Dies**e** Gruppe gefällt mir.
neuter: Dies**es** Buch ist interessant.
plural: Dies**e** DVDs sind langweilig.

## welcher/welche/welches …?

To say 'which', you use:

masculine: Welch**er** Film gefällt dir?
feminine: Welch**e** Gruppe ist das?
neuter: Welch**es** Buch liest du?
plural: Welch**e** DVDs gefallen dir?

## Reading longer texts

You don't have to know every word in order to understand a longer text. Here are some strategies to help you:

- Before you start reading, look at any clues to figure out what the text is about: photos and illustrations, for example. Also look at the title and introduction.
- Read through the questions and tasks – they will also give you an idea of what the text is about.

- Then quickly read through the text to get the gist of it. Skim over any words you don't understand.
- Do any words look similar to English or another German word you know?
- Try to guess the meaning of unknown words by looking at the words before and after them.

### Hop: Ein Kinospaß für die ganze Familie

Der Super-Zeichentrickfilm zum Osterfest: ein „**rockiger**" **Osterhase** und ein 29-jähriger **Faulenzer** werden – auf Umwegen – Freunde …

E.B. ist ein Osterhase und wohnt auf den weit entfernten Osterinseln, am „Ende der Welt". Er soll – wie sein Vater und Großvater – allen Kindern zu Ostern Schokolade und Süßigkeiten **bringen**. Aber E.B. will lieber Schlagzeuger werden.

Er fährt in die **Filmstadt** Hollywood und sucht dort Arbeit als **Musiker**. In Hollywood trifft er Fred. Fred ist faul und sitzt den ganzen Tag zu Hause auf dem Sofa. E.B. kann bei Fred wohnen, aber das gibt Probleme: E.B. räumt nie auf, putzt nie, wäscht nie ab …

Aber bald sind E.B. und Fred gute Freunde und zusammen suchen sie nun Arbeit. Das ist nicht einfach, aber mit Freds Hilfe bekommt E.B. sogar einen Auftritt bei einer berühmten Castingshow – und **gewinnt**! Jetzt ist er Schlagzeuger bei den „Blind Boys of Alabama".

Aber auch auf den Osterinseln gibt es Probleme: das gemeine **Küken** Carlos will Osterhase Nummer 1 werden! Nur E.B. kann helfen. Seine Osterhasen-Freunde müssen nach Hollywood fahren und E.B. zurück nach Hause bringen …

**4** Work out the meaning of the **bold** words in the text. Which of the strategies above did you use?

**5** Answer these questions in English.
  **a** What kind of film is 'Hop'?
  **b** What does E.B. want to be?
  **c** Why does he go to Hollywood?
  **d** What are the problems when he stays with Fred?
  **e** How does Fred help E.B.?
  **f** What problems are there back at home?

## Pronunciation of *ei* and *ie*

**6** Listen carefully. Do you hear *ei* or *ie*? (1–10)

- Vocabulary: talk about different forms of media
- Grammar: practise the structures of the unit
- Skills: build answers from questions

**SCHREIBEN 1**

**Schreib die Wörter richtig auf.**

What types of TV programme are these? Unscramble the words.

*Beispiel:* **a** *Seifen…*

a OPIESERFEN
b NECHTRICHNA
c SENZIUQNGUD
d KIGNUNESDSUM
e EIRESDOKRATUMEN
f CHENEIZEICKTRISER

**LESEN 2**

**Finde zehn Wörter zum Thema „Musik".**

Find ten words on the topic of music in the wordsearch. Make a list.

*Beispiel: Sänger, …*

| S | Ä | N | G | E | R | X | C | Ö | H |
|---|---|---|---|---|---|---|---|---|---|
| C | H | J | L | T | J | A | Z | Z | E |
| H | S | C | H | E | R | I | G | R | A |
| L | I | E | D | C | O | E | R | E | V |
| A | S | P | C | H | Z | N | U | U | Y |
| G | E | S | H | N | A | Z | P | A | M |
| Z | W | I | E | O | S | T | P | D | E |
| E | B | A | N | D | P | O | E | U | T |
| U | F | S | C | H | I | L | K | J | A |
| G | P | O | P | M | U | S | I | K | L |

**LESEN 3**

**NC 2–3**

**Finde die passenden Antworten für die Fragen.**

Find the correct answers to the questions.

*Beispiel:* **a** *4*

a Was siehst du gern im Fernsehen?
b Welche Musik hörst du gern?
c Welche Medien nutzt du?
d Was liest du im Internet?
e Was ist dein Lieblingsfilm?
f Warum gefällt dir dieser Film?

1 Webseiten.
2 Eine Komödie aus Deutschland.
3 Klassische Musik.
4 Eine Sportsendung.
5 Die Schauspieler sind gut.
6 Das Radio.

**SCHREIBEN 4**

**NC 4**

**Du bist dran! Beantworte die Fragen aus Übung 3.**

Write your own answers to the questions in activity 3.

*Beispiel:* **a** *Ich sehe gern Quizshows und die Nachrichten.*

- Vocabulary: talk about different forms of media
- Grammar: use demonstrative adjectives; use the perfect tense and the imperfect
- Skills: practise reading skills

**SCHREIBEN 1**

**„Dieser/Diese/Dieses … gefällt mir (nicht) gut." Schreib Sätze.**

*Beispiel:* **a** *Diese Zeichentrickserie gefällt mir gut!*

**a** Zeichentrickserie
**b** Zeitschrift
**c** MP3-Player
**d** Quizsendung
**e** Roman
**f** Fernseher

**SCHREIBEN 2**

**„Welche Medien nutzt du?" Schreib Sätze.**

*Beispiel:* **a** *Ich chatte im Internet.*

**SCHREIBEN 3**

**Beantworte die Fragen auf Deutsch für a und b.**

NC 5

*Beispiel:* **a 1** *Ich habe … gesehen.*

1 Welchen Film hast du gesehen?
2 Was für ein Film war das?
3 Wie hat dir der Film gefallen?

1 Welche Fernsehsendung hast du gesehen?
2 Was für eine Sendung war das?
3 Wie hat dir die Sendung gefallen?

**a** Shrek ✓ weil HA! HA!

**b** Die Griechen ✗ weil

**LESEN 4**

**Lies Davids Nachricht und beantworte die Fragen auf Englisch.**

NC 5

a What TV programmes does David like to watch? Why?
b What did he used to watch? Why doesn't he watch this any more?
c What music did he listen to this summer? Why?
d Where does he listen to music?
e What does he say about downloading videos? (2)

Ich sehe sehr gern Seifenopern, weil sie lustig sind. Früher habe ich gern Sportsendungen gesehen, aber jetzt finde ich Sport langweilig.

Ich höre auch gern Musik. Im Sommer war ich auf Jamaika und habe dort am liebsten Reggae gehört, weil diese Musik cool ist. Ich höre Musik meistens am Computer in meinem Zimmer. Ich lade auch Videos herunter, am liebsten Pop-Videos, weil sie unterhaltsam sind.

**HÖREN 1**
**NC 4**

🎧 **Listen to Sira and answer the questions in German. (See pages 52–59.)**

*Beispiel:* **a** *„Germany's Next Topmodel", weil …*

a Was ist ihre Lieblingssendung? Warum?
b Wer ist ihre Lieblingssängerin?
c Warum mag sie Silbermond?
d Welche Medien nutzt sie? Warum?
e Was liest sie im Internet?
f Warum findet sie „Wickie und die starken Männer" gut?

**SPRECHEN 2**
**NC 4**

**Answer these questions for yourself. (See pages 52–53, 56–57.)**

*Beispiel: Ich sehe gern …, weil …*

- Was siehst du gern im Fernsehen? Warum?
- Was ist deine Lieblingssendung?
- Was siehst du nicht gern im Fernsehen? Warum nicht?
- Was ist deine Lieblingsband?
- Welche Musik hörst du gern? Warum?
- Welche Musik hörst du nicht gern? Warum nicht?

**LESEN 3**
**NC 5**

**Read Arne's message and answer the questions in English. (See pages 52–59.)**

*Beispiel:* **a** *He saw a German film for …*

a What kind of film did he see last weekend?
b What was his opinion of the film? Why?
c What other type of media does he use? Why?
d What type of music doesn't he like? Why not?
e What does he like to watch on TV? Why?

Ich habe am Wochenende einen tollen Film gesehen – „Die Wilden Kerle 5". Das war ein deutscher Film für Kinder und Jugendliche. Der Film hat mir sehr gut gefallen, weil er spannend war – und die Schauspieler waren super.

Ich höre auch Radio auf meinem MP3-Player, weil das praktisch ist. Aber ich höre nicht gern klassische Musik, weil sie langweilig ist …

Und im Fernsehen sehe ich gern Musiksendungen, weil ich Gitarre und Schlagzeug spiele.

**SCHREIBEN 4**
**NC 5**

**Write at least ten sentences about yourself. (See pages 54–59.)**

Say:

- what music you like to listen to, and why
- what music you don't like to listen to, and why not
- what you like to read on the internet, and why
- what films you like to watch, and why
- what films you don't like to watch, and why not
- what the last film you saw was like

### Im Fernsehen — On TV

| | |
|---|---|
| eine Castingshow | *a talent show* |
| eine Dokumentarserie | *a documentary* |
| eine Musiksendung | *a music programme* |
| die Nachrichten (*plural*) | *the news* |
| eine Quizsendung | *a quiz show* |
| eine Realityshow | *a reality show* |
| eine Seifenoper | *a soap opera* |
| eine Sportsendung | *a sports programme* |
| eine Zeichentrickserie | *a cartoon* |
| Ich sehe (nicht) gern … | *I (don't) like watching …* |
| Meine Lieblingssendung ist … | *My favourite programme is …* |

### Neue Medien, alte Medien — New media, old media

| | |
|---|---|
| das Chatten auf Skype | *chatting on Skype* |
| der Fernseher | *television set* |
| das Handy, das Telefon | *mobile phone, telephone* |
| der Kassettenrekorder | *cassette recorder* |
| die Schreibmaschine | *typewriter* |
| die Tageszeitung | *daily paper* |
| die Webseite | *web page* |

| | |
|---|---|
| Ich höre Radio auf meinem MP3-Player. | *I listen to the radio on my MP3 player.* |
| Ich sehe Filme auf meinem Computer. | *I watch films on my computer.* |
| Ich lese im Internet. | *I read on the internet.* |
| Ich lade Videoclips aus dem Internet herunter. | *I download video clips from the internet.* |
| Ich chatte mit Freunden im Internet. | *I chat with friends on the internet.* |

| | |
|---|---|
| weil das schnell/langsam geht | *because it's fast/slow* |
| bequem | *convenient* |
| billig, teuer | *cheap, expensive* |
| einfach, kompliziert | *easy, complicated* |
| langweilig | *boring* |
| praktisch, unpraktisch | *practical, impractical* |
| Das kostet nichts/viel. | *It costs nothing/a lot.* |

| | |
|---|---|
| morgens, mittags | *in the mornings, at midday* |
| nachmittags, abends | *in the afternoons/evenings* |
| jeden Tag/Abend, jede Woche | *every day/evening/week* |
| oft, manchmal, selten, nie | *often, sometimes, seldom, never* |

### Techno ist toll! — Techno is great!

| | |
|---|---|
| Welcher/Welche/Welches … gefällt dir (am besten)? | *Which … do you like (best)?* |
| … gefällt mir gut/gar nicht. | *I like … /don't like … at all.* |
| Ich höre am liebsten … | *I prefer listening to …* |

| | |
|---|---|
| die Band, die Gruppe | *band, group* |
| das Lied | *song* |
| der Sänger/die Sängerin | *singer (male/female)* |
| der Schlagzeuger | *drummer* |

### Wie war der Film? — What was the film like?

| | |
|---|---|
| Welchen Film hast du gesehen? | *What film have you seen?* |
| Ich habe … gesehen. | *I saw …* |
| Was für ein Film ist/war das? | *What kind of film is/was it?* |
| ein Actionfilm | *an action film* |
| ein Dokumentarfilm | *a documentary* |
| ein Fantasyfilm | *a fantasy film* |
| eine Komödie | *a comedy* |
| ein Liebesfilm | *a love story* |
| ein Musical | *a musical* |
| ein Science-Fiction-Film | *a science fiction film* |
| ein Zeichentrickfilm | *a cartoon* |

| | |
|---|---|
| Dieser Film gefällt mir (nicht), … | *I (don't) like this film, …* |
| Dieser Film hat mir (nicht) gefallen, … | *I liked/didn't like this film …* |
| weil er lustig ist/war. | *because it is/was funny.* |
| weil die Spezialeffekte toll sind/waren. | *because the special effects are/were great.* |

| | |
|---|---|
| die Dialoge (*plural*) | *dialogue/script* |
| die Geschichte | *story/plot* |
| der Schauspieler/die Schauspielerin | *actor/actress* |
| romantisch | *romantic* |
| spannend | *exciting* |
| unterhaltsam | *entertaining* |

### ◉ I can …

- ◉ talk about TV programmes
- ◉ talk about old and new forms of media
- ◉ talk about my favourite music, singers and bands
- ◉ talk about films and describe the plot of a film
- ◉ talk about my reading habits
- ◉ use possessive adjectives
- ◉ use *dieser/diese/dieses* and *welcher?/welche?/welches?*
- ◉ use the perfect tense and the imperfect
- ◉ use strategies to help me understand longer texts
- ◉ pronounce the *ei* and *ie* sounds

- Vocabulary: talk about your favourite hobby
- Grammar: use the present tense of regular and irregular verbs
- Skills: use knowledge of language patterns

**LESEN 1** **Finde die passenden Bilder (1–6) für die Sätze (a–f) .**

*Beispiel:* **a 6**

a Ich sammle Karten.
b Ich fahre Schlittschuh.
c Ich singe in einem Chor.
d Ich fotografiere.
e Ich spiele Theater.
f Ich mache Leichtathletik.

**HÖREN 2** 🎧 **Ist alles richtig? Hör zu.**

**SPRECHEN 3** 👥 **„Was ist dein Hobby?" Macht Dialoge. A ↔ B.**

*Beispiel:* **A** *Was ist dein Hobby? Bild 1!*
**B** *Ich singe in einem Chor.*

**LESEN 4** 👥 **Wie heißen diese Hobbys auf Englisch?**
What strategies can you use to work these out?
Discuss with your partner.

| Rollschuh  Saxofon  Rennrad  Tischtennis  Golf  Wasserski |
|---|

**SCHREIBEN 5** **„Ich spiele …" oder „Ich fahre …"? Schreib Sätze für die Hobbys in Übung 4.**

**LESEN 6** **Noch mehr Hobbys! Finde die passenden Wörter (1–7) für a–g.**

*Beispiel:* **a 2**

a Ich höre
b Ich surfe
c Ich sehe
d Ich lese
e Ich besuche
f Ich tanze
g Ich mache

1 Freunde.
2 Musik.
3 Bücher.
4 Sport.
5 fern.
6 im Internet.
7 in der Disco.

**? Think**

- In German, you often use the verbs *spielen* and *fahren* to talk about hobbies:
  Ich spiele Theater.
  *I'm in a drama group.*
  Ich fahre Schlittschuh.
  *I go ice-skating.*

- You know all the hobbies below – but do they use *spielen* or *fahren*? Test your partner – who gets the most answers right?
  Tennis    Skateboard
  Fußball    Gitarre    Ski
  Computerspiele
  Schlagzeug    Rad

**HÖREN 7** NC 4

🎧 **Schreib die Tabelle ab. Hör zu und mach Notizen auf Deutsch für Katja, Arne, Mila und Sven.**

*Beispiel:*

|       | Lieblingshobby? | Gern?            | Nicht gern? | Warum nicht?     |
|-------|-----------------|------------------|-------------|------------------|
| Katja | *Lesen*         | *Freunde besuchen* | *Singen*  | *nicht musikalisch* |

**SPRECHEN 8** NC 4

**Macht eine Klassenumfrage und schreibt die Resultate auf.**

*Beispiel: Lieblingshobby? 12 = Musik hören; 10 = …*

- Was ist dein Lieblingshobby?
- Was machst du gern?
- Was machst du nicht gern?
- Warum nicht?

**? Think**

- What are the other forms (*du, er/sie/es, wir, ihr, sie/Sie*) of regular verbs? What endings do you add? (*ich mache, du mach_…*)
- *Lesen, sehen* and *fahren* are irregular verbs. What changes do you make for their *du* and *er/sie/es* forms?

(See pages 162–163.)

Was ist dein Lieblingshobby?
Was machst du gern/nicht gern?

Mein Lieblingshobby ist …
Ich sammle (am liebsten) Karten.
Ich fotografiere (gern).
Ich singe in einem Chor.
Ich mache (nicht) gern … Sport/Leichtathletik.
Ich spiele …
Computerspiele/Fußball/Gitarre/Golf/Saxofon/Schach/Schlagzeug/Tennis/Tischtennis.
Ich fahre …
Rad/Rennrad/Rollschuh/Schlittschuh/Skateboard/Ski/Wasserski.

**LESEN 9**

**Lies Susis Text und schreib die richtigen Verbformen auf.**

*Beispiel: spielt, …*

Meine Familie ist sehr musikalisch! Ich spiele Geige und mein Bruder _____ Gitarre. Meine Schwester s_____ in einem Chor. Abends h_____ wir oft Musik im Wohnzimmer.

Ich bin auch sportlich: ich mache Leichtathletik. Aber mein Bruder _____ nicht gern Sport. Das ist zu anstrengend, findet er.

Mein Lieblingshobby? Ich sehe am liebsten fern und ich fahre gern Rad. Und ich lese gern, am liebsten Jugendbücher.

Und du? _____ du auch gern fern und _____ du auch gern Rad? Und _____ du auch gern Bücher?

Susi

**Challenge**

Talk to the class in German for at least 30 seconds about your hobbies!
- What is your favourite hobby?
- What else do you like doing? Why?
- What don't you like? Why?

NC 4

**SCHREIBEN 10** NC 4

**Schreib einen Text wie Susi (Übung 9) – über dich, deine Familie und Freunde.**

- Vocabulary: talk about why you like your hobby
- Grammar: use adjective endings correctly
- Skills: use linking words

**HÖREN 1**

**NC 5**

🎧 **Hör zu und lies Daniels Text. Finde die richtige Reihenfolge für die Bilder.**

*Beispiel:* **f,** …

> ungewöhnlich
> *unusual*

### Daniel (16): „Mein ungewöhnliches Hobby"

Mein **großes** Hobby sind Computer, und vor allem Computerspiele. Ich sitze jeden Tag vor dem Computer!

Mein Hobby ist jetzt sogar ein **toller** „Job" – ich bin Spieletester. Ich teste **neue** Computer- und Videospiele!

Ich habe eine Anzeige in einem **deutschen** Computermagazin gesehen und habe eine **kurze** E-Mail geschickt. Danach habe ich einen **schweren** Online-Test gemacht und dann habe ich den Job bekommen!

Jede Woche bekomme ich zwei bis drei **neue** Spiele. Ich spiele sie und danach schreibe ich einen **langen** Bericht über jedes Spiel: Wie funktioniert es? Was sind die Spielregeln? War es ein **langweiliges** oder ein **interessantes** Spiel? Normalerweise finde ich die Spiele super!

**LESEN 2**

**NC 5**

**Lies Daniels Text noch einmal. Sind die Sätze a–f richtig (R), falsch (F) oder nicht im Text (NiT)?**

a Daniel sieht den ganzen Tag fern.
b Er hat eine Anzeige in einer Zeitschrift gelesen.
c Er hat die Zeitschrift im Supermarkt gekauft.
d Er hat einen Telefon-Test gemacht.
e Jetzt testet er Video- und Computerspiele.
f Er muss einen Report über die Spiele schreiben.

**? Think**

Look at the **adjectives** in Daniel's text. What do you notice about their position and their endings?

**SCHREIBEN 3**

**Füll die Lücken aus.**

*Beispiel:* **a** *interessant**es***

a Ich habe ein interessant____ Hobby.
b Das Quizspiel ist ein toll____ Spiel!
c Tom schreibt eine lang____ E-Mail.
d Ich habe einen neu____ Job.
e Das Spiel hat schwer____ Regeln.
f Er hat einen billig____ Computer.

### Grammatik → p.160

**Adjective endings**

| Das ist/sind … | Ich teste … |
|---|---|
| ein neu**er** Computer | einen neu**en** Computer |
| eine neu**e** Spielregel | eine neu**e** Spielregel |
| ein neu**es** Spiel | ein neu**es** Spiel |
| neu**e** Spiele | neu**e** Spiele |

**HÖREN 4**

NC 4

🎧 **Hör zu und lies Annas Text.**

Mein Hobby ist Musik. Ich bin total happy, wenn ich Musik mache!
Als Kind habe ich Geige gespielt, aber jetzt singe ich in einer Band
und ich spiele Schlagzeug. Ich schreibe auch Lieder selber, oder
manchmal schreibt die ganze Band zusammen ein Lied.

Das ist ein tolles Hobby, weil es Spaß macht. Die Band ist sehr wichtig
für mich, aber ich habe leider keine Zeit für andere Hobbys mehr, denn
wir üben jeden Tag. Das finde ich nicht so gut.

*Anna*

Anna

**? Think**

- Search Anna's text for sentences that use *weil* and *wenn*. Compare them with sentences that use *aber*, *denn*, *und* and *oder*. How is the word order different?
- Why do you think it's useful to use linking words?

**LESEN 5**

NC 5

**Lies noch einmal. Beantworte die Fragen auf Englisch.**

a   What did Anna play as a child?
b   What does she do and play now? (2)
c   What does she say about the songs? (2)
d   What is so great about her hobby?
e   What is the downside of it?

| Mein Hobby ist Musik/Sport. Mein Hobby sind Computerspiele. Ich mache/spiele/fahre … und/oder ich … | |
|---|---|
| Das ist/interessant/super, … | weil ich musikalisch/sportlich/… bin. |
| Das ist ein tolles Hobby, … | denn es ist interessant/billig/… |
| Das Hobby macht Spaß, … | aber es ist teuer. |
| | aber ich habe keine Zeit für andere Hobbys. |

**SPRECHEN 6**

NC 4

👥 **A beschreibt Hobby 1 (auf Deutsch!). B beschreibt Hobby 2.**

*Beispiel:*   **B**   *Was ist dein Hobby?*
              **A**   *Mein Hobby ist …*

My hobby is **1** sport **2** music.
I **1** go cycling **2** play guitar.
It's **1** fun **2** great because (*weil*) I'm very
  **1** sporty **2** musical.
**1** It's a great hobby because (*denn*) it's cheap.
**2** But I don't have time for other hobbies.

**Challenge**

👥 How long a sentence can you build about hobbies? Play this game!

**A** begins a sentence, but finishes with a linking word.

**B** continues the sentence and finishes with another linking word.

Carry on for as long as you can!

*Beispiel:*

**A**   *Ich spiele gern Fußball, aber …*

**B**   *… aber ich schwimme nicht gern, weil …*

NC 4

**SCHREIBEN 7**

NC 4

**Du bist dran! Beschreib dein Hobby wie in Übung 6.**

Use as many linking words and opinions as you can.

- Vocabulary: talk about what hobbies you do in different kinds of weather
- Grammar: use the correct word order
- Skills: build longer sentences

**HÖREN 1** 🎧 **Hör zu (1–5) und finde die passenden Bilder.**

*Beispiel:* **1 e**

**HÖREN 2** 🎧 **Hör noch einmal zu (1–5). Wie ist das Wetter? Schreib die passenden Buchstaben auf (a–j).**

*Beispiel:* **1 b, d**

**Wie ist das Wetter?**

a Es ist sonnig.
b Es ist heiß. **32°**
c Es ist warm. **22°**
d Es ist windig.
e Es ist kalt.

f Es ist neblig.
g Es schneit.
h Es friert.
i Es regnet.
j Es gewittert.

**? Think**

- Can you remember how to say 'in spring', 'in summer', etc? Fill in the gaps:
  i_ Frü_ _ _ _g
  i_ S_ _ _ _r
  i_ He_ _ _t
  i_ Wi_ _ _r
- You know how to say the weather in the present tense, for example *Es **ist** sonnig*. So how would you say 'It **was** sunny'?

**SPRECHEN 3** 👥 **„Wie ist das Wetter?" Macht Dialoge. A ↔ B.**

*Beispiel:* **A** *Bild d! Wie ist das Wetter?* **B** *Es ist windig!*

**SCHREIBEN 4** **Wie ist das Wetter in deiner Gegend – im Frühling, Sommer, Herbst und Winter?**

**NC 3–4** Write a weather report, with three sentences per season. Use lots of linking words!

*Beispiel:* *Es schneit im Winter und es friert. Aber es …*

**LESEN 5**

NC 4

**Lies die Texte und finde die passenden Wörter.**

Ich fahre im Herbst Motocross, wenn es nicht heiß ist, aber im Winter fahre ich Ski, wenn es ▭ und ▭.

Im Sommer mache ich Cheerleading, wenn es nicht ▭. Im ▭ mache ich nicht Cheerleading, sondern ich spiele Theater.

Ich mache im ▭ Streetdance in der Stadt, wenn es sonnig und ▭ ist. Aber im Winter mache ich nicht Streetdance, sondern ich tanze im Tanzstudio.

**? Think**

Can you work out the meaning of *sondern* in the texts?

| Winter | friert | regnet | Sommer | warm | schneit |

**Grammatik → p.167**

**Word order**

**Ich fahre** im Winter Ski.
Im Winter **fahre ich** Ski.

**Ich spiele** Badminton, wenn es warm ist.
Wenn es warm ist, **spiele ich** Badminton.

**HÖREN 6** 🎧 **Ist alles richtig? Hör zu.**

**SPRECHEN 7**

NC 4

👥 **Was machst du wann? Was machst du nicht? Macht Dialoge mit den Informationen a–d. A ↔ B.**

Beispiel: *A Was machst du im Winter?*
*B Im Winter …, wenn …*

a Winter ▭ , wenn ▭

b Sommer ▭ X , sondern ▭

c Herbst ▭ , wenn ▭

d Frühling ▭ X , sondern ▭

**SCHREIBEN 8**

NC 4

**Du bist dran! Was machst du (oder nicht) im Frühling, Sommer, Herbst und Winter?**

• Write eight sentences.
• Use as many linking words as you can.

**Challenge**

Expand your answer for activity 8! For example, say why you do/don't do these activities. Then describe yesterday's weather and say what you did.

*Beispiel: Im Winter fahre ich Ski, wenn es schneit, weil es Spaß macht … Es war gestern sonnig und …*

NC 5

- Vocabulary: talk about what you will do next weekend
- Grammar: use the future tense
- Skills: identify grammar patterns

**HÖREN 1**

🎧 **Hör zu und mach das Freizeit-Quiz. Welche Sätze wählst du? Schreib die Symbole auf.**

### FREIZEIT-QUIZ

**Was wirst du nächstes Wochenende machen?**

- \* Ich werde spät aufstehen.
- # Ich werde Musik auf meinem MP3-Player hören.
- + Ich werde Fußball spielen.
- # Ich werde mit meinem Chor ein Musical singen.
- \* Ich werde zu Hause ein Buch lesen.
- + Ich werde im Park Inliner fahren.
- \* Ich werde fernsehen – das ganze Wochenende lang!
- # Ich werde auf einer Party Gitarre spielen.
- + Ich werde im Hallenbad schwimmen.

**? Think**

Look at the quiz: all the sentences begin with *Ich werde*. Later, in the video, you will hear:

- Du <u>wirst</u> es mögen.
- Nein, ich <u>werde</u> es nicht mögen.
- Ich <u>werde</u> bei meinen Bananenaufklebern bleiben.

What tense uses *werden*?

**Was hast du am meisten?**

- \* Du bist ziemlich faul und nicht sehr aktiv …
- # Du bist musikalisch – Musik ist dein Leben!
- + Du bist fit und sehr aktiv – bravo!

**SPRECHEN 2**

👥 **Macht Dialoge: „Was wirst du nächstes Wochenende machen?" Benutzt die Informationen a–f.**

*Beispiel:* **A** *Was wirst du nächstes Wochenende machen?*
**B** *Ich werde Tennis spielen.*

a  b  c  d  e  f

**SCHREIBEN 3**

**NC 4**

**Du bist dran! Was wirst du nächstes Wochenende machen? Schreib neun Sätze wie im Freizeit-Quiz.**

*Beispiel: Ich werde in die Stadt fahren ….*

**⚙ Grammatik → p.166**

**Talking about the future**

Remember that you use the verb *werden* to talk about the future. *Werden* sends the main verb to the end of the sentence in its infinitive form:

Ich gehe ins Kino. → Ich **werde** ins Kino gehen.

Sira spielt Tennis. → Sira **wird** Tennis spielen.

Wir fahren Ski. → Wir **werden** Ski fahren.

▶ *Die Video-Aufgabe*

**VIDEO 4**

**Sieh dir das Video an. Finde die passenden Sätze (a–e) für die Bilder (1–5).**

a   Die Handgelenke kreisen!
b   Jetzt springen!
c   Auf alle Viere und weiterlaufen!
d   Jetzt balancieren!
e   Hier landen und rollen!

**VIDEO 5**

**Lies die Sätze. Sind sie richtig (R), falsch (F) oder nicht im Video (NiV)?**

*Beispiel:* **a** F

a   Siras Hobby ist Nordic Walking.
b   Für Parkour braucht man sportliche Kleidung.
c   Leo und Sira fahren mit dem Bus zum Parkour-Training.
d   Um 13 Uhr 15 beginnt das Parkour-Training.
e   Parkour-Sportler klettern über Mauern und Häuser.
f   Sie fliegen auch mit dem Flugzeug.
g   Leo macht einmal pro Monat Parkour in Zürich.
h   Leo mag Parkour, weil es spannend ist.

Ich werde bei meinen Bananenaufklebern bleiben. Oder was denkt ihr? Welches ist das coolere Hobby?

**VIDEO 6**

**What do you think? Which is the best hobby?**

**Challenge**

You're a journalist for a teenage magazine and you have found the diary of a famous person (for example, a pop star, TV star, sports personality, …). Write an article about his/her activities for next weekend!

*Beispiel: … wird am Freitagabend ein Konzert machen. Sie wird am Samstagmorgen …*

NC 5

- Vocabulary: learn about other unusual hobbies
- Grammar: use different tenses and linking words
- Skills: practise reading skills

**LESEN 1**

**Lies die Texte und finde die passenden Bilder.**

**1**

Alex James ist der Bassist in der englischen Britpop-Band „Blur". Vor zwölf Jahren hat er sich ein Bauernhaus auf dem Land gekauft und hat seitdem ein neues Hobby: er produziert Käse! Er hat viele Kühe auf dem Bauernhof und das heißt: er hat sehr viel Milch … und aus Milch macht man Käse!

Alex produziert jetzt sogar Käse für Prince Charles. Der Prinz ist ein großer Fan von Alex' Käse.

**2**

David Beckham ist ein englischer Fußballstar. Doch was macht er in seiner Freizeit?

Sein ungewöhnliches Hobby ist Lego. Er möchte den ganzen Tag mit seinen Legosteinen spielen! Er hat jetzt sogar ein Set mit 6 000 Steinen gekauft und er will das indische Tadsch Mahal bauen.

Und dürfen seine vier Kinder auch mit Papas Legosteinen spielen? Manchmal – wenn er keine Zeit hat …

**3**

Gisele Bündchen kommt aus Brasilien und fliegt oft mit dem Flugzeug, denn sie ist ein erfolgreiches Model. Doch jetzt will sie selbst fliegen. Das ist ihr neues Hobby: sie will Pilotin werden!

Sie hat schon viele Flugstunden gemacht und ist eine sehr gute Schülerin auf der privaten Flugschule Shoreline Aviation in Los Angeles.

**4**

Der Schauspieler Brad Pitt mag Kinder und kleine Tiere. Für 100 000 Dollar hat er deshalb ein großes „Haus" für seine vielen Wüstenrennmäuse (diese Mäuse sind sehr schnell) gekauft. Sie können dort spielen, klettern und laufen, den ganzen Tag!

Er hat das Haus zusammen mit seinen Kindern gebaut. Sie finden sein Hobby toll!

**5**

Kelley Deal spielt in der amerikanischen Indie-Band „The Breeders" Gitarre. Sie ist modern und trendy, aber sie hat ein ziemlich altmodisches Hobby: am liebsten strickt sie in ihrer Freizeit! Vor Konzerten und auf Tournee hat man viel freie Zeit und das ist oft langweilig. Stricken kann man überall und es macht Spaß!

Sie strickt am liebsten Pullover, Schals und Taschen. Ihre Taschen heißen „Bags That Rock".

**6**

Mladen Petrić ist professioneller Fußballer beim deutschen HSV, aber in seiner Freizeit zaubert er Hasen und Blumen. Die Magie ist sein Hobby! Er hat einen Kurs bei einem richtigen Magier gemacht und er zaubert für seine Freunde und Familie.

Und was zaubert er alles? Am liebsten macht er Kartentricks, weil das spannend ist!

**LESEN 2**

**Finde a–j in Übung 1. Wie heißt das auf Englisch? Finde die Paare.**

*Beispiel:* **a 4**

a Kuh
b produzieren
c indisch
d bauen
e erfolgreich
f Pilotin
g stricken
h Schal
i zaubern
j Magie

| | | | |
|---|---|---|---|
| **1** to knit | | **6** to produce | |
| **2** magic | | **7** to do magic tricks | |
| **3** to build | | **8** Indian | |
| **4** cow | | **9** female pilot | |
| **5** scarf | | **10** successful | |

**LESEN 3** · NC 5

**Lies die Texte (Übung 1) noch einmal. Sind a–h richtig (R), falsch (F) oder nicht im Text (NiT)?**

a Alex James wohnt auf dem Land und macht Käse.
b Er isst am liebsten Käse.
c David Beckhams Hobby ist nichts für Kinder.
d Gisele Bündchen fliegt am liebsten nach Brasilien.
e Brad Pitts Hobby sind kleine Tiere.
f Er hat ein Haus für seine Kinder gebaut.
g Kelley Deal macht Pullover, Schals und Taschen.
h Mladen Petrićs Hobby ist Kartensammeln.

**HÖREN 4** · NC 5

**Hör zu. Was ist Katjas Hobby? Wähle die passenden Antworten.**

*Beispiel:* **a 2**

a Die „fünfte" Jahreszeit in Köln ist
  1 Frühling.
  2 Karneval.

b Katja geht jede Woche
  1 in den Karnevalsverein.
  2 ins Jugendzentrum.

c Die Funkenmariechen
  1 tanzen.
  2 spielen Fußball.

d Sie arbeiten auch
  1 an den Faschingswagen.
  2 an den Kostümen und Figuren.

e Am Rosenmontag gibt es
  1 einen Faschingsumzug.
  2 schlechtes Wetter.

f Katja mag ihren Verein, weil
  1 einige Jugendliche nett sind.
  2 sie dort viel Spaß hat.

Katja

**SPRECHEN 5** · NC 4

**Beantwortet die Fragen (a–f) für Katja. A ↔ B.**

*Beispiel:* **A** *Was ist dein Lieblingshobby?*
**B** *Mein Lieblingshobby ist Karneval.*

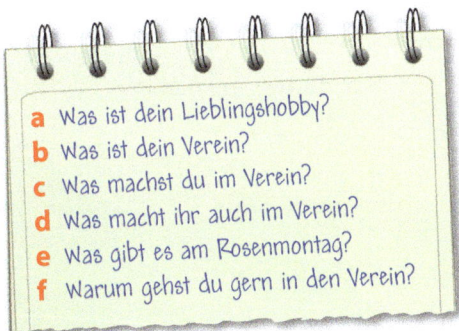

a Was ist dein Lieblingshobby?
b Was ist dein Verein?
c Was machst du im Verein?
d Was macht ihr auch im Verein?
e Was gibt es am Rosenmontag?
f Warum gehst du gern in den Verein?

**Challenge**

Professional footballer Andreas Görlitz plays guitar in the rock band Room77. Do you know of any stars with unusual hobbies? Choose someone and write a short magazine article about their hobby.

Try to include the past, present and future tenses and as many linking words as you can. Write about 80–100 words

NC 5–6

# 2B.6 Sprachlabor

## Adjective endings, the future tense

### Adjective endings

When an adjective is placed in front of a noun, it adds an extra ending. This ending depends on the gender of the noun (masculine, feminine, neuter), the article (der/die/das or ein/eine/ein) and the case:

| | Nominative case (subject)<br>Das ist/sind … | Accusative case (object)<br>Ich kaufe … |
|---|---|---|
| m. | ein toller Fußball<br>der tolle Fußball | einen tollen Fußball<br>den tollen Fußball |
| f. | eine tolle CD<br>die tolle CD | eine tolle CD<br>die tolle CD |
| n. | ein tolles Buch<br>das tolle Buch | ein tolles Buch<br>das tolle Buch |
| pl. | tolle Schuhe<br>die tollen Schuhe | tolle Schuhe<br>die tollen Schuhe |

**1 Write sentences with *Das ist/sind …***

*Beispiel:* **a** *Das ist ein moderner MP4-Player.*

**a** ein MP4-Player – modern
**b** ein Computerspiel – interessant
**c** eine DVD – langweilig
**d** eine Konzertkarte – billig
**e** Sammelkarten – neu
**f** eine CD – deutsch
**g** die Zeitschrift – interessant
**h** das Handy – neu
**i** der Computer – modern
**j** die DVDs – billig
**k** die Schreibmaschine – altmodisch
**l** der Krimi – spannend

**2 Now rewrite the sentences from activity 1 with *Ich kaufe …***

*Beispiel:* **a** *Ich kaufe einen modernen MP4-Player.*

**3 Fill in the correct forms of *werden*.**

*Beispiel:* **a** *werden*

**a** Jan und Ina _____ eine Party machen.
**b** _____ ihr auch ins Kino gehen?
**c** Wir _____ im Winter Ski fahren.
**d** Ich _____ in die Stadt fahren.
**e** Was _____ du am Sonntag machen?
**f** Lisa _____ Karaoke singen.

### Talking about the future

You use the verb *werden* to talk about the future. *Werden* sends the main verb to the end of the sentence in its infinitive form:

Ich spiele Tennis. → Ich **werde** Tennis spielen.

Here are the forms of *werden*:

| ich werde | I will | wir werden | we will |
|---|---|---|---|
| du wirst | you will | ihr werdet | you (pl.) will |
| er/sie/es wird | he/she/it will | sie/Sie werden | they/you will |

**4** Write new sentences in the future tense.

*Beispiel:* **a** *Ich werde im Park Fahrrad fahren.*

**a** Ich fahre im Park Fahrrad.
**b** Wir machen ein Picknick.
**c** Du schreibst eine E-Mail.
**d** Jana hört die neue CD.
**e** Ich spiele Tischtennis.
**f** Wir gehen ins Kino.

## Using linking words

Linking words (also called connectives) are small words that link sentences together. They are useful for making longer and more complex sentences in speaking or writing. Remember that there are two kinds:

- und, aber, oder, denn, sondern

  These words don't change the word order of the sentence they introduce:

  Ich spiele Tennis und ich fahre Rad. *I play tennis and I ride my bike.*
  Tennis macht Spaß, aber es ist teuer. *Tennis is fun but it is expensive.*

- weil, wenn

  These words send the verb to the end of the sentence they introduce:

  Das macht Spaß, weil es spannend ist. *It's fun because it's interesting.*
  Ich jogge, wenn es warm ist. *I jog when it's warm.*

**5** Join each pair of sentences with a different linking word.

*Beispiel:* **a** *Ich spiele Gitarre und ich singe.*

**a** Ich spiele Gitarre. Ich singe.
**b** Ich mag Tennis. Ich finde Fußball langweilig.
**c** Ich mag Sport. Ich bin sportlich.
**d** Im Winter fahre ich nicht Fahrrad. Ich fahre Ski.
**e** Ich höre Musik. Ich mache Hausaufgaben.
**f** Ich trinke morgens Kaffee. Ich trinke Orangensaft.

**6** Describe what you are doing this weekend using all the linking words from this section.

## Pronunciation of *v* and *w*

**7** Listen carefully (1–12). Which sound do you hear: *v* or *w*?

*Beispiel:* **1** *w*

The *v* and *w* sounds are different in German and English:
- The German *v* is pronounced like an English *f*.
- And the German *w* is pronounced like an English *v*.

**LESEN 1**

**Finde acht Hobbys und schreib sie auf.**

Find and write down the eight hobbies in the word snake.

*Beispiel: Musik, …*

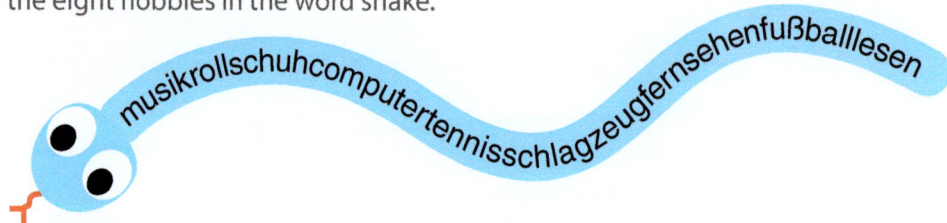

musikrollschuhcomputertennisschlagzeugfernsehenfußballlesen

**LESEN 2**

**Finde die Paare (a–f und 1–6).**

Match up the sentence halves.

*Beispiel:* **a 4**

| | | | |
|---|---|---|---|
| **a** | Ich spiele | **1** | in der Disco. |
| **b** | Ich mache | **2** | in einem Chor. |
| **c** | Ich singe | **3** | Schlittschuh. |
| **d** | Ich sammle | **4** | Gitarre. |
| **e** | Ich fahre | **5** | Leichathletik. |
| **f** | Ich tanze | **6** | Fußballkarten. |

**SCHREIBEN 3**

**NC 3**

**Schreib die Sätze richtig auf.**

Unscramble the sentences and write them out using the correct word order.

*Beispiel:* **a** *Ich fahre Inliner, wenn es nicht zu kalt ist.*

| | | | |
|---|---|---|---|
| **a** | Inliner / ich / fahre / , | wenn | zu kalt / es / ist / nicht / . |
| **b** | spiele / ich / Tennis / gern / , | aber | nicht / ich / gern / Rad / fahre / . |
| **c** | ist / ein / Hobby / tolles / das / , | weil | ist / interessant / es / . |
| **d** | Musik / höre / ich / , | wenn | schneit / es / . |
| **e** | spiele / ich / Computerspiele | oder | im / surfe / Internet / ich / . |
| **f** | mein / das / Lieblingshobby / ist / , | weil | macht / es / Spaß / . |

**SCHREIBEN 4**

**NC 2**

**Schreib Sätze für die Bilder.**

Write a sentence to describe the weather in each picture.

*Beispiel:* **a** *Es regnet.*

- Vocabulary: talk about hobbies and the weather
- Grammar: use correct word order with linking words; use the future tense
- Skills: build longer sentences

**SCHREIBEN 1**

**Schreib Sätze für die Bilder.**

*Beispiel:* **a** *Ich singe in einem Chor.*

**a**  **b**  **c**  **d**  **e**

**SCHREIBEN 2**

NC 3

**Schreib Sätze im Futur für Übung 1.**

*Beispiel:* **a** *Ich werde in einem Chor singen.*

**SCHREIBEN 3**

**Du bist dran! Beschreib deine Hobbys (a–f).**

*Beispiel:* **a** *Ich spiele Tennis oder Basketball, wenn es sonnig und warm ist.*

**a** Ich spiele _____, wenn _____.
**b** Ich _____ gern _____, aber _____.
**c** _____ ist ein tolles Hobby, weil _____.

**d** Ich spiele gern _____ oder _____.
**e** _____ ist mein Lieblingshobby, weil _____.
**f** Im Winter fahre ich nicht _____, sondern _____.

**LESEN 4**

NC 5

**Lies Rebekkas E-Mail und beantworte die Fragen auf Englisch.**

**a** What does she say about her favourite hobby? (2)
**b** What does she do in the summer? When?
**c** What doesn't she like to do? Why not?
**d** What does she say about her friends' hobby? (2)
**e** What does she say about her third hobby? (3)
**f** What will she do at the weekend?

Mein Lieblingshobby ist ein ungewöhnliches Hobby für Mädchen: Fußball! Ich mag Fußball, weil ich sehr sportlich bin. Im Sommer mache ich auch Leichtathletik, wenn es nicht kalt ist und es nicht regnet. Aber ich singe nicht gern, weil ich leider nicht musikalisch bin!

Meine Freundinnen sammeln alle Karten, aber ich nicht, weil sie zu teuer sind. Fotografieren ist auch mein Hobby. Im Sommer, wenn die Sonne scheint, fotografiere ich meine Freunde im Park und Tiere im Wald. Und im Winter, wenn es kalt ist und es schneit, mache ich Fotos im Schnee.

Am Wochenende werde ich Computerspiele spielen und ich werde Schlittschuh fahren.

Rebekka

**HÖREN 1**

NC 5

🎧 **Listen and answer the questions in English about Verena's hobbies. (See pages 68–75.)**

*Beispiel:* **a** *dancing, because …*

**a** What is Verena's favourite hobby? Why?
**b** What does she do in summer? In what weather?
**c** Where does she do that?
**d** What does Verena say about bad weather in summer?
**e** What does she do in winter? Where?
**f** What is she going to do in the holidays?

Verena

**LESEN 2**

NC 5

**Read Jan's message and answer the questions in English. (See pages 68–75.)**

*Beispiel:* **a** *He plays computer games every day when …*

**a** What does he say about his first hobby? (3)
**b** What does he do in the summer? (3)
**c** What does he do when it's cold?
**d** What does he say about music? (3)
**e** Where will he go next year?
**f** What hobby doesn't he like – and why not?

> Ich habe viele Hobbys! Ich spiele jeden Tag Computerspiele, wenn es regnet oder kalt ist. Im Sommer, wenn es warm und sonnig ist, mache ich Sport: ich spiele Tennis oder ich fahre Skateboard. Im Winter mache ich auch Sport: ich fahre auf dem See Schlittschuh, wenn es friert.
>
> Musik ist auch mein Hobby: ich spiele Gitarre und ich singe in einem Chor. Das macht Spaß, weil ich das mit meinen Freunden mache. Und nächstes Jahr werden wir mit dem Chor nach England fahren!
>
> Und welche Hobbys finde ich nicht gut? Ich sehe nicht gern fern, weil das langweilig ist.

Jan

**SPRECHEN 3**

NC 5

**Choose five different hobbies and say something different about each of them! (See pages 68–75.)**

*Beispiel:* Ich spiele nicht gern Basketball, weil ich zu klein bin.
Ich werde im Sommer … machen, wenn …

**? Think**

If you want to aim for level 5–6, be sure to include some other tenses as well as the present, for example the perfect tense, the imperfect or the future.

**SCHREIBEN 4**

NC 5

**Write at least six sentences about your hobbies. (See pages 68–75.) Say:**

- what your favourite hobby is – and why: *Mein Lieblingshobby ist …, weil/denn …*
- what you do or don't do in different types of weather: *Im Winter/Wenn es schneit, mache ich nicht …, sondern ich …*
- what you are going to do next weekend: *Ich werde …*

## Mein Lieblingshobby — My favourite hobby

| Mein Lieblingshobby | My favourite hobby |
|---|---|
| Was machst du gern/nicht gern? | What do/don't you like doing? |
| Ich besuche Freunde. | I visit friends. |
| Ich fotografiere. | I do photography. |
| Ich höre Musik. | I listen to music. |
| Ich lese Bücher. | I read books. |
| Ich mache Leichtathletik/Sport. | I do athletics/sport. |
| Ich sammle Karten. | I collect cards. |
| Ich sehe fern. | I watch TV. |
| Ich singe in einem Chor. | I sing in a choir. |
| Ich spiele Theater. | I'm in a drama group. |
| Ich surfe im Internet. | I surf the internet. |
| Ich tanze. | I go dancing. |

| Ich spiele … | I play … |
|---|---|
| Computerspiele. | computer games. |
| Fußball. | football. |
| Gitarre. | guitar. |
| Golf. | golf. |
| Saxofon. | saxophone. |
| Schach. | chess. |
| Schlagzeug. | drums. |
| Tennis. | tennis. |
| Tischtennis. | table tennis. |

| Ich fahre … | I go … |
|---|---|
| Rad. | cycling. |
| Rennrad. | cycle racing. |
| Rollschuh. | roller-skating. |
| Schlittschuh. | ice-skating. |
| Skateboard. | skateboarding. |
| Ski. | skiing. |
| Wasserski. | waterskiing. |

## Das ist ein tolles Hobby! — That's a great hobby!

| Das ist ein tolles Hobby! | That's a great hobby! |
|---|---|
| Mein Hobby ist … | My hobby is … |
| Das ist ein tolles Hobby, … | It's a great hobby, … |
| Das Hobby macht Spaß, … | It's a fun hobby, … |
| weil es billig ist. | because it's cheap. |
| weil ich musikalisch/sportlich bin. | because I'm musical/sporty. |
| denn es ist interessant. | because it's interesting. |
| denn es ist ungewöhnlich. | because it's unusual. |
| aber es ist teuer. | but it's expensive. |
| aber ich habe keine Zeit für andere Hobbys. | but I have no time for other hobbies. |

## Wenn es heiß ist, … — When the weather's hot, …

| Wenn es heiß ist, … | When the weather's hot, … |
|---|---|
| Es ist … | It's … |
| heiß. | hot. |
| kalt. | cold. |
| sonnig. | sunny. |
| warm. | warm. |
| windig. | windy. |
| Es friert. | It's freezing. |
| Es gewittert. | It's stormy/There's thunder and lightning. |
| Es ist neblig. | It's foggy. |
| Es regnet. | It's raining. |
| Es schneit. | It's snowing. |
| im Frühling | in spring |
| im Sommer | in summer |
| im Herbst | in autumn |
| im Winter | in winter |

| | |
|---|---|
| Wenn es windig ist, gehe ich Windsurfen. | When it's windy, I go windsurfing |
| Ich fahre Inliner, wenn es warm ist. | I go rollerblading when it's warm. |

## Nächstes Wochenende — Next weekend

| Nächstes Wochenende | Next weekend |
|---|---|
| Ich werde … | I will … |
| spät aufstehen. | get up late. |
| Musik hören. | listen to music. |
| Fußball spielen. | play football. |
| in einem Musical singen. | sing in a musical. |
| ein Buch lesen. | read a book. |
| Inliner fahren. | go rollerblading. |
| fernsehen. | watch TV. |
| Gitarre spielen. | play guitar. |
| schwimmen. | go swimming. |

## I can …

- talk about my favourite hobby and explain why I like it
- talk about what hobbies I do in different kinds of weather
- talk about what I will do next weekend
- use regular and irregular verbs in the present tense
- use adjective endings correctly
- use the future tense
- use the correct word order with linking words
- pronounce the v and w sounds

- Vocabulary: name the parts of the body
- Grammar: use possessive adjectives; use noun plurals
- Skills: identify language patterns

**HÖREN 1**

🎧 **Hör zu und lies (1–12). Welcher Körperteil (a–l) ist das?**

*Beispiel:* **1 i**

1. Mein **Körper** ist klein.
2. Mein **Kopf** ist groß.
3. Ich habe drei **Augen**.
4. Meine **Füße** sind sehr lang, …
5. … aber ich habe kurze **Beine**.
6. Ich habe eine rote **Nase**.
7. Mein **Mund** ist blau …
8. … und ich habe vier **Zähne**.
9. Ich habe zwei rechte **Hände**, …
10. … ein knubbeliges **Knie**, …
11. … große **Ohren** …
12. … und muskulöse **Arme**.

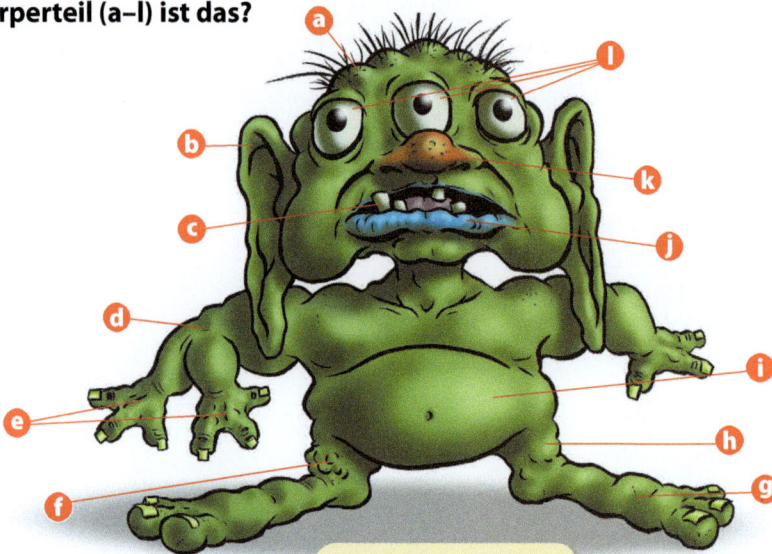

knubbelig *knobbly*

**LESEN 2**

**Finde die Pluralformen.**

*Beispiel:* **1 i**

1. der Fuß
2. der Mund
3. der Kopf
4. der Körper
5. der Arm
6. der Zahn
7. die Nase
8. die Hand
9. das Ohr
10. das Auge
11. das Bein
12. das Knie

a die Knie
b die Arme
c die Augen
d die Ohren
e die Zähne
f die Köpfe
g die Münder
h die Hände
i die Füße
j die Körper
k die Nasen
l die Beine

**? Think**

Look at the different ways in which the plural is formed.
Can you identify any patterns?

**HÖREN 3**

🎧 **Ist alles richtig? Hör zu und wiederhole.**

**SPRECHEN 4**

👥 **Beschreib ein Monster! A ↔ B.**
Describe a monster! Your partner listens carefully and draws it.

*Beispiel:* Es ist klein und grün. Es hat ein Auge. Es hat zwei Arme und …

## LESEN 5

**Beantworte die Fragen auf Englisch.**

NC 4

**a** What is the problem with Insektosaurus's eyes?
**b** What does he think of his body?
**c** Whose body and eyes would he like?
**d** What does Insektosaurus say about his hands, feet and fingers?
**e** In his opinion, who has better hands and feet than him?
**f** How does he describe Dr. Kakerlake's eyes and head?

Hallo!

Ich habe ein Problem. Ich mag meinen Körper nicht. Meine Augen sind zu groß und mein Körper ist zu dick.

Warum kann ich nicht schön sein? Vielleicht so wie Gigantika? Ihr Körper ist nicht dick und ihre Augen sind schön.

Meine Arme und Beine sind zu kurz. Ich möchte Finger haben. Meine Hände und Füße sind unpraktisch!

Dr. Kakerlake hat bessere Hände und Füße. Aber seine Augen sind sehr groß und er hat zwei lange, unpraktische Antennen auf dem Kopf.

Insektosaurus

dick  *fat*

## SCHREIBEN 6

**Füll die Lücken aus.**

*Beispiel:* **a** *mein*

**a** _____ Vater hat lange Beine.   (mein/meine/meinen)
**b** _____ Nase ist groß.   (dein/deine/deinen)
**c** Ich finde _____ Körper prima.   (mein/meine/meinen)
**d** _____ Füße sind klein.   (ihr/ihre/ihren)
**e** _____ Augen sind blau.   (sein/seine/seinen)

## SCHREIBEN 7

**Wie ist das Monster?**

NC 3–4

- Imagine a monster! List his or her main body parts in English.
- Swap your list with your partner.
- Describe your partner's monster in German!

*Beispiel:*

two heads,
ten ears – small,
one long leg, ...

Er hat zwei Köpfe und zehn Ohren. Seine Ohren sind klein. Sein Bein ist lang ...

### Think

- Do you remember how to say 'my', 'his', 'her' and 'your' in German? Some of these words are in Insektosaurus's letter.
- What other word do you know that behaves in the same way?

### Grammatik → p.161

**Possessive adjectives**

| | Masc. | Fem. | Neut. | Pl. |
|---|---|---|---|---|
| my | mein<br>*acc* meinen | meine | mein | meine |
| your | dein<br>*acc* deinen | deine | dein | deine |
| his | sein<br>*acc* seinen | seine | sein | seine |
| her | ihr<br>*acc* ihren | ihre | ihr | ihre |

### Challenge

You are going to give Insektosaurus a makeover!

Write a description of his new body and illustrate your work.

*Beispiel:* Er hat ... Sein Körper ist ... Seine Hände sind ...

NC 4

# 3A.2 Was fehlt dir?

- Vocabulary: talk about illness and injuries
- Grammar: use *seit* to say 'since' and 'for'; use dative pronouns
- Skills: adapt language to build new words and phrases

## LESEN 1 Was passt zusammen?

*Beispiel:* **a 5**

**①** **②** **③** **④** **⑤** **⑥** **⑦**

| | |
|---|---|
| **a** | Ich habe Bauchschmerzen. |
| **b** | Ich habe Halsschmerzen. |
| **c** | Ich habe eine Grippe. Ich habe Fieber. |
| **d** | Ich habe Ohrenschmerzen. |
| **e** | Ich habe Rückenschmerzen. |
| **f** | Ich habe Knieschmerzen. |
| **g** | Ich habe Kopfschmerzen. |

## HÖREN 2 🎧 Ist alles richtig? Hör zu.

### ? Think

Look at activity 1: what is the word for 'aches' or 'pains'? Can you work out how to say other ailments?

You know what 'tooth' is in German, so what is 'toothache'?

## LESEN 3 Leo macht eine Party, aber Carla kann nicht kommen! Lies den Telefon-Dialog. Was ist die richtige Reihenfolge?

NC 4

*Beispiel:* **c** *Hallo! Hier ist Leo.*

| | |
|---|---|
| **a** | Was? Warum nicht? Was fehlt dir? |
| **b** | Danke. Tschüs! |
| **c** | Hallo! Hier ist Leo. |
| **d** | Oh nein. Gute Besserung! |
| **e** | Hallo Leo. Ich bin's, Carla! Es tut mir leid, aber ich kann am Samstag nicht zu deiner Party kommen. |
| **f** | Danke, tschüs. Viel Spaß auf der Party! |
| **g** | Es geht mir nicht gut. Ich bin krank! Ich habe eine Grippe mit Halsschmerzen, Kopfschmerzen und Fieber. |

Was fehlt dir?
Es geht mir nicht gut.
Ich bin krank.
Es tut mir leid.
Gute Besserung.

## HÖREN 4 🎧 Ist alles richtig? Hör zu.

## SPRECHEN 5 👥 Macht Dialoge wie in Übung 3.

NC 4

### ⚙ Grammatik

**Dative pronouns**

*Mir* and *dir* are dative pronouns. They often come up in set phrases:
Wie geht es **dir**? – Es geht **mir** gut.
*How are you? – I'm well.*

| Ich habe | eine Allergie gegen Katzen. Migräne. | |
|---|---|---|
| Ich habe mir | die Nase/das Bein/… | gebrochen. |
| Mein Kopf tut weh. | | |

## ? Think

You can adapt the expressions in the language box to talk about different ailments:

| | | |
|---|---|---|
| I'm allergic to <u>cats</u>. | → | Ich habe eine Allergie gegen <u>Katzen</u>. |
| I'm allergic to dogs. | → | |
| I've broken my <u>leg</u>. | → | Ich habe mir <u>das Bein</u> gebrochen. |
| I've broken my nose. | → | |
| My <u>head</u> hurts. | → | Mein <u>Kopf</u> tut weh. |
| My foot hurts. | → | |

How many of these expressions can you spot when you listen to activity 6?

## ⚙ Grammatik → p.159–60

**seit (since, for)**

Seit always takes the dative case:

seit **einem** Monat    seit **einer** Woche

seit **einem** Jahr    seit Samstag

You use it with the present tense in German:

Er **ist** seit sechs Tagen krank.
He **has been** ill for six days.

### HÖREN 6
**Hör zu (1–5). Warum können sie nicht zu Leos Party kommen?**

NC 5    *Beispiel:*

| | 1 Paul | 2 Liv | 3 Caro | 4 Claas | 5 Timo |
|---|---|---|---|---|---|
| Problem? | *broken leg* | | | | |
| Seit wann? | *last Saturday* | | | | |
| Wie passiert? | *playing football* | | | | |

### SPRECHEN 7
**Macht Dialoge. A ⟷ B.**

NC 4–5    *Beispiel:*

A  *Was fehlt dir?*    B

A  *Seit wann?*    B

### SCHREIBEN 8
**Deine Freunde gehen ins Kino, aber du bist krank. Schreib eine Nachricht.**

NC 4–5    Say what is wrong and how long you've been ill or injured.

*Beispiel:*

> Ich kann nicht
> kommen. Ich bin
> total krank. Ich
> habe seit Mittwoch
> Grippe...

## ◎ Challenge

You are unwell and can't go on a school trip. Write a note for school saying:

- you're sorry you can't come on the trip: *Es tut mir leid. Heute kann ich leider keinen Ausflug machen, …*
- what the problem is: *denn …*
- when and how it happened: *Gestern …*
- how you're feeling today (e.g. headache, fever): *Heute …*

NC 4–5

- Vocabulary: talk about what sports you do to keep fit
- Grammar: use *um ... zu ...* (in order to ...)
- Skills: give more detailed responses

**LESEN 1** **Finde die Paare.**

*Beispiel:* **1 d**

a Ich spiele Volleyball und Basketball.  b Ich mache Pilates.
c Ich gehe mit dem Hund spazieren.  d Ich gehe zu Fuß in die Schule.
e Ich mache Yoga.  f Ich mache Karate.  g Ich jogge.  h Ich spiele Tischtennis.

1

2

3

4

5

6

7

8

**HÖREN 2** 🎧 **Ist alles richtig? Hör zu.**

**HÖREN 3** 🎧 **„Was machst du?" Hör zu und füll die Tabelle aus. (1–8)**

*Beispiel:*

|   | Was? | Wie oft? |
|---|------|----------|
| 1 | jogging | seldom |

**SPRECHEN 4** 👥 **Macht Dialoge. A ↔ B.**

**NC 3**

*Beispiel:* **A** *Was machst du?*
**B** *Ich mache zweimal pro Woche Karate.*

**SCHREIBEN 5** **Was machst du? Wie oft? Schreib Sätze.**

**❓ Think**

How can you give a more detailed answer to *Was machst du?* – Add details of when or how often! Match the English to the German:

oft
manchmal
hin und wieder
selten
nie
einmal pro Woche
zweimal pro Monat

seldom   once a week
twice a month   never
sometimes   often
now and then

Where do you put these phrases in a sentence? Look at a–h in activity 1 and try to work out the word order.

## ▶ Die Video-Aufgabe

**VIDEO 6** **Sieh dir das Video an und beantworte die Fragen auf Englisch.**

a What are Leo and Sira doing in this video clip?
b What is Sira's main task? And what is Leo's?
c What kind of sport does Moritz do?
d How often does he practise?
e What tips does Moritz have for a healthy lifestyle?
f What other sport does he do and why?

**VIDEO 7** Is Leo pleased to get the tickets? Why do you think this is?

**VIDEO 8** Would you like to try white-water canoeing? Why?

---

**LESEN 9**
NC 4
**Lies Ninas Text. Wer macht was? Wie oft? Und warum?**

*Beispiel: Klaus: sometimes goes surfing, to stay young; Birgit: …*

Meine Familie ist sehr sportlich und gesund. Wir machen oft Sport, um fit zu bleiben. Ich finde das toll!

Mein Opa Klaus surft manchmal, um jung zu bleiben. Meine Oma Birgit macht oft Yoga, um hip zu sein.

Um nicht dick zu werden, isst mein Vater Oliver nie Kuchen oder Fastfood. Um gesund zu bleiben, joggt meine Mutter Hanna dreimal pro Woche. Sie hat viel Energie!

Und ich? Ich gehe fünfmal pro Woche zu Fuß in die Schule!

*Nina*

**SPRECHEN 10**
NC 4
**Macht eine Klassenumfrage: „Was machst du, um fit zu bleiben?"**

*Beispiel:* A *Was machst du, um fit zu bleiben?*
B *Ich spiele Fußball, um fit zu bleiben.*
C *Um fit zu bleiben, mache ich …*

**SCHREIBEN 11**
NC 4
**Du bist ein Fitnessfanatiker/eine Fitnessfanatikerin! Was machst du, um fit zu bleiben? Wie oft? Warum? (um … zu …)**
Mention at least four activities.

### ⚙ Grammatik → p.167

**um … zu … (in order to …)**

- Ich mache oft Sport, **um** fit **zu bleiben.**
  *I often do sport, in order to keep fit.*

- **Um** fit **zu bleiben, mache** ich oft Sport.
  *In order to keep fit, I often do sport.*

  We call this a verb sandwich: verb–comma–verb.

How many *um … zu …* phrases can you spot in Nina's text?

**Challenge**
Your head teacher has asked you to interview some sportspeople about their active lifestyles. Write up the interviews as an article for the school website. Include:
- your questions and their answers
- at least two tenses
- two sentences in which you use *um … zu …*

NC 4–5

- Vocabulary: talk about healthy eating; give advice on a healthy lifestyle
- Grammar: use the imperative
- Skills: use previously learned language

**LESEN 1**

**Was passt zusammen?**

*Beispiel:* **1 b**

a die Pommes    b die Chips
c die Süßigkeiten
d das Mineralwasser
e das Schwarzbrot
f das Weißbrot    g die Kekse
h die Cola    i das Eis    j der Käse
k das Fastfood    l die Milch
m das Obst    n das Gemüse
o die Wurst

**HÖREN 2**

🎧 **Ist alles richtig? Hör zu.**

**? Think**

Look at these two sentences. What do you think *gesund* and *ungesund* mean?

- Obst und Gemüse sind gesund.
- Cola und Kekse sind ungesund.

**SPRECHEN 3**

👥 **Macht Dialoge. Ist das gesund oder ungesund (1–15 in Übung 1)? A ↔ B.**

*Beispiel:* **A** *Nummer 14!*
        **B** *Das Eis. Das ist ungesund!*

**HÖREN 4**

🎧 **Hör zu. Wie oft essen und trinken Freddie und Fiona das? Füll die Tabelle (mit 1–15 aus Übung 1) aus.**

*Beispiel:*

| | Oft | Selten | Nie |
|---|---|---|---|
| Freddie: | 5, … | | |
| Fiona: | 7, … | | |

**SPRECHEN 5**

👥 **Macht Dialoge. Isst dein Partner/deine Partnerin gesund? A ↔ B.**

*Beispiel:*

**A** *Was isst und trinkst du oft?*
**B** *Ich esse oft Kekse und ich trinke oft Cola.*
**A** *Das ist ungesund! Was isst und trinkst du selten?*
**B** *Ich esse selten …*

Freddie

Fiona

## Gesundheits-Quiz!

Was ist gesund? Was ist ungesund?
Wähle G oder U.

| | | G | U |
|---|---|---|---|
| a | Trink oft Cola! | G | **U** |
| b | Mach viel Sport! | **G** | U |
| c | Geh nicht oft zu Fuß! | G | **U** |
| d | Iss kein Obst und Gemüse! | G | **U** |
| e | Machen Sie Yoga! | **G** | U |
| f | Rauchen Sie nicht! | **G** | U |
| g | Trinken Sie keinen Alkohol! | **G** | U |
| h | Essen Sie Fastfood! | G | **U** |

### Grammatik → p.166

**The imperative**
To tell someone what to do, use the imperative:

- **Talking to a friend**
  du trinkst → du trinkst → trink (*drink*)
  du isst → du isst → iss (*eat*)

- **Talking to an adult**
  Sie trinken → Sie trinken → trinken Sie (*drink*)
  Sie essen → Sie essen → essen Sie (*eat*)

rauchen *to smoke*

**LESEN 6** **Mach das Gesundheits-Quiz!**

Beispiel: **a** U

**HÖREN 7** 🎧 **Ist alles richtig? Hör zu.**

**SCHREIBEN 8** **Schreib a–d aus dem Quiz in der Sie-Form auf. Schreib e–h in der Du-Form auf. Korrigiere die ungesunden Tipps!**

Beispiel: **a** Trinken Sie keine Cola!

**SPRECHEN 9** NC 4–5 👥 **Du bist Person a, b oder c! Wie bist du? A ↔ B.**
Imagine you are a, b or c! Tell your partner about your lifestyle and what you eat and drink. Your partner gives you advice.

Beispiel: **A** Ich heiße Freddie und ich bin ziemlich faul. Ich esse oft Fastfood … Gestern habe ich … gegessen.
**B** Iss kein Fastfood, …

### ? Think

How do you tell someone what **not** to eat, drink or do?

Trinken Sie **keinen** Alkohol!

Trink **keine** Cola!

Essen Sie **kein** Fastfood!

Iss **keine** Süßigkeiten!

Rauchen Sie **nicht**!

### Challenge

Imagine you are someone with a very unhealthy lifestyle. You want to be healthier so you write to a lifestyle adviser for help. Say:
- what you usually eat and drink, how often, and why
- what sports you do, how often, and why
- what you ate/drank and did yesterday

Now imagine you are the lifestyle adviser! Write a reply offering some advice (using the imperative).

NC 4–5

Freddie Faul

Fiona Fit

Bastian Schweinsteiger

- Vocabulary: give a detailed description of a healthy diet
- Grammar: learn more about infinitive structures
- Skills: develop your dictionary skills and expand your vocabulary

tierische Fette    Süßigkeiten
Fleisch    Eier
Fisch    Milchprodukte
Gemüse    Obst
Getreideprodukte
Getränke

**SCHREIBEN 1**

**Schreib die Produkte aus der Pyramide auf Deutsch auf.**
Make a list, in German, of the food and drink shown in each section of the pyramid. Use a dictionary to help you.

*Beispiel:*

| Getränke | Getreideprodukte | Gemüse |
|---|---|---|
| das Wasser, … | das Brot, … | die Karotte (–n), … |

**HÖREN 2**  🎧 **Ist alles richtig? Hör zu.**

**SPRECHEN 3**  👥 **Gedächtnis-Spiel!**

- Close your books and try to remember as many words as you can from each section of the pyramid.
- Your partner checks to see how many you get right.
- Who remembers the most?

*Beispiel:*  **A** Getreideprodukte!  **B** Brot, Kartoffeln, …

**SCHREIBEN 4**

**Was isst du aus der Pyramide? Wie oft? Isst du gesund?**

NC 3

*Beispiel:* Getränke: Ich trinke selten Wasser, aber ich trinke oft Cola. Das ist ungesund.
Getreideprodukte: Ich esse jeden Tag Brot und …

**? Think**

How do you find a word in a bilingual dictionary? What other information does the dictionary give you apart from the word itself?

When you do activity 1, remember to make a note of the gender and plural of each word.

| Ich esse/trinke … | |
|---|---|
| jeden Tag oft hin und wieder nie … | Fleisch, … Wasser, … |

**HÖREN 5**

NC 5

🎧 **Moritz ist Kanufahrer und ist sehr fit. Hör zu, lies und füll die Lücken aus.**

*Beispiel: essen, …*

> zwei  Äpfel  Energie  Fastfood  Süßigkeiten  essen
> Vitamine  Gemüse  Wasser  Obst

Hallo! Ich heiße Moritz und ich bin Kanufahrer. Hier sind meine Tipps für ein gesundes Leben!

Es ist wichtig, gesund zu ▭, um gesund zu bleiben. Man soll viel ▭ und viel Gemüse essen, zum Beispiel Karotten, Tomaten und ▭. Gestern habe ich viel Obst und ▭ gegessen und ich hatte viel Energie!

Es ist wichtig, viel ▭ zu trinken. Man soll mindestens ▭ Liter pro Tag trinken.

Man soll auch nicht so viele ▭ essen, weil sie ungesund sind und viel Zucker enthalten. Man soll selten ▭, Chips und Pommes essen, weil sie auch sehr ungesund sind.

Fruchtsäfte sind gut, weil sie viele Vitamine enthalten. Es ist sehr wichtig, jeden Tag ▭ zu essen, um gesund zu bleiben und um ▭ zu haben!

Isst du gesund?

> der Zucker  *sugar*
> enthalten  *to contain*

⚙️ **Grammatik**

To say that it is important to do something, use *Es ist wichtig, … zu …*

**Es ist wichtig**, gesund **zu** essen.
**Es ist wichtig**, viel Wasser **zu** trinken.

How many times can you spot this structure in Moritz's text?

**SPRECHEN 6**

NC 4

👥 **Was ist wichtig? Macht Dialoge.**
Talk to your partner about what is important for a healthy diet.

*Beispiel:* **A** *Was ist wichtig?*
**B** *Es ist wichtig, viel Gemüse zu essen.*
**A** *Ja, richtig. Und man soll …*

| Es ist wichtig, | (nicht) viel Fleisch/Obst/… | zu essen/trinken. |
|---|---|---|
| Man soll | (nicht) viel Wasser/Cola/… (nicht) viele Süßigkeiten/… | essen/trinken. |
| jeden Tag, oft, selten, nie mindestens zwei Liter pro Tag | | |

**SCHREIBEN 7**

NC 4–5

**Schreib einen Gesundheits-Blog für deine Schulwebseite.**

*Beispiel:*

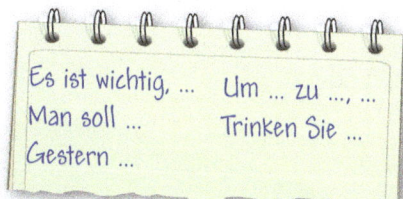

Es ist wichtig, …  Um … zu …, …
Man soll …  Trinken Sie …
Gestern …

🎯 **Challenge**

Homer Simpson is going on a strict diet! Draw up a plan for him:

- First, think of what different structures you could use, including the new ones you have learned in this unit.
- Write up your plan for Homer. Tip: As well as telling him what to do, explain why he should do it!

*Beispiel:*
*Diätplan für Homer Simpson:*

**1** Trink kein Bier!

**2** …

NC 4

**Seit, the imperative, um … zu …**

**seit (since, for)**

Seit always takes the dative case:

seit **einem** Monat  seit **einer** Woche

seit **einem** Jahr  seit Samstag

You use it with the present tense in German:

Ich **bin** seit fünf Tagen krank.
I **have been** ill for five days.

Es **geht** mir seit Donnerstag nicht gut.
I **have been** unwell since Thursday.

**1** Translate these sentences into German.

Beispiel: **a** Ich bin seit Freitag krank.

**a** I have been ill since Friday.
**b** I have had backache for ten days.
**c** He has had a fever since Saturday.
**d** I have been living in Hamburg for a year.
**e** She has had earache for a week.
**f** He has been living in Berlin for a month.

**The imperative**

If you want to tell someone what to do or give a command in German, you use the imperative form:

Trink viel Wasser.  Drink lots of water.
Essen Sie kein Fastfood.  Don't eat fast food.

- **Talking to a friend**

  Use the du form of the verb but drop the word du and the -st ending:

  du trinkst  →  d̶u̶ trinks̶t̶  →  trink

  du machst  →  d̶u̶ machs̶t̶  →  mach

  If the stem (main part) of the verb ends in -s, just drop the -t ending:

  du isst  →  d̶u̶ iss̶t̶  →  iss

- **Talking to an adult**

  Use the Sie form of the verb but swap the position of Sie and the verb:

  Sie trinken  →  Sie trinken  →  trinken Sie

  Sie machen  →  Sie machen  →  machen Sie

**2** Give advice to a good friend and to an adult.

Beispiel: **a** Rauch nicht. Rauchen Sie nicht.

**a** Ich rauche zu viel.
**b** Ich mache nie Sport.
**c** Ich esse kein Obst.
**d** Ich trinke Alkohol.
**e** Ich fahre mit dem Auto in die Schule.
**f** Ich spiele nie Fußball, Tennis oder Basketball.
**g** Ich gehe selten mit dem Hund spazieren.

## um … zu … (*in order to …*)

Use *um … zu …* to say why you do something. There are two ways to use it:

- Put *um* at the beginning of the second clause (after the comma) and put *zu* at the end followed by an infinitive:

  Ich mache oft Sport, **um** fit **zu bleiben**.
  *I often do sport, **in order to keep** fit.*

- Or you can start the sentence with *um … zu …* If you do this, the verb must be the first item in the next clause:

  **Um** fit **zu bleiben**, **mache** ich oft Sport.
  ***In order to keep** fit, I often **do** sport.*

  We call this a verb sandwich (verb–comma–verb).

**3** Unscramble these sentences. Start each sentence with the highlighted word.

*Beispiel:* **a** *Ich fliege nach Spanien, um zu relaxen.*

a  fliege Ich nach Spanien, relaxen um zu
b  nach Deutschland fahre Ich, zu sprechen um Deutsch
c  hart trainieren Sie, um zu gewinnen das Spiel
d  fahren nach Paris Meine Familie und ich, sehen um zu den Eiffelturm
e  Wir ins Restaurant gehen, um essen zu chinesisches Essen

**4** Now rewrite activity 3 so that *Um … zu …* starts each sentence.

*Beispiel:* **a** *Um zu relaxen, fliege ich nach Spanien.*

## Learning plurals of nouns

**5** Find all the plural nouns in this text. Write them out with their singular forms.

*Beispiel: die Augen – das Auge, …*

Das ist Gigantika. Sie ist ziemlich schön. Ihre Augen sind groß, ihre Nase klein und ihr Mund toll geformt. Gigantika hat sehr lange Beine und muskulöse Arme. Ihre Haare sind weißblond.

In German, there are different ways to form plurals of nouns. So when you learn a new noun, the best thing to do is to learn its plural at the same time. You can also look up noun plurals in a dictionary.

## Pronunciation of *z* and *g*

Letter *z* is sharp like the 'ts' sound in the English 'fits'.

**6** Listen (1–12). Do you hear *g* or *z*? If it's *g*, look at the pronunciation tips: is it a, b, c or d?

*Beispiel:* **1** *a*

**7** Listen again and repeat.

There are different ways to pronounce *g* in German:
a  *-ig* at the end of words like *nervig* sounds like *ich*.
b  Letter *g* at the end of words like *Tag* is sharp like the 'k' in 'kick'.
c  It can also be soft like in the English word 'sing'.
d  In the middle of a word or at the beginning, it usually sounds like the 'g' in 'good'.

- Vocabulary: practise words for parts of the body; talk about health and fitness
- Grammar: form plurals of nouns
- Skills: use a dictionary

**SCHREIBEN 1**

**Finde ein Foto und schreib die Körperteile auf.**
Find a photo of a person, animal or monster (or draw one) and label it. Write the plural forms too. Use a dictionary to help.

die Hand

der Bauch

das Bein

der Fuß

**LESEN 2**

**NC 2**

**Was passt zusammen?**
Match the sentences to the pictures.

*Beispiel:* **a 6**

a   Ich habe Zahnschmerzen.
b   Ich habe Fieber und eine Grippe.
c   Ich habe Halsschmerzen. Mein Hals tut weh.

d   Ich habe mir das Bein gebrochen.
e   Ich habe seit vier Tagen Rückenschmerzen.
f   Seit Samstag habe ich Kopfschmerzen.

1    2    3    4    5    6

**LESEN 3**

**NC 4**

**Füll die Lücken aus.**
Fill in the gaps using the words provided.

*Beispiel: Obst, …*

> Süßigkeiten   gesund   gehe   Obst   trinke
> oft   sehr   Sport   Mineralwasser
> ungesund

> Um fit zu bleiben, esse ich viel ▭ und Gemüse. Ich trinke ▭ Milch und ▭, aber ich ▭ selten Cola. Ich esse nie ▭, weil sie sehr ▭ sind. Um ▭ zu bleiben, mache ich viel ▭. Ich ▭ oft zu Fuß, weil das ▭ gesund ist!

**SCHREIBEN 4**

**NC 3**

**Schreib Sätze für die Bilder.**
Write a sentence to go with each picture. Use words from the box or your own ideas.

*Beispiel:* **a** *Trinken Sie viel Wasser, um gesund zu bleiben!*

> Ich spiele   Trinken Sie   Essen Sie   Iss
> jeden Tag   oft   nie   viel
> um gesund/fit zu bleiben
> weil das gesund/ungesund ist

1    2    3    4

# 3A.7 / Extra Plus

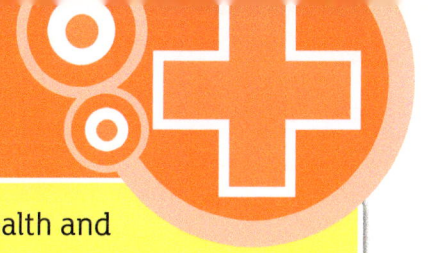

- Vocabulary: practise food words; talk about health and fitness
- Grammar: form plurals of nouns; use *um ... zu ...*
- Skills: use a dictionary; understand more complex texts

## SCHREIBEN 1

**Wie heißen 1–5 auf Deutsch? Schreib die Singular- und Pluralformen auf.**

Use a dictionary to help you. Add five more foods of your own choice.

*Beispiel:* **1** der Apfel – die Äpfel

## LESEN 2

NC 5

**Richtig (R) oder falsch (F)?**

*Beispiel:* **a** R

a Philipp is a racing driver.
b Rice and fish are a big part of his diet.
c Yesterday he ate steak with carrots.

d He must drink at least five litres of water per day.
e He starts his day with jogging and weight training.
f Yesterday he spent three hours training in the car.

---

Für die Weltmeisterschaft trainiere ich viel. Um erster in der Tabelle zu sein, muss man viel Disziplin haben und gesund essen. Jeden Tag esse ich Nudeln oder Kartoffeln mit Fleisch und

**Philipp Fahn, Rennfahrer**

Gemüse, um gesund zu bleiben. Am liebsten esse ich Karotten und Bohnen. Gestern habe ich zum Mittag Hähnchen mit Karotten gegessen.

Ich muss mindestens fünf Liter Wasser pro Tag trinken. Cola und Limonade enthalten zu viel Zucker und diese extra Kalorien sind ungesund.

Morgens beginnt mein Trainingsprogramm mit Joggen und Krafttraining. Ich mache oft Yoga, um zu relaxen.

Natürlich fahre ich auch viel Auto. Gestern bin ich sechs Stunden gefahren. Das ist sehr anstrengend und gar nicht einfach, denn man muss sich stark konzentrieren.

Ich muss topfit sein, wenn ich an den Start gehe!

---

## SCHREIBEN 3

NC 4–5

**Das ist die Familie Gesund! Was macht sie, um gesund zu bleiben?**

- Benutze *um ... zu ...*
- Schreib Sätze im Präsens, im Perfekt und im Futur.

*Beispiel: Um gesund zu bleiben, macht Frau Gesund Pilates. Gestern war sie drei Stunden im Park ...*

**HÖREN 1**

**NC 3–5**

🎧 **Listen (1–6) and note down the following information for each person. (See pages 86–87.)**

- What is wrong with each person?
- Any other details, e.g. how long they've been ill or injured, how it happened, what it is stopping them from doing.

| | What is wrong? | Other details |
|---|---|---|
| 1 | *stomach ache* | … |

**LESEN 2**

**NC 6**

**Read the text about Freddie Faul and answer the questions in English. (See pages 88–91.)**

*Beispiel:* **a** *He is very unhealthy*

- **a** What is Freddie like at the moment?
- **b** Describe his diet. (Mention what he does and doesn't eat.)
- **c** What exercise does he do?
- **d** What was his lifestyle like last year? (Mention diet and sport.)
- **e** What will he do in future to get fit?
- **f** What does he say about crisps and cola?

**SPRECHEN 3**

**NC 5**

**Give a mini-presentation about your lifestyle. (See pages 88–91.)**

Say:

- what you do to keep fit: *Um fit zu bleiben, …*
- what you eat normally: *Normalerweise esse/trinke ich …*
- what you did to keep fit yesterday: *Gestern habe ich …*

**SCHREIBEN 4**

**NC 5**

**Choose your favourite cartoon monster and imagine that he or she is going to be the focus of a healthy lifestyle campaign! (See pages 84–85 and 88–91.)**

Describe:

- what your monster looks like
- his or her healthy lifestyle (diet and activities)
- what he or she ate/drank and did yesterday

**? Think**

- Remember that if you use one tense only, you can achieve a level 4.
- To aim for level 6, include some present, past and future tenses.
- To aim beyond level 6, add some new ideas and structures, and use reference materials.

Ich bin Freddie und im Moment bin ich total ungesund. Ich esse zu viel Schokolade, Pommes und Chips. Das finde ich schlecht. Jeden Tag esse ich Süßigkeiten, aber ich esse nie Gemüse, zum Beispiel Salat oder Tomaten. Ich mache auch keinen Sport.

Letztes Jahr habe ich viel Obst und Gemüse gegessen und oft Mineralwasser getrunken. Im Schulsport war ich der Beste und ich habe Basketball gespielt. Ja, ich war richtig fit.

In Zukunft werde ich mehr Sport machen und gesund essen, um fit zu werden. Ich werde selten Fastfood essen. Ich werde nur am Wochenende Cola trinken und Chips essen, zum Beispiel auf Partys.

| Der Körper | The body |
|---|---|
| der Arm (-e) | arm |
| das Auge (-n) | eye |
| das Bein (-e) | leg |
| der Finger (-) | finger |
| der Fuß (Füße) | foot |
| die Hand (Hände) | hand |
| das Knie (-) | knee |
| der Kopf (Köpfe) | head |
| der Körper (-) | body |
| der Mund (Münder) | mouth |
| die Nase (-n) | nose |
| das Ohr (-en) | ear |
| der Zahn (Zähne) | tooth |

| Was fehlt dir? | What's wrong with you? |
|---|---|
| Ich habe … | I have … |
| Bauchschmerzen | stomach ache |
| Halsschmerzen | a sore throat |
| Knieschmerzen | a sore knee |
| Kopfschmerzen | a headache |
| Ohrenschmerzen | earache |
| Rückenschmerzen | backache |
| Zahnschmerzen | toothache |
| Fieber | a fever, a high temperature |
| eine Grippe | flu |
| Wie geht es dir? | How are you? |
| Es geht mir (nicht) gut. | I'm (not) well. |
| Ich bin krank. | I'm ill. |
| Mein Bein tut weh. | My leg hurts. |
| Ich habe mir die Nase gebrochen. | I've broken my nose. |
| Ich habe eine Allergie gegen Katzen. | I'm allergic to cats. |
| Ich habe Migräne. | I've got a migraine. |
| seit einer Woche/vier Tagen | for a week/four days |
| Es tut mir leid. | I'm sorry. |

| Topfit! | Superfit! |
|---|---|
| Ich mache … | I do … |
| Karate/Pilates. | karate/Pilates. |
| Sport/Yoga. | sport/yoga. |
| Ich spiele … | I play … |
| Basketball. | basketball. |
| Tischtennis. | table tennis. |
| Volleyball. | volleyball. |
| Ich jogge. | I go jogging. |
| Ich gehe (mit dem Hund) spazieren. | I go walking (with the dog). |

| | |
|---|---|
| Ich gehe zu Fuß in die Schule. | I walk to school. |
| Ich mache Sport, um fit zu bleiben. | I do sport in order to keep fit. |
| hin und wieder | now and then |
| manchmal | sometimes |
| nie | never |
| oft | often |
| selten | seldom |
| einmal/zweimal pro Woche | once/twice a week |
| dreimal pro Monat | three times a month |

| Du bist, was du isst! | You are what you eat! |
|---|---|
| die Chips | crisps |
| die Cola | cola |
| das Eis | ice cream |
| das Fastfood | fast food |
| das Gemüse | vegetables |
| der Käse | cheese |
| die Kekse | biscuits, cookies |
| die Milch | milk |
| das Obst | fruit |
| die Pommes | chips |
| die Süßigkeiten | sweets |
| das Mineralwasser | mineral water |
| das Schwarzbrot | rye bread |
| das Weißbrot | white bread |
| die Wurst | sausage |

| | |
|---|---|
| Ich esse normalerweise/oft/selten/nie … | I usually/often/rarely/never eat … |
| Iss kein Fastfood! | Don't eat fast food! |
| Trinken Sie viel Wasser! | Drink lots of water! |

**I can …**
- name parts of the body
- talk about illness and injuries
- talk about what sports I do to keep fit
- talk about healthy eating
- use possessive adjectives
- use plural forms of nouns
- use *seit*
- use the infinitive structure *um … zu …*
- use the imperative
- pronounce the *g* and *z* sounds

# 3B.1 Wir brauchen Infos!

- Vocabulary: plan a trip and ask for tourist information
- Grammar: use the accusative case
- Skills: write a formal letter

**HÖREN 1**
**NC 5**

🎧 **Hör zu und lies. Finde die passenden Bilder (a–g) für 1–7.**

*Beispiel:* **1 c**

**Leo**: Puuhh, die Arbeit war heute anstrengend, ich bin kaputt! Ich möchte Urlaub machen!

**Sira**: Ferien sind erst im Juli! Aber ich habe eine gute Idee, schau mal …

**Leo**: Am Samstag gibt es in Düsseldorf im Open-Air-Kino „Parkour" – der Filmhit zum Extremsport … Super!

**Sira**: Genau, also, hier ist mein Plan: wir werden einen Ausflug nach Düsseldorf machen, für ein Wochenende! Wir werden ins Kino gehen und wir werden die Stadt besuchen!

**Leo**: Ja, toll! Aber wir brauchen mehr Informationen …

**Sira**: Ja, wir brauchen **1 einen Fahrplan** für die Zugfahrt von Köln. Und wir brauchen **2 eine Broschüre über die Stadt** mit allen Sehenswürdigkeiten!

**Leo**: Gute Idee! Und wir brauchen **3 eine Liste von Jugendherbergen** und auch **4 eine Liste von billigen Hotels**.

**Sira**: Ja, und **5 eine Liste von Campingplätzen**! Und was brauchen wir noch?

**Leo**: Ich weiß, wir brauchen **6 einen Stadtplan**! Und natürlich **7 eine Liste von billigen Restaurants**.

a Düsseldorf

b Jugendherbergen

c 5 Fahrplan

d Hotels

e Düsseldorf

f Essen & Trinken

g Camping

**SPRECHEN 2**
**NC 3–4**

👥 **Du willst mit deinem Partner/deiner Partnerin nach Düsseldorf fahren: „Was brauchen wir?" (a–g in Übung 1) A ⟷ B.**

*Beispiel:* **A** Also, was brauchen wir? (Bild b!)
**B** Wir brauchen eine Liste von Jugendherbergen. Und was brauchen wir noch? (Bild …)
**A** Wir brauchen …

**? Think**

Look at the conversation between Leo and Sira. Can you work out what *brauchen* (*Ich brauche …*, *wir brauchen …*) means? Use the context to help you.

Which case do you use with it? Nominative or accusative?

**LESEN 3**

**Leo schreibt an die Touristeninformation in Düsseldorf. Lies seine E-Mail und füll die Lücken aus.**

> Köln, 3. Juni
>
> Sehr geehrte Damen und Herren,
> wir werden vom 17. bis 19. Juni Düsseldorf besuchen.
>
> Wir hätten gern [ ] . Wir möchten auch [ ] . Haben Sie auch [ ] ?
>
> Wir sind Jugendliche und haben nicht viel Geld. Wir möchten deshalb gern
>
> [ ] . Gibt es auch [ ] ? Und wir hätten gern [ ] . Wir möchten auch
>
> gern [ ] . Vielen Dank im Voraus für Ihre Hilfe.
>
> Mit freundlichen Grüßen
> Leo Dürlewanger

**? Think**

Look at *Wir hätten gern* in Leo's email. What do you think it means? Which verb is it?

**HÖREN 4** 🎧 **Ist alles richtig? Hör zu.**

**? Think**

**Writing formal letters**

- Put your town and the date in the top right-hand corner.
- Start your letter with *Sehr geehrte Damen und Herren,* (including the comma).
- If you know the person's name, use it: *Sehr geehrte Frau Braun, Sehr geehrter Herr Braun.*
- Start the first line of the letter with a small letter (unless it's a noun).
- Always use *Sie*: *Haben Sie einen Fahrplan?*

- You can add one of the following polite phrases before you end the letter:
  *Vielen Dank im Voraus für Ihre Hilfe.* (Many thanks in advance for your help.)
  *Ich freue mich auf eine baldige Antwort.* (I look forward to hearing from you soon.)
- End your letter with *Mit freundlichen Grüßen* and your name.

**SCHREIBEN 5**

**NC 5**

**Schreib einen Brief an die Touristeninformation in Berlin.**

- Say you're going to visit Berlin (3.9. – 6.9.).
- Say you'd like a city brochure.
- Say you'd also like a map and a list of restaurants.
- Ask if they also have a list of hotels.

**Challenge**

You're a famous star and you're very rich. Write a letter requesting information for your dream holiday, where only the best and the most expensive will do!

**NC 5**

- Vocabulary: say what you can see and do in a town, and what you're going to do
- Grammar: use *in* + accusative and dative; use the future tense
- Skills: think about language patterns; adapt a text

**HÖREN 1** NC 3

🎧 **Was können Sira und Leo in Düsseldorf machen? Hör zu und finde die passenden Bilder (1–6) für die Sätze (a–f).**

*Beispiel:* **a 4**

Wir können …
a eine Stadtrundfahrt machen.
b einen Einkaufsbummel machen.
c den Rheinturm besichtigen.
d ins Spektakulum gehen.
e in den Südpark gehen.
f das Filmmuseum besuchen.

**HÖREN 2** NC 4

🎧 **Hör noch einmal zu und beantworte die Fragen auf Deutsch.**

*Beispiel:* **a** *Man kann die Attraktionen der Stadt besichtigen.*

Was kann man …
a bei der Stadtrundfahrt machen?
b in der Königsallee machen?
c vom Rheinturm aus sehen?
d im Spektakulum machen?
e im Südpark machen?
f im Filmmuseum machen?

**SPRECHEN 3** NC 4

👥 **„Was können wir machen?" A wählt ein Bild (Übung 1). B antwortet. A ↔ B.**

*Beispiel:* **A** *Bild 1. Was können wir machen?*
**B** *Wir können ins Spektakulum gehen.*

**SCHREIBEN 4**

**„Man kann in den/in die/ins … gehen." Schreib Sätze für a–f.**

*Beispiel:* **a** *Man kann in die Disco gehen.*

a die Disco          c die Pizzeria          e das Museum
b das Open-Air-Kino   d der Freizeitpark      f der Zoo

**? Think**

- What does *man* mean? When do you use it?
- What kind of verb is *können* (*man kann, wir können*)? What do you need to use with it?
- Look at the sentences below. Why do you think *in* is followed by different words for 'the'?

|     | Man kann …          | Was kann man …        |
| --- | ------------------- | --------------------- |
| m.  | in den Park gehen.  | im Park machen?       |
| f.  | in die Stadt gehen. | in der Stadt machen?  |
| n.  | ins Museum gehen.   | im Museum machen?     |

**⚙ Grammatik → p.160**

**in**

The preposition *in* is followed by the **accusative** case or the **dative**:

- **with accusative**: it tells you where someone or something is **going to**:
  Ich gehe **in die** Stadt.
- **with dative**: it tells you where someone or something **is**:
  Ich bin **in der** Stadt.

**LESEN 5**
NC 5

**Lies Siras Blog. Finde die richtige Reihenfolge für a–g.**

*Beispiel:* **c**, …

> Wir werden heute Düsseldorf zu Fuß entdecken!
>
> Wir werden zuerst die Sehenswürdigkeiten besichtigen, zum Beispiel den Schlossturm. Danach werden wir sicher hungrig sein. Wir werden auf dem Carlsplatz eine Bratwurst essen. Und danach werden wir das Senfmuseum besuchen, weil das gut zur Bratwurst passt! Dort werden wir lustige Souvenirs für die Familie und Freunde kaufen.
>
> Danach werden wir eine Bootsfahrt auf dem Rhein machen. Das wird bestimmt interessant sein! Und wir werden einen Eiskaffee in einem Café am Rheinufer trinken.
>
> Am Nachmittag werden wir zum Unterbacher See fahren, weil man dort schwimmen und segeln kann. Wir werden mit dem Zug fahren. Und am Abend werden wir in eine Disco in der Altstadt gehen.

**LESEN 6**
NC 5

**Lies Siras Blog noch einmal. Sind die Sätze richtig (R), falsch (F) oder nicht im Text (NiT)?**

*Beispiel:* **a** *NiT*

a Sira und Leo werden eine Stadtrundfahrt machen.
b Die Bratwürste auf dem Carlsplatz schmecken sehr gut.
c Im Senfmuseum kann man keine Geschenke kaufen.
d Der Unterbacher See ist sehr groß.
e Sie werden mit der U-Bahn zum See fahren.
f Abends werden sie in einer Disco tanzen.

**SCHREIBEN 7**
NC 5

**Dein Brieffreund/Deine Brieffreundin aus Deutschland wird dich besuchen. Schreib einen Plan für eine Stadtrundfahrt.**

**? Think**

**Adapting a text**

Sira's blog contains lots of phrases that you can use to describe a tour of your town. Use them as a framework and change the highlighted sections.

**Grammatik → p.166**

**The future tense**

Ich fahre nach Berlin. →
Ich **werde** nach Berlin fahren.

Wir schwimmen. →
Wir **werden** schwimmen.

**Challenge**

Write a similar plan for a sightseeing tour of another German, Swiss or Austrian city or town, like in activity 7.

NC 5

# 3B.3 Zwei Fahrkarten, bitte!

- Vocabulary: ask for and give directions; buy train tickets
- Grammar: use the imperative
- Skills: use knowledge of grammar to help you understand texts

**LESEN 1**
**NC 3**

**Lies die Dialoge (a und b) und sieh dir den Stadtplan an. Wohin gehen sie? Ist das 1 oder 2?**

**a**
- Wie komme ich am besten zur nächsten S-Bahn-Station?
- ▲ Nehmen Sie die erste Straße rechts – an der Ampel. Gehen Sie immer geradeaus und nehmen Sie dann die zweite Straße links.

**b**
- ◆ Wo ist die nächste Bushaltestelle?
- ■ Geh geradeaus und nimm die erste Straße links. Dann geh über die Brücke und an der Kreuzung geh rechts.

**Du bist hier**

**HÖREN 2**
🎧 **Ist alles richtig? Hör zu.**

**SPRECHEN 3**
👥 **Macht Dialoge. Benutzt den Stadtplan. A ↔ B.**

**NC 3**

*Beispiel:* **A** *Wie komme ich am besten zur Post?*
**B** *Geh geradeaus und dann …*

## ▶ Die Video-Aufgabe

**VIDEO 4**

**Lies a–g. Richtig (R), falsch (F) oder nicht im Video (NiV)?**

a  Sira kann mit der U-Bahn Nummer 3 und 5 fahren.
b  Die Fahrt mit der U-Bahn dauert zu lange.
c  Die Fahrt mit der S-Bahn ist langsamer.
d  Die S-Bahn-Station ist neben der Post.
e  Die Fahrt mit dem Zug ist am schnellsten.
f  Siras Fahrkarte kostet 2,50 Euro.
g  Leo fährt mit dem Bus.

**VIDEO 5**
👥 **What do you think? Was the competition fair?**

### ⚙ Grammatik → p.166

**The imperative**
- Talking to a friend:
  du gehst → **Geh** links!
- Talking to an adult:
  Sie nehmen → **Nehmen Sie** …!

Wo ist **die** nächste Bushaltestelle?
Wie komme ich am besten …
  zum Bahnhof? zum Park?
  zum Zoo?
  zur U-Bahn-Station?
  zur S-Bahn-Station? zur Post?
  zum Kino? zum Stadion?
  zum Schwimmbad?
Geh/Gehen Sie …
  links/rechts/immer geradeaus.
  über die Brücke.
Nimm/Nehmen Sie die erste/zweite
  Straße links/rechts.
an der Ampel/Kreuzung

**LESEN 6** · NC 4

**Sira kauft Fahrkarten. Lies den Dialog und finde die passenden Wörter.**

> Was erster ab Fahrkarten kommt einfach umsteigen

- Guten Tag. Ich möchte zwei ▢ nach Düsseldorf, bitte.
- ▢ oder hin und zurück?
- Hin und zurück, bitte.
- Und ▢ oder zweiter Klasse?
- Zweiter Klasse, bitte. ▢ kosten die Fahrkarten?
- Eine Fahrkarte kostet 45 Euro. Das macht 90 Euro.
- Und fährt der Zug direkt oder müssen wir ▢?
- Nein, der Zug fährt direkt.
- Wann fährt der Zug ▢? Am Samstagmorgen?
- Um 8:45 Uhr.
- Und wann ▢ er an?
- Um 9:20 Uhr. Die Fahrt wird also 35 Minuten dauern.

**? Think**

Your knowledge of German grammar can help you to understand texts. Use these strategies to help you do activity 6:

- Look at the missing words. Are they nouns, verbs, adjectives, …?
- If they are verbs: what form or tense are they in? Are they infinitives, past participles, etc.?
- Or are they parts of verbs, for example a prefix that belongs to a separable verb?
- Do any words start with a capital letter? If so, either they are nouns or they go at the beginning of a sentence.
- Are there any question words like *wer, wie, wann*? If so, look for sentences with question marks at the end.

**HÖREN 7** 🎧 **Ist alles richtig? Hör zu.**

**HÖREN 8** · NC 4 🎧 **Hör zu (1–3) und mach Notizen.**

*Beispiel:* **1** *3 Personen, einfach, 1., …*

- Wie viele Personen?
- Einfach? Hin und zurück?
- Klasse?
- Was kostet das?
- Direkt oder umsteigen?
- Abfahrt? Ankunft?

**SPRECHEN 9** · NC 4 👥 **Im Hauptbahnhof. Macht Dialoge.**

A ↔ B.

*Beispiel:* **A** *Guten Tag. Ich möchte zwei Fahrkarten nach …, bitte.*
**B** *Einfach oder hin und zurück?*

**a** 1. **München** 38€ ← → ... 38€
Abfahrt: 8:25 Uhr  Ankunft: 10:50 Uhr
Direkt

**b** 2. **Köln** 24€ →
Abfahrt: 15:30 Uhr  Ankunft: 18:05 Uhr
Umsteigen in Dresden

**Challenge** · NC 4

Your German penfriend is coming to visit. Send an email explaining how to get to where you live after arrival in the UK. Give the following details:

- best way to travel (*Zug, Bus, …*)
- ticket destination and price
- is the bus/train direct?
- journey time
- directions from the railway station or bus stop to your house (use the imperative!)

*Beispiel: Du fährst am besten mit dem Zug. Du kaufst eine Fahrkarte nach …*

- Vocabulary: say where clothes are in a room; describe a trip
- Grammar: use prepositions; use the perfect tense and the imperfect
- Skills: write creatively

**LESEN 1**

**Wieder zu Hause – Sira packt ihren Rucksack aus. Was passt zusammen?**

*Beispiel: a 5*

a das Hemd
b die Jacke
c die Jeans
d der Kapuzenpullover
e der Pullover
f die Schuhe
g die Shorts
h das T-Shirt

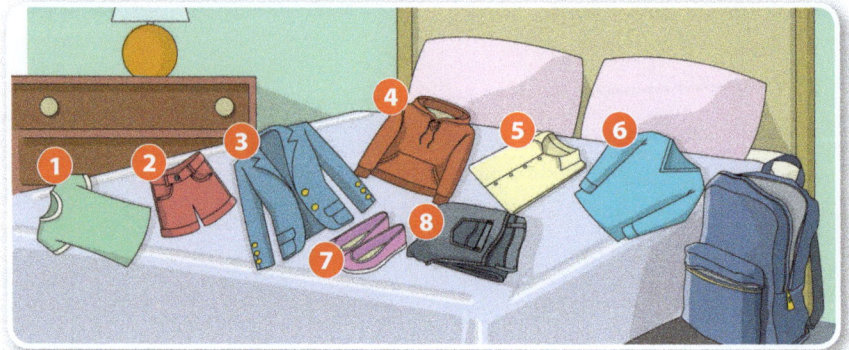

**LESEN 2**

**Chaos in Leos Zimmer! Finde die passenden Bilder (1–8) für die Sätze (a–h) – und die passenden Wörter in Übung 1.**

*Beispiel: a 4 – die Jeans*

a _____ ist unter dem Bett.
b _____ ist neben dem Computer.
c _____ ist auf dem Regal.
d _____ sind zwischen dem Bett und dem Stuhl.
e _____ ist vor dem Schreibtisch.
f _____ hängt an der Tür.
g _____ sind im Schrank.
h _____ ist hinter dem Bett.

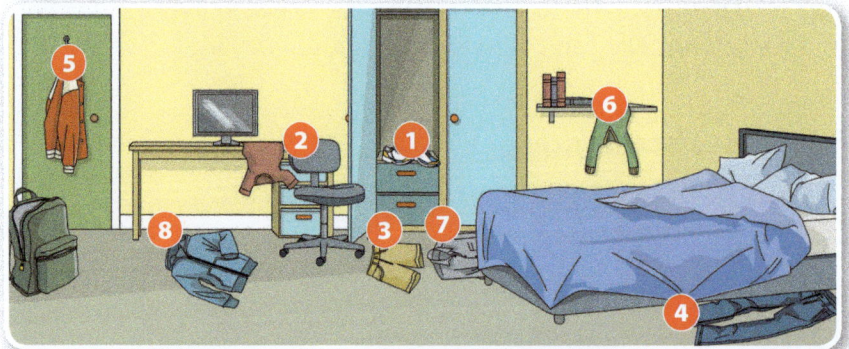

**HÖREN 3**

🎧 **Ist alles richtig? Hör zu.**

**SPRECHEN 4**

👥 **Wo ist Leos Kleidung? Macht Dialoge. A ↔ B.**

*Beispiel:* **A** *Wo ist die Jeans?*
**B** *Die Jeans ist unter dem Bett. Wo ist …?*

**? Think**

- What do prepositions tell you?
- What happens to the articles (*der*/*die*/*das*) when they follow a preposition? Why is this?

> **Grammatik → p.159–60**
>
> **Prepositions with the dative case**
> Like *in*, the following prepositions take the **dative** case to say where something **is**:
>
> **an auf hinter neben unter vor zwischen**
>
> Das Handy ist **neben dem** Computer.
> Das T-Shirt ist **vor der** Tür. Das Buch ist **auf dem** Regal.

**LESEN 5**

NC 5

**Lies Siras Text und finde die passenden Perfekt-Partizipien.**

Wir sind mit dem Zug **1** _____ und sind am Samstagmorgen um 9:20 Uhr **2** _____. Wir sind dann zu Fuß zu unserer Jugendherberge **3** _____. Wir haben nachmittags im Südpark Volleyball **4** _____. Danach haben wir das Filmmuseum **5** _____!

Am Sonntag haben wir die Sehenswürdigkeiten **6** _____ und danach haben wir eine Bratwurst **7** _____. Dann haben wir im Senfmuseum Souvenirs **8** _____. Am Nachmittag haben wir nach der Bootsfahrt auf dem Rhein am Rheinufer Eis-Kaffee **9** _____ und sind dann im Unterbacher See **10** _____! Und abends haben wir bis spät in einer Disco **11** _____!

getanzt   besichtigt   gegangen   geschwommen   gekauft   gefahren
gegessen   angekommen   getrunken   besucht   gespielt

**HÖREN 6**

NC 5

🎧 **Ist alles richtig in Übung 5? Hör zu. Und wie war es? Schreib die passenden Adjektive auf.**

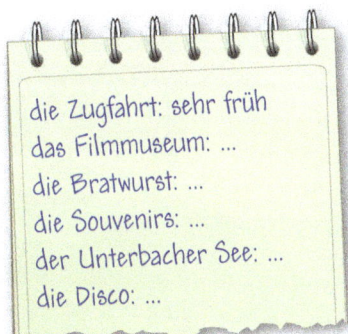

die Zugfahrt: sehr früh
das Filmmuseum: ...
die Bratwurst: ...
die Souvenirs: ...
der Unterbacher See: ...
die Disco: ...

**SPRECHEN 7**

👥 **„Wie war …?" Macht Dialoge. Benutzt die Informationen aus Übung 6. A ↔ B.**

*Beispiel:* **A**  *Wie war die Zugfahrt?*
**B**  *Sie war sehr früh – zu früh!*

**SCHREIBEN 8**

NC 5

**Du hast auch Düsseldorf besucht. Was hast du alles gemacht? Wähle acht Perfekt-Partizipien aus Übung 5 und schreib neue Sätze.**

*Beispiel:  Ich habe in einer Pizzeria Pizza gegessen. Dann sind wir …*

**Challenge**

🎯 You're writing an article about a sightseeing tour of your own town/region for a German holiday website:

- Describe what you did and what you saw on your tour last week (using the perfect tense).
- Give your opinions too (using the imperfect tense).
- And be sure to use as many linking words as possible!

*Beispiel: Ich habe … Das war super, weil …*

NC 5

- Vocabulary: say what you can see and do in a town, and what you're going to see and do
- Grammar: use modal verbs and the future tense
- Skills: read for gist and detail

## Mein Wochenende in Köln

Viele Blog-Leser fragen: „Was kann man in Köln in der Freizeit und am Wochenende machen?" Ich habe deshalb mein bestes „Köln-Freizeit-und-Wochenend-Programm" zusammengestellt – viel Spaß!

Sira

**1 Der Kölner Strandklub**
Du willst dich am Meer entspannen? Dann komm hierher: mitten in Köln gibt es am Rhein einen künstlichen Sandstrand. Hier kann man sich sonnen, faulenzen oder Beach-Volleyball spielen!

**2 Die Lanxess Arena**
Dieses riesige Stadion ist schon Grund genug, um nach Köln zu kommen! Dort gibt es Top-Konzerte von weltberühmten Bands und Sängerinnen und Sängern, Sportveranstaltungen, Zirkus, Musicals …

**3 Die Einkaufsmeilen**
Köln ist ein wahres Einkaufsparadies – hier macht Einkaufen Spaß! Das Angebot in all den tollen Läden und Boutiquen ist riesig. Und die Schildergasse ist Deutschlands Einkaufsstraße Nummer eins!

**4 Die Grünanlagen**
Hier ist Erholung angesagt: man kann am Aachener Weiher spazieren gehen, Inliner durch den Rheinpark fahren oder dort eine Wanderung machen. Danach kann man dort ein Picknick machen oder grillen.

**5 Der Tanzbrunnen**
Musikfans, Theaterfreunde und Tanzfreaks lieben den Tanzbrunnen: hier gibt es Konzerte unter freiem Himmel, Theater oder Open-Air-Disco. Dieser Freizeitpark bietet jedem etwas!

**LESEN 1**
NC 4

**Lies Siras Blog (Seite 108). Finde die passenden Fotos (a–e) für die Texte 1–5.**

**LESEN 2**
NC 5

**Was wollen diese Touristen (a–e) machen? Finde die passenden Aktivitäten (1–5) in Siras Blog.**

*Beispiel:* **a 3**

a Ich habe zum Geburtstag 100 Euro bekommen! Was kann ich damit machen?
b Ich möchte gern draußen sein, wenn es sonnig ist. Ich will aber nicht faulenzen, sondern tanzen!
c Ich interessiere mich für Sport – aber was mache ich, wenn es regnet?
d Ich mag die Natur, und ich mag es gern grün – aber ich bin auch gern aktiv.
e Wenn es total heiß ist, will ich nur ein Sonnenbad nehmen.

**SPRECHEN 3**
NC 4

**„Was kann man in Köln machen?" Macht Notizen für 1–5 in Siras Blog. Dann macht Dialoge. A ←→ B.**

*Beispiel:* *Lanxess Arena: Konzerte, Sportveranstaltungen, …*

A *Was kann man in der Lanxess Arena machen?*
B *Man kann Konzerte besuchen …*

**HÖREN 4**
NC 4

**„Hier ist die Touristeninformation …"**
**Hör zu und mach Notizen auf Deutsch für a und b.**

*Beispiel:* **a** *jede Stunde, 10–17 Uhr; vom …*

**HÖREN 5**
NC 4

**Hör noch einmal zu und beantworte die Fragen auf Englisch.**

a How long has the Düsseldorf CityTour-Bus been operating?
b Where can you buy tickets?
c On what days is the Aquazoo open between November and March?
d What else can you do in the Aquazoo?

**SCHREIBEN 6**
NC 5

**Nächstes Wochenende wirst du Köln besichtigen! Beschreib, was du machen wirst.**

*Beispiel:* *Ich werde die Lanxess Arena besuchen. Ich werde ein Konzert besuchen, weil es Spaß macht.*

**? Think**

What tense do you need to use in activity 6?

**a**

**CityTour-Bus:**
- Fährt wann? …
- Von wo? …
- Die Fahrt dauert …?
- Wo endet die Fahrt? …
- Kosten für Erwachsene/ Kinder? …

**b**

**Aquazoo:**
- Geöffnet: welche Monate? …
- Um wie viel Uhr? …
- Eintritt: Erwachsene/ Kinder/Familien? …

**Challenge**

Write a guide to leisure and weekend activities in your town or area, like Sira.

- Es gibt …
- Man kann in den/in die/ins … gehen.
- Man kann einen/eine/ein … machen.
- Man kann … besuchen/ sehen.

NC 4

# 3B.6 Sprachlabor

## Prepositions with the accusative case and the dative case

### Prepositions: accusative or dative?

Prepositions are little words like 'in' and 'on' that tell you the position of someone or something:

Leo ist im Wohnzimmer.
*Leo is in the living room.*

Die DVDs sind auf dem Tisch.
*The DVDs are on the table.*

Most prepositions are followed by either the accusative case or the dative case:

|  | masc. | fem. | neut. |
|---|---|---|---|
| **accusative** | den | die | das |
| **dative** | dem | der | dem |

Remember to use these shortened forms after *in*:

- masculine and neuter dative:
  **im** (in + dem) → **im** Schrank, **im** Hotel

- neuter accusative: **ins** (in + das) → **ins** Hotel

| Akkusativ | Dativ + Akkusativ | Dativ |
|---|---|---|
| für | an auf hinter in neben über unter vor zwischen | aus bei mit nach seit von zu |

- When these prepositions are followed by the **accusative**, they tell you where someone or something is **going to**.
- When these prepositions are followed by the **dative**, they tell you where something or someone **is**.

### 1 Fill in the correct prepositions from the box.

*Beispiel:* **a** *aus*

a  Leo kommt _____ der Schweiz.
b  Wir gehen _____ einem Freund.
c  Sira fährt _____ dem Rad zur Schule.
d  Sie sind _____ Düsseldorf gefahren.
e  Ich habe _____ Samstag Fieber.
f  Sira kauft Souvenirs _____ ihre Familie.

seit   zu   für   aus   nach   mit

### 2 Accusative or dative? Choose the correct word to complete each sentence.

*Beispiel:* **a** *die*

a  Ich gehe auf die / dem Straße.
b  Susi wohnt neben den / dem Supermarkt.
c  Wir sind in der / die Küche.
d  Ich fahre über der / die Brücke.
e  Sira ist vor die / der Tür.
f  Die Katze springt unter den / dem Tisch.

### 3 Where is everything? Fill in the missing word for 'the' in each sentence.

*Beispiel:* **a** *dem*

a  Die CDs sind auf _____ Schreibtisch.
b  Die Jacke ist unter _____ Bett.
c  Die Schuhe sind hinter _____ Tür.
d  Das T-Shirt ist neben _____ Stuhl.
e  Das Buch ist vor _____ Lampe.
f  Der MP3-Player ist in _____ Tasche.

## Writing in different styles

**?**

Not everything you read in German is written in the same style. Like in English, you will come across a variety of different styles. Here are some of them (a–f). Match them up with their explanations (1–6):

*Beispiel:* **a 4**

a a formal letter
b an informal letter
c a newspaper article
d a magazine article
e a literary text
f instructions

1 the imperative or the infinitive is used – in recipes, for example
2 a factual account which often describes past events in the imperfect tense
3 a usually more informal account which may contain slang
4 a reservation letter or a demand for information from an organisation
5 a short story, a poem or song lyrics
6 an email message to a friend

**4** Match up the following text extracts (1–6) with the styles in the box above (a–f).

**1**
**Justin Bieber** ist ein toller Typ – total entspannt! Wir haben den Star aus Kanada zu Hause besucht.

**2**
In Köln war es gestern sehr heiß: über 35 Grad am Rheinufer und 32 Grad in der Innenstadt.

**3**
Geben Sie ein Ei, 100 Gramm Butter, 125 Gramm Zucker und 75 Gramm Mehl in eine Schüssel.

**4**
*Hey, du bist mein Superstar, Du bist einfach wunderbar!*

**5**
Hallo Sandra!
Na, wie geht's? Du, ich habe Tom gestern getroffen – Tom aus deiner Klasse!! Er ist sooo super …

**6**
*Sehr geehrte Damen und Herren, wir hätten gern eine Broschüre über Ihr Hotel. Haben Sie auch Zimmer mit Telefon und Fernseher?*

## Pronunciation of *pf* and *zw*

**5** 🎧 **Listen and repeat.**

- Vocabulary: follow directions; ask for tourist information; buy tickets
- Grammar: practise the imperative
- Skills: practise reading skills

## LESEN 1

**Finde die passenden Bilder für die Sätze.**
Find the correct pictures for the sentences.

*Beispiel:* **a 2**

a  Nehmen Sie die erste Straße rechts.
b  Gehen Sie über die Brücke und dann links.
c  Nimm die zweite Straße links.
d  Geh geradeaus und an der Ampel rechts.
e  Nimm die zweite Straße rechts und geh dann links.
f  Gehen Sie geradeaus und an der Kreuzung rechts.

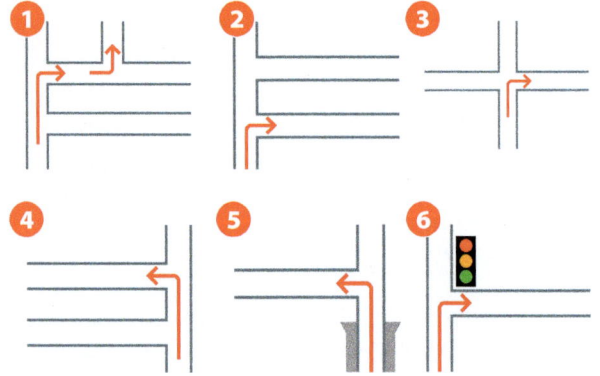

## SCHREIBEN 2

**Was brauchen Sira und Leo? Schreib die passenden Wörter auf.**
Fill in the gaps in a–d using the pictures as clues.

Wir brauchen …

a  einen         .
b  eine Liste von         .
c  eine         über         .
d  einen         .
e  eine Liste von         .
f  eine Liste von         .

## LESEN 3

**NC 3**

**Finde die richtige Reihenfolge für den Dialog.**
Work out the correct sequence for the dialogue.

*Beispiel:* **g**, …

a  Nein, Sie müssen in Köln umsteigen.
b  Das kostet 120 Euro.
c  Hin und zurück.
d  Erster Klasse. Was kostet das?
e  Einfach oder hin und zurück?
f  120 Euro – bitte. Fährt der Zug direkt?
g  Guten Tag! Eine Fahrkarte nach Bonn, bitte.
h  Und erster oder zweiter Klasse?

## LESEN 4

**NC 5**

**Beantworte die Fragen auf Englisch.**
Answer the questions in English.

a  Where was Sven at the weekend? And with whom?
b  What did they do on Saturday morning?
c  What did they do at lunchtime?
d  What did he do in the afternoon?
e  What did they do on Sunday?
f  What does he say about next year?

Ich war am Wochenende mit meiner Familie in Zürich! Wir haben am Samstagmorgen eine Schiffsfahrt auf dem Zürichsee gemacht und wir haben mittags am Bahnhofsplatz Pizza gegessen. Am Nachmittag habe ich einen Einkaufsbummel in der Bahnhofstraße gemacht. Ich habe einen Rucksack gekauft.

Am Sonntag haben wir eine Stadtrundfahrt gemacht. Wir haben die Sehenswürdigkeiten besichtigt.

Der Ausflug nach Zürich war super! Nächstes Jahr werden wir wieder in die Schweiz fahren. Wir werden Luzern besuchen.

*Sven*

- Vocabulary: describe where things are; give directions
- Grammar: use the dative case and the accusative; use the imperative
- Skills: practise reading skills

**SCHREIBEN 1** NC 3

**Wo ist die Kleidung? Schreib Sätze für die Bilder.**

*Beispiel:* **a** *Die Jeans ist auf dem Regal.*

**SCHREIBEN 2** NC 3

**„Die Katze springt …" Schreib neue Sätze für Übung 1.**

*Beispiel:* **a** *Die Katze springt auf das Regal.*

**SCHREIBEN 3** NC 3

**Frau Braun fragt: „Wo ist der Bahnhof, bitte?" Beschreib den Weg.**

*Beispiel:* *Gehen Sie geradeaus und dann …*

**Du bist hier**

**LESEN 4** NC 6

**Beantworte die Fragen auf Englisch.**

**a** Where is Tina going and with whom?
**b** What does she say about the journey?
**c** What did she do last year?
**d** What did they do first?
**e** What does she say about the museum?
**f** What does she say about the park?
**g** What will she do with her sister? Why?
**h** Where else do they want to go? Why?

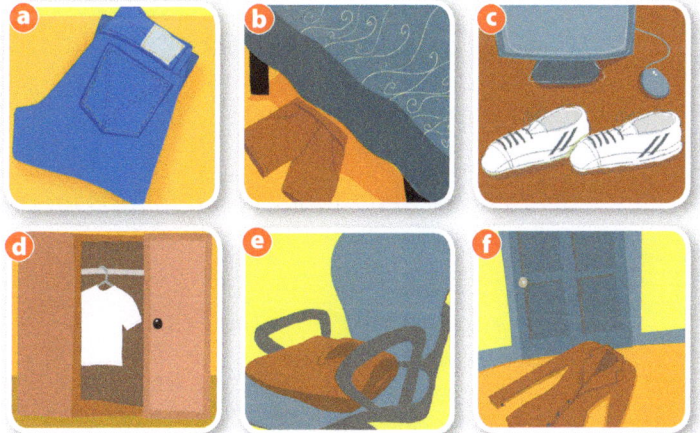

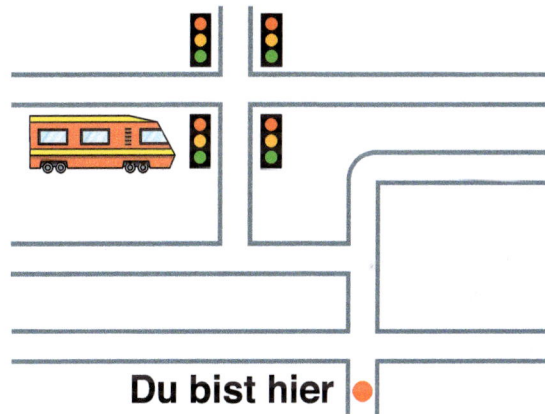

Ich fahre am Wochenende nach München! Ich fahre mit meiner Schwester. Wir werden mit dem Zug fahren, weil das am schnellsten ist.

Ich war letztes Jahr mit meiner Klasse in München und wir haben viel gemacht. Wir haben eine Stadtrundfahrt gemacht und wir haben die Sehenswürdigkeiten besichtigt. Wir haben auch ein Museum besucht, aber das war ziemlich langweilig. Und wir haben im Englischen Garten – das ist ein Park – Frisbee gespielt! Das war super!

Ich werde mit meiner Schwester auch einen Einkaufsbummel machen. In München gibt es tolle Geschäfte! Wir werden auch einen Ausflug zum Chiemsee machen, weil man da schwimmen kann.

*Tina*

## HÖREN 1 — NC 5

🎧 **Listen to the telephone conversation at the tourist information centre. Answer the questions in English. (See pages 100–101.)**

*Beispiel:* **a** *Berlin, …*

**a** Where is the girl going? When?
**b** What does she want to know?
**c** What does the man suggest? (2)
**d** What else does the girl want? (2)
**e** What is she asking for in terms of accommodation? (3)
**f** What is the last item she asks for?

## SPRECHEN 2 — NC 5

**Give a presentation about what there is for tourists in your town. (See pages 102–103, 107.)**

Say:
- what sights there are to see: *Es gibt …*
- what you can visit: *Man kann …*
- where you can go
- what else you can do
- what you can eat/drink, and where
- what you did there last weekend, and your opinion of it (using the perfect and imperfect tense): *Ich habe/bin …*

## LESEN 3 — NC 6

**Read Daniel's message and answer the questions in English. (See page 107.)**

*Beispiel:* **a** *Hamburg, with …*

**a** Where did Daniel go? And with whom?
**b** How did they travel? Why?
**c** What does he say about the journey? (2)
**d** What is there to do? (2)
**e** What does he say about the museums? (2)
**f** What does he say about the zoo?
**g** What is he going to do next weekend? (2)

> Das letzte Wochenende war super. Ich bin mit meinen Eltern nach Hamburg gefahren. Wir sind mit dem Zug gefahren, weil das schnell ist. Die Fahrt war gar nicht langweilig, weil ich Musik gehört und meine Zeitschrift gelesen habe.
>
> Wir haben meine Tante besucht und die Sehenswürdigkeiten besichtigt. Man kann viel in Hamburg machen: man kann eine Bootsfahrt auf der Alster machen und man kann am Alster-Ufer spazieren gehen.
>
> Wir haben auch Museen besichtigt, aber das war ziemlich langweilig, denn es gab dort nur alte Bilder. Und ich habe den Hagenbeck-Zoo besucht – das war super, weil ich Tiere mag!
>
> Nächstes Wochenende werden wir einen Ausflug nach München machen und auch dort alle Touristenattraktionen besuchen – ich freue mich schon sehr darauf!
>
> *Daniel*

## SCHREIBEN 4 — NC 6

**Describe an excursion to Düsseldorf. Write at least five sentences. (See page 107.)**

Say:
- when you went: *am Wochenende, im Sommer, …*
- who you went with: *mit meinem/meiner/meinen …*
- what you did: *Ich habe … gemacht/besucht/…*
- what you ate and drank: *Ich habe … gegessen/getrunken.*
- what you thought of it, and why: *Das war …, weil ich …*
- where you're going on another excursion: *Ich werde …*

## Wir brauchen Infos! — *We need info!*

| | |
|---|---|
| Wir brauchen … | *We need …* |
| eine Broschüre über die Stadt. | *a brochure about the town.* |
| einen Fahrplan. | *a timetable.* |
| eine Liste von billigen Hotels/Restaurants. | *a list of cheap hotels/ restaurants.* |
| eine Liste von Campingplätzen/ Jugendherbergen. | *a list of campsites/ youth hostels.* |
| einen Stadtplan. | *a map of the town.* |

## Was kann man machen? — *What can you do?*

| | |
|---|---|
| Man kann/Wir können … | *You/We can …* |
| einen Einkaufsbummel machen. | *go on a shopping expedition.* |
| das Filmmuseum besuchen. | *visit the Film Museum.* |
| den Rheinturm besichtigen. | *visit the Rhine Tower.* |
| eine Stadtrundfahrt machen. | *do a tour of the town.* |
| in den Südpark gehen. | *go to the South Park.* |

## Zwei Fahrkarten, bitte! — *Two tickets, please!*

| | |
|---|---|
| Wie komme ich am besten … | *What's the best way …* |
| zum Bahnhof? | *to the railway station?* |
| zur nächsten U-Bahn-Station? | *to the nearest underground station?* |
| zum Kino? | *to the cinema?* |
| Wo ist die nächste … | *Where's the nearest …* |
| Bushaltestelle? | *bus stop?* |
| S-Bahn-Station? | *S-Bahn station?* |
| Geh/Gehen Sie … | *Go …* |
| Nimm/Nehmen Sie … | *Take …* |
| links/rechts/geradeaus | *left/right/straight on* |
| die erste Straße rechts | *the first road on the right* |
| die zweite Straße links | *the second road on the left* |
| über die Brücke | *over the bridge* |
| an der Ampel/Kreuzung | *at the traffic lights/crossroads* |

| | |
|---|---|
| Ich möchte zwei Fahrkarten nach …, bitte. | *I'd like two tickets to …, please.* |
| Einfach oder hin und zurück? | *One-way or return?* |
| Erster oder zweiter Klasse? | *First or second class?* |
| Was kosten die Fahrkarten? | *How much are the tickets?* |
| Eine Fahrkarte kostet … Euro. | *One ticket costs … euros.* |
| Fährt der Zug direkt? | *Is this a direct train?* |
| Nein, Sie müssen in … umsteigen. | *No, you have to change in …* |
| Wann fährt der Zug ab? | *When does the train leave?* |
| Und wann kommt er an? | *When does it arrive?* |
| Die Fahrt wird … Minuten dauern. | *The journey will take … minutes.* |

## Wieder zu Hause! — *Home again!*

| | |
|---|---|
| das Hemd | *shirt* |
| die Jacke | *jacket* |
| die Jeans | *jeans* |
| der Kapuzenpullover | *hooded jumper* |
| der Pullover | *jumper* |
| die Schuhe | *shoes* |
| die Shorts | *shorts* |
| das T-Shirt | *T-shirt* |

| | |
|---|---|
| unter dem Bett | *under the bed* |
| neben dem Computer | *next to the computer* |
| auf dem Regal | *on the shelf* |
| zwischen dem Bett und dem Stuhl | *between the bed and the chair* |
| vor dem Schreibtisch | *in front of the desk* |
| an der Tür | *on the door* |
| im Schrank | *in the wardrobe* |
| hinter dem Bett | *behind the bed* |

| | |
|---|---|
| Wir sind … | *We …* |
| gefahren/gegangen/ angekommen/ geschwommen. | *travelled/went/ arrived/ swam …* |
| Wir haben … | *We …* |
| besichtigt/besucht. | *visited …* |
| gekauft/gespielt. | *bought/played …* |
| gesehen/gemacht. | *saw/did …* |
| getanzt. | *danced.* |
| gegessen/getrunken. | *ate/drank …* |

### I can …

- plan a trip and write a formal letter
- say what there is to see and do in a town, and what I'm going to do
- ask for and give directions
- buy train tickets
- say where items of clothing are in a room
- describe a trip using past tenses
- use the accusative case
- use prepositions with the accusative and dative
- use the imperative
- identify different styles of writing
- pronounce the *pf* and *zw* sounds

# 4A.1 Meine Gegend

- Vocabulary: describe in detail where you live and give your opinion of it
- Grammar: use correct word order with *weil*
- Skills: use knowledge of language patterns

**LESEN 1** **Wo wohnst du? Finde die Paare (a–h und 1–8).**

*Beispiel:* **a 6**

a am Stadtrand
b in einer Stadt
c auf dem Land
d in einer Kleinstadt
e in einer Großstadt
f in einer Industriestadt
g in einem Dorf
h an der Küste

| | | | |
|---|---|---|---|
| **1** | at the coast | **5** | in a small town |
| **2** | in a town | **6** | in the suburbs |
| **3** | in a village | **7** | in the countryside |
| **4** | in a city | **8** | in an industrial town |

**HÖREN 2** 🎧 **Hör zu und lies (1–4). Wo wohnen sie (a–d)?**

**1**
Ich wohne in Hamburg im Norden von Deutschland. Hamburg ist eine Großstadt und liegt an einem großen Fluss. In Hamburg gibt es einen Hafen. Ich wohne gern hier, weil man viel machen kann. Früher habe ich in einer Industriestadt gewohnt. Dort war es laut und schmutzig.

*Anne*

**2**
Ich wohne in Rostock im Osten von Deutschland. Rostock ist eine mittelgroße Stadt an der Küste. Es gibt hier viele alte, traditionelle Häuser und Gebäude. Das finde ich schön. Aber in Zukunft werde ich auf dem Land wohnen, weil es dort ruhig und sauber ist.

*Henning*

**3**
Meine Familie wohnt in einem Dorf in den Bergen. Hier ist es total langweilig. Ich möchte in einer Stadt wohnen, weil man dort viel machen kann. Hier gibt es nichts für Jugendliche.

*Jan*

**4**
Ich wohne am Stadtrand von Frankfurt. In Frankfurt kann man einkaufen und ins Kino gehen. Das finde ich sehr praktisch! Aber leider gibt es in Frankfurt viel Kriminalität und zu viele Autos. Hier am Stadtrand ist es sicher und man kann mit dem Fahrrad fahren.

*Eva*

**LESEN 3**
NC 4

**Lies 1–4 (Übung 2) noch einmal. Wie sagt man das auf Deutsch?**

*Beispiel:* **a** *an einem großen Fluss*

**a** on a big river
**b** harbour
**c** noisy and dirty
**d** a medium-sized town
**e** buildings
**f** quiet and clean
**g** in the mountains
**h** nothing for young people
**i** a lot of crime
**j** too many cars
**k** safe

**LESEN 4**
NC 5–6

**Lies 1–4 (Übung 2) noch einmal. Richtig (R), falsch (F) oder nicht im Text (NiT)?**

**a** In Annes Stadt kann man Boote und Schiffe sehen.
**b** Anne mag ihre Stadt nicht.
**c** Hennings Stadt ist nicht groß und nicht klein.
**d** Früher hat Jan in einer Stadt gewohnt.
**e** Eva wohnt in der Stadtmitte.
**f** In Evas Stadt gibt es nichts für Jugendliche.

**SCHREIBEN 5**

**Schreib die Sätze richtig auf.**

*Beispiel:* **a** *Ich wohne gern hier, weil es nicht viel Kriminalität gibt.*

**a** Ich wohne gern hier, weil es / gibt / nicht viel Kriminalität / .
**b** Wir wohnen gern auf dem Land, weil ruhig / es / ist / .
**c** Ich wohne nicht gern in London, weil zu laut / ist / es / .
**d** Ich wohne nicht gern in einer Großstadt, weil es / gibt / zu viele Autos / .
**e** Wir wohnen gern an der Küste, weil schwimmen / wir / gern / .

**HÖREN 6**
NC 4

🎧 **Wo wohnen sie? Hör zu (1–5) und füll die Tabelle auf Deutsch aus.**

*Beispiel:*

| | Wo? | Gern? | Warum? |
|---|---|---|---|
| 1 | Kleinstadt, Küste | ✓ | schwimmt gern |

**SPRECHEN 7**
NC 4

👥 **Macht eine Klassenumfrage. Fragt drei Personen:**

● Wo wohnst du?
● Wohnst du gern da? Warum? Warum nicht?

**SCHREIBEN 8**
NC 4

**Du bist 1, 2, 3, 4 oder 5 aus Übung 6. Wo wohnst du? Wohnst du gern da? Warum? Benutze deine Antworten aus Übung 6.**

*Beispiel: Nummer 3: Ich wohne am Stadtrand von Wolfsburg. Ich …*

**? Think**

● How many sentences using *weil* can you spot in activity 2? What happens to the word order after *weil*?
● What other linking words do you know? Which ones affect word order?

Ich wohne (nicht) gern hier, weil …
… es langweilig/laut/praktisch/ruhig/sauber/schmutzig/schön/sicher ist.
… es viel Kriminalität gibt.
… es zu viele Autos gibt.
… es nichts für Jugendliche gibt.
… man viel machen kann.

**Challenge**

Write an email to your German friend, describing:
● where you live
● what it is like
● whether you like it and why
● Try to add where you will live in the future and/or where you lived in the past.

To help you reach level 7, use reference materials and more complex structures.

NC 4–7

# 4A.2 Bus und Bahn

- Vocabulary: talk about ways to travel
- Grammar: use the dative case
- Skills: identify language patterns

**HÖREN 1**

🎧 **Hör zu (1–9). Welche Verkehrsmittel benutzen sie?**

NC 3  *Beispiel:* **1 b**

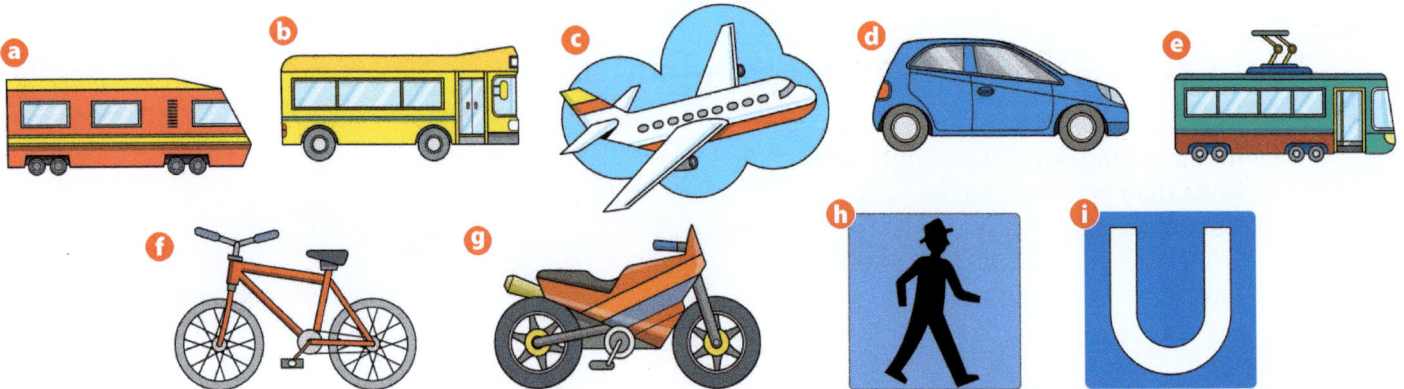

**Ich fahre mit …**
  dem Bus/Zug
  der Straßenbahn/U-Bahn
  dem Auto/Fahrrad/Motorrad
Ich fliege mit dem Flugzeug
Ich gehe zu Fuß

  zum Flughafen/Park.
  zur Arbeit/Schule.
  zum Kino/Stadion.
  nach Berlin/Frankreich.
  in den Urlaub.

**? Think**

- Look at the different ways to travel. What happens to the word for 'the' when it follows *mit*? Why do you think this is?
- Look at the destinations. What happens when *zu* is used? How does it affect the word for 'the'?

**SPRECHEN 2**

👥 **Macht eine Klassenumfrage. Fragt acht Personen: „Wie kommst du zur Schule?"**
Draw a diagram to show the results.

*Beispiel:* **A** *Wie kommst du zur Schule?*
**B** *Ich fahre mit dem Auto zur Schule.*
**C** *Ich …*

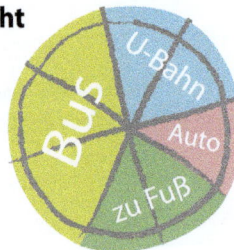

**SCHREIBEN 3**

**Füll die Lücken aus:** *dem, der, zum* **oder** *zur*?

*Beispiel:* **a** *dem*

a Mein Vater fährt mit _____ Auto.
b Ich fahre mit _____ Fahrrad _____ Schule.
c Meine Mutter geht zu Fuß _____ Arbeit.
d Wir fahren mit _____ Bus _____ Park.
e Fahren Sie am besten mit _____ Straßenbahn.
f Ich fahre mit _____ U-Bahn _____ Flughafen.

**⚙ Grammatik → p.159**

**The dative case**
*Mit* and *zu* take the dative case. *Zu* is usually added to the word for 'the' (*dem* or *der*) to give *zum* (zu + dem) and *zur* (zu + der):

| m. | mit **dem** Bus | **zum** Flughafen (zu + dem) |
|----|-----------------|------------------------------|
| f. | mit **der** U-Bahn | **zur** Schule (zu + der) |
| n. | mit **dem** Auto | **zum** Kino (zu + dem) |

**LESEN 4** **Wie ist Bremen? Füll die Lücken aus: _dem_, _der_, _zum_ oder _zur_?**

*Beispiel:* **a** *der*, …

**a** In Bremen gibt es keine U-Bahn, sondern eine Straßenbahn. Am besten fährt man mit [____] Straßenbahn oder mit [____] Bus.

**b** Es gibt in Bremen eine große Universität. Die meisten Studenten sind umweltfreundlich und gehen zu Fuß oder fahren mit [____] Fahrrad [____] Universität.

**c** Wenn du ein Fußballfan bist, hast du schon von Bremen gehört! Bremens Klub heißt „Werder Bremen" und das Stadion heißt „Weser-Stadion". Viele Fans kommen mit [____] Auto [____] Stadion. Sehr umweltfeindlich!

**d** Am Stadtrand von Bremen gibt es einen großen internationalen Flughafen. Man kann dort mit [____] Flugzeug in den Urlaub fliegen.

**LESEN 5** **Lies den Text (Übung 4) noch einmal.**

**NC 4**

**a** Wie sagt man auf Deutsch: **1** „environmentally friendly"?
**2** „environmentally unfriendly"?

**b** Welche Verkehrsmittel findest du im Text? Schreib zwei Listen: **1** und **2**.

**SCHREIBEN 6** **Schreib Sätze für a–e.**

**NC 3–4**

Write a sentence for each of a–e. Try to use a different subject (e.g. *ich*, *er*, *meine Mutter*, …) in each sentence. Try to use different tenses too!

*Beispiel:* **a** *Mein Vater fährt am Montag mit der Straßenbahn zur Arbeit.*

**a** on Monday

**b** often

**c** every day

**d** at the weekend

**e** in the evening

> **⚙ Grammatik →** p.162–6
>
> **Present:**
> ich fahre       wir fahren
> du fährst       ihr fahrt
> er/sie fährt    sie/Sie fahren
>
> **Past:**
> Ich bin … gefahren.
>
> **Future:**
> Ich werde … fahren.

**Challenge**

Your exchange partner from Bremen is coming to visit you. He/She is very environmentally friendly and wants to know how you travel around. Write an email, saying:

• how you and your family travel to different places
• how often you use different means of transport
• how you used to travel
• how you are going to travel in future

**NC 6–7**

# 4A.3 Umweltschutz

- Vocabulary: talk about ways to be environmentally friendly
- Grammar: use compound nouns
- Skills: evaluate language tasks; identify language patterns

**Bist du umweltfreundlich? Finde die Paare (1–8 und a–h).**

*Beispiel:* **1 c**

1. Ich spare Strom.
2. Ich nehme keine Plastiktüten, sondern Stofftaschen.
3. Meine Familie nutzt alternative Energien, z.B. Sonnenenergie und Windenergie.
4. Ich bade nicht. Ich dusche.
5. Wir haben vier Mülleimer. Wir trennen unseren Müll.
6. Ich recycle Papier und Dosen.
7. Ich bringe Glasflaschen zum Container.
8. Ich fahre mit dem Rad oder gehe zu Fuß.

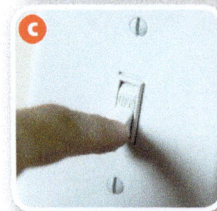

🎧 **Hör zu (1–5). Welches Bild (a–h) passt?**

*Beispiel:* **1 b**, …

**Umweltfeindlich oder umweltfreundlich? Mach zwei Listen.**

*Beispiel: Umweltfreundlich: a, …*
*Umweltfeindlich: …*

a. Ich nehme Stofftaschen.
b. Ich bade morgens und abends.
c. Wir trennen unseren Müll nicht.
d. Ich recycle Papier, Plastik, Dosen und Glas.
e. Mein Computer ist immer im Stand-by.
f. Ich gehe zu Fuß zur Schule.

## Grammatik → p.158

**Compound nouns**

- Compound nouns are formed by putting two or more shorter nouns together:

  der Wind + die Energie → die Windenergie
  das Plastik + die Tüte → die Plastiktüte
  der Müll + der Eimer → der Mülleimer

- How can you work out the gender of a compound noun? Look at the examples above and try to come up with a rule.

👥 **Klassenumfrage: „Was machst du für die Umwelt?"**
**Ist eure Klasse umweltfreundlich?**

*Beispiel:*

A. Was machst du für die Umwelt?
B. Ich gehe zu Fuß zur Schule.
C. Ich …

**HÖREN 5** NC 6

🎧 **Hör zu und lies. Was machen Jan und Anna für die Umwelt? Was haben sie gemacht? Was werden sie machen?**

| | Präsens | Perfekt | Futur |
|---|---|---|---|
| Jan | *Ich recycle …* | *Letztes Jahr haben wir …* | *In Zukunft werde ich …* |
| Anna | | | |

**Anna:** Was machst du für die Umwelt?

**Jan:** Ich recycle Papier, Dosen und Glas. Und zu Hause nutzen wir alternative Energien.

**Anna:** Cool! Nächstes Jahr werden wir zu Hause Sonnenenergie nutzen. Letztes Jahr haben wir Strom gespart, immer geduscht und nicht gebadet. Ich bin immer mit dem Rad zur Schule gefahren.

**Jan:** Ich gehe oft zu Fuß zur Schule. Letztes Jahr haben wir zu Hause unseren Müll getrennt und viel recycelt. Aber ich habe oft Plastiktüten genommen. In Zukunft werde ich Stofftaschen nehmen.

**Anna:** Ich nehme nie Plastiktüten. In Zukunft werde ich mehr recyceln. Ich werde Papier, Dosen und Glasflaschen zum Container bringen.

**SCHREIBEN 6** NC 5–6

**Du bist dran! Was machst du für die Umwelt? Was hast du gemacht? Was wirst du machen? Schreib einen Blog.**

Letztes Jahr habe ich …
   gebadet/gebracht/geduscht/genommen/
   genutzt/recycelt/gespart/getrennt.
Letztes Jahr bin ich … gefahren/gegangen.

Nächstes Jahr/In Zukunft werde ich …
   baden/bringen/duschen/fahren/gehen/
   nehmen/nutzen/recyceln/sparen/trennen.

**? Think**

What language features do you need to use for level 6 or above?

**Challenge**

Write an article for a Swiss school magazine about what people in the UK do for the environment, e.g. recycling, energy saving. Try to use different tenses.

NC 5–6

▶ *Die Video-Aufgabe*

**VIDEO 7**

**Sieh dir das Video an und beantworte die Fragen auf Englisch.**

*Beispiel:* **a** *Four*

**a** How many bins are used for recycling?

**b** What do you put in the blue bin? And in the yellow bin?

**c** Sira says *Essensreste* and *Biomüll* go into the brown 'Bio' bin. What do you think *Essensreste* and *Biomüll* are?

**d** The fourth bin is the grey *Restmüll* bin. What do you think *Restmüll* is?

**e** What does Leo do to protect the environment?

**f** What does Sira think you can do to protect the environment?

**g** What is recycled in the recycling centre?

**h** What is Leo's first step to becoming more environmentally friendly?

**VIDEO 8** 👥 **What do you think of the German recycling system?**

# 4A.4 Fünf vor zwölf

- Vocabulary: talk about environmental problems and solutions
- Grammar: use comparatives and superlatives
- Skills: work out the meaning of new words

**LESEN 1**

**Welche Umweltprobleme gibt es? Finde die Paare (a–i und 1–9).**

*Beispiel:* **a 5**

a nuclear waste
b a lot of traffic
c deforestation
d hole in the ozone layer
e greenhouse effect
f extinction of animals
g rubbish mountains
h air pollution
i climate change

**1** die Müllberge

**2** die Luftverschmutzung

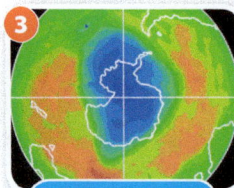
**3** das Ozonloch

**4** viel Verkehr

**5** der Atommüll

**6** die Entwaldung

**7** der Klimawandel

**8** der Treibhauseffekt

**9** das Aussterben von Tieren

**HÖREN 2**

🎧 **Hör zu (1–5). Welche Umweltprobleme gibt es (1–9 aus Übung 1)? Und was muss man machen?**

*Beispiel:*

| | Problem? | Was muss man machen? |
|---|---|---|
| **1** | 5 | *alternative Energien nutzen, …* |

**? Think**

There are a lot of new German words in activity 1. Try to work out their meaning by looking at the pictures. What else helps you to understand them?

**SPRECHEN 3**

**NC 3–4**

👥 **Macht Dialoge. Welche Umweltprobleme gibt es? Was muss man machen?**

*Beispiel:*

A *Welche Umweltprobleme gibt es?*
B *Ein großes Problem sind die Müllberge. Man muss …*

Welche Umweltprobleme gibt es?
Ein großes Problem ist/sind …
Was muss man machen?
Man muss …
    mehr zu Fuß gehen/mit dem Rad fahren.
    nicht so viel mit dem Auto fahren.
    alternative Energien nutzen.
    Strom sparen.
    mehr recyceln.
    die Natur schützen.

**HÖREN 4** · NC 4

🎧 **Hör zu und lies. Was glauben Sira und Leo? Welche Umweltprobleme ☹ gibt es? Und welche Lösungen ☺?**

| | ☹ | ☹☹ | ☹☹☹ | ☺ | ☺☺ | ☺☺☺ |
|---|---|---|---|---|---|---|
| Sira | Müllberge | | | Recycling | | |
| Leo | | | | | | |

**Sira:** Ich finde, die Müllberge sind <u>schlimm</u> für die Umwelt. Aber die Luftverschmutzung ist <u>schlimmer als</u> die Müllberge. Der Atommüll ist <u>am schlimmsten</u>.

**Leo:** Die Entwaldung ist ein <u>großes</u> Problem. Aber es gibt auch zu viel Verkehr – das ist ein <u>größeres</u> Problem. Ich glaube, das <u>größte</u> Problem ist die Luftverschmutzung.

**Sira:** Alternative Energien sind <u>am wichtigsten</u> für die Umwelt, finde ich. Ich recycle Papier, Dosen und Glas. Das ist auch sehr <u>wichtig</u>. Und ich spare Strom. Ich glaube, das ist <u>wichtiger als</u> Recycling.

**Leo:** Ich dusche immer und bade nicht – das ist <u>gut</u> für die Umwelt. Ich nehme keine Plastiktüten, weil Stofftaschen <u>besser</u> für die Umwelt sind. Und ich gehe oft zu Fuß. Das finde ich <u>am besten</u>.

**? Think**

- Look at the conversation between Sira and Leo. Find two verbs you can use to give your opinion.
- Look at the <u>underlined</u> words. Can you work out what they mean?

## Grammatik → p.161

- **The comparative:** 'bigger', 'better', 'worse', etc.

  schlimm → schlimm**er** (bad → **worse**)
  gut → **besser** (good → **better**)
  groß → gr**öß**er (big → big**ger**)
  wichtig → wichtig**er als** … (important → **more** important **than** …)

- **The superlative:** 'the biggest', 'the best', etc.

  das gr**öß**t**e** Problem → the big**gest** problem
  **am** wichtig**sten** → the **most** important **of all**
  **am besten** → the **best of all**

**SPRECHEN 5** · NC 4

👥 **Macht Dialoge. Welche Umweltprobleme gibt es? Und welche Lösungen?**

*Beispiel:* **A** Ich finde, die Luftverschmutzung ist das größte Problem für die Umwelt.

**B** Nein, der Atommüll ist schlimmer als die Luftverschmutzung. Ich glaube, alternative Energien sind am wichtigsten …

**SCHREIBEN 6** · NC 4–5

**Du bist dran! Welche Umweltprobleme gibt es? Was ist schlimm/schlimmer/am schlimmsten? Schreib acht Sätze wie in Übung 5.**

**Challenge**

Design a poster or leaflet showing the state our environment is in. Use the comparative and superlative to explain what the problems and solutions are. Use *man muss* … to explain what must be done.

NC 4–6

- Vocabulary: talk about environmental issues
- Grammar: use the present tense, the past and the future
- Skills: think about language patterns

**Umweltschutz statt Umweltschmutz**

Früher

Heute

**LESEN 1**

NC 5

**Früher (F) oder heute (H)?**

*Beispiel:* **a F**

a Das Licht war immer an.
b Es gibt viele Pflanzen. Wir haben einen Bio-Garten.
c Wir haben Solarzellen auf dem Schuldach.
d Wir sparen Strom.
e Es gab überall Müll.
f Die Schüler kommen mit dem Schulbus, mit dem Rad oder zu Fuß zur Schule.

g Wir trennen den Müll. Es gibt Mülleimer für Plastik, Glas, Papier und Dosen.
h Wir haben ein Recyclingsystem. Wir können unser Papier recyceln.
i Es war schmutzig.
j Es ist sauber.
k Alles war grau. Es gab keine Pflanzen oder Bäume.
l Die Schüler sind mit dem Auto zur Schule gefahren.

**HÖREN 2**

🎧 **Hör zu (1–5). Was sind die Zukunftspläne? (a–l, Übung 1)**

*Beispiel:* **1 b**

**SPRECHEN 3**

👥 **A zeigt auf etwas auf dem Bild (Übung 1). B wählt einen Satz aus a–l. A ↔ B.**

*Beispiel:* **A** *(points to pupils arriving at school by car)*
**B** *Die Schüler sind mit dem Auto zur Schule gefahren.*

**? Think**

Activity 2 asks: *Was sind die Zukunftspläne?* So which tense are you going to hear? Can you remember how to form this tense?

**HÖREN 4**

NC 6

🎧 **Hör zu. Wie war es früher? Wie ist es heute? Wie wird es sein? Schreib die Tabelle ab und mach Notizen auf Deutsch.**

*Beispiel:*

| Früher | Heute | In Zukunft |
|---|---|---|
| … | *Die Schüler kommen mit dem Rad …* | … |

# Initiative „Grüne Schule"

Früher war unsere Schule nicht sehr umweltfreundlich. Recycling war ein großes Problem. Es gab keine Mülleimer für Papier, Dosen oder Glas. Aber seit einem Jahr hat die Schule ein Recyclingsystem. Jetzt trennen wir den Müll.

Wir recyceln nicht nur Papier, Dosen, Plastik und Glas, sondern auch Druckerpatronen! Wir schicken die Druckerpatronen an die Computerfirmen zurück und sie geben uns Geld dafür. Wir geben das Geld einem Tierheim in unserer Stadt und das Tierheim kauft Futter und Medikamente für die Tiere. Eine tolle Idee!

In Zukunft werden wir Solarzellen auf dem Schuldach haben. Es wird auch mehr Schulbusse geben, weil zu viele Schüler mit dem Auto zur Schule kommen. Und wir werden einen Fahrradkeller haben! Das finde ich super, weil ich jeden Tag mit dem Rad zur Schule fahre.

Wir hatten früher keine Bäume oder Pflanzen in unserer Schule, aber jetzt haben wir einen Bio-Garten. Nächstes Jahr werden wir viel Gemüse für die Schulkantine haben!

Oliver (16)

## LESEN 5

**Lies Olivers Text. Finde a–e im Text.**

**a** printer cartridges **c** animal food **e** bike cellar
**b** animal shelter **d** medicines

## LESEN 6
NC 6

**Lies Olivers Text noch einmal. Richtig (R), falsch (F) oder nicht im Text (NiT)?**

**a** In Olivers Schule kann man nur Papier, Dosen, Plastik und Glas recyceln.
**b** Man sammelt Druckerpatronen, um Geld für das Tierheim zu bekommen.
**c** Viele Schüler haben Hunde und Katzen aus dem Tierheim.
**d** In Zukunft wird Olivers Schule Sonnenenergie nutzen.
**e** Oliver fährt normalerweise mit dem Schulbus zur Schule.
**f** Die Schüler werden Gemüse aus dem Schulgarten essen.

> Früher …
> war es/gab es/hatten wir …
> haben wir … recycelt/getrennt/…
> sind wir … gefahren/gegangen.
>
> Heute …
> ist es/gibt es/haben wir …
> recyceln wir/trennen wir …
> fahren/gehen wir …
>
> In Zukunft …
> wird es … sein/geben.
> werden wir … haben/recyceln/ …

## SCHREIBEN 7

**„Ist deine Schule umweltfreundlich?" Mach Notizen.**

*Beispiel:*

| Früher | Heute | In Zukunft |
|---|---|---|
| kein Recyclingsystem, … | wir trennen den Müll, … | wir werden … |

## SPRECHEN 8
NC 4–6

**„Ist deine Schule umweltfreundlich?" Mach eine Präsentation. Benutze deine Notizen aus Übung 7.**

*Beispiel: Früher war meine Schule … Heute … In Zukunft …*

**Challenge**

You are entering an international competition:

- The prize: a trip to a wildlife sanctuary.
- The task: design a leaflet or write a report describing how environmentally friendly your school is, what it used to be like and what it will do in future.

NC 6

**The linking word *weil*, comparatives and superlatives, the dative case**

**1** Build sentences from these phrases, using *Ich wohne gern/nicht gern …, weil …*

✓ = *Ich wohne gern …*
✗ = *Ich wohne nicht gern …*

*Beispiel:* **a** *Ich wohne gern am Stadtrand, weil es praktisch ist.*

**a** ✓ / am Stadtrand / es ist praktisch
**b** ✗ / auf dem Land / es ist langweilig
**c** ✓ / in einer Stadt / es gibt viel für Jugendliche
**d** ✗ / in einer Großstadt / es gibt zu viele Autos
**e** ✓ / in einem Dorf / es gibt keine Kriminalität

> **weil**
>
> The word *weil* smells so vile – it makes the verb run a mile!
>
> Remember that *weil* sends the verb to the end of the clause.

**2** Write the comparative and superlative form of each adjective.

*Beispiel:* **a** *kleiner, am kleinsten*

**a** klein
**b** schmutzig
**c** groß
**d** sauber
**e** wichtig
**f** umweltfreundlich
**g** interessant
**h** schön
**i** ruhig

> **Comparatives and superlatives**
>
> - Use the comparative when you want to say something is 'bigger', 'better', 'worse', etc. Like in English, you usually add *-er* to the adjective in German:
>
>   klein → klein**er** (*small → smaller*)
>   ruhig → ruhig**er** (*quiet → quieter*)
>
> - For some short adjectives, you also add an umlaut to the first vowel:
>
>   groß → gr**ö**ß**er** (*big → bigger*)
>
> - Some comparatives are irregular:
>
>   gut → **besser** (*good → better*)
>
> - To say 'than', use *als*:
>
>   Der Atommüll ist schlimmer **als** die Luftverschmutzung.
>   *Nuclear waste is worse **than** air pollution.*
>
> - Use the superlative when you want to say something is 'the biggest (of all)', 'the best (of all)', etc. You usually put *am* before the adjective and add *-sten* to the end, or *-esten* if the adjective ends in *t, d, s, sch* or *z*:
>
>   **am** wichtig**sten** → *the most important of all*
>   **am** laut**esten** → *the loudest of all*
>
> - Some superlatives are irregular:
>
>   am **besten** → *the best of all*
>   am gr**ö**ß**ten** → *the biggest of all*

**3** Write sentences using some of the adjectives from activity 2. Try to use at least three comparatives and three superlatives.

*Beispiel: Meine Stadt ist <u>kleiner als</u> London.*

**4** Fill in the gaps with *dem*, *der*, *zum* or *zur*.

*Beispiel:* **a** *dem, zum*

**a** Meine Mutter fährt oft mit _____ Bus _____ Supermarkt.
**b** Meine Familie fliegt gern mit _____ Flugzeug.
**c** Ich gehe zu Fuß _____ Schule.
**d** Wir fahren mit _____ Straßenbahn in die Stadt.
**e** Meine Mutter fährt mit _____ Auto _____ Arbeit.
**f** Ich fahre gern mit _____ Fahrrad _____ Park.
**g** Wir bringen die Glasflaschen _____ Container.

### The dative case

The prepositions *mit* and *zu* take the dative case. *Zu* is usually added to the word for 'the' (*dem* or *der*) to give *zum* (*zu* + *dem*) and *zur* (*zu* + *der*):

| m. | mit **dem** Bus | **zum** Flughafen (zu + dem) |
|----|-----------------|------------------------------|
| f. | mit **der** U-Bahn | **zur** Schule (zu + der) |
| n. | mit **dem** Auto | **zum** Kino (zu + dem) |

## Evaluating and improving your written work

**?**

To get a high mark for your writing, you need to be accurate. Always check your work very carefully for the following:

**a** **Spellings**. Use capital letters for nouns, and umlauts where needed.
**b** **Verbs**. Check irregular verbs in a verb table.
**c** **Tenses**. Have you used the correct tenses (past, present, future) and have you formed them correctly?
**d** **Plurals**. Check these in a dictionary.
**e** **Word order**. Remember the verb comes second, but other things affect word order too, e.g. past participles go to the end, and *weil* sends the verb to the end.

**5** **Read Leo's text. There is <u>one</u> mistake in every sentence.**

- Identify each mistake: is it a, b, c, d or e from the checklist above?
- Write out each sentence correctly.

*Beispiel: Sentence 1 = mistake b. It should be: 'In der Schweiz <u>ist</u> man sehr umweltfreundlich.'*

> In der Schweiz sind man sehr umweltfreundlich. Die Schweizer trennen ihren Hausmüll und den industriellen müll. Papier, Metall, Plastik und Biomüll kommen in getrennte Mülleimers.
>
> Gestern bin ich im Supermarkt eingekauft. Ich habe keine Plastiktüten genommen, weil sie sind nicht gut für die Umwelt.
>
> Es gibt viele alternative Energien. Meine Familie wird in Zukunft Sonnenenergie nutzt.

## Pronunciation of long *u* and short *u*

**6** The letter *u* can be long or short. Listen to these words, repeat and decide: long or short?

**a** gut     **b** Natur     **c** Umwelt     **d** U-Bahn
**e** Zug     **f** Bus     **g** Luft     **h** Wohnung

- Vocabulary: talk about transport, the environment and where you live
- Grammar: practise the dative case and different tenses
- Skills: use a text as a model

**LESEN 1**

**Was passt zusammen?**
**Finde die Paare.**
Match the words and pictures.

*Beispiel:* **a 2**

a   mit dem Auto
b   mit dem Fahrrad
c   mit dem Flugzeug
d   mit der U-Bahn
e   mit der Straßenbahn
f   zu Fuß

**SCHREIBEN 2**

**Schreib diese Umwelt-Wörter richtig auf.**
Unscramble these words for things that affect the environment.

*Beispiel:* **a** *das Ozonloch*

a   das lozOchon
b   der Altomülm
c   viel Vkerehr
d   der Treffekteibusah
e   die eMbülergl
f   die Lgufschtvermnutzu

**LESEN 3**

NC 4–5

**Füll die Lücken aus.**
Fill in the gaps.

*Beispiel: Früher haben wir in einer kleinen* <u>Wohnung</u> *in …*

> Bergen   laut   Wohnung   Müll   sauber   gewohnt

Früher haben wir <u>in einer kleinen</u> ▢ in einer Großstadt ▢. Die Stadt war viel zu ▢ und schmutzig, weil es <u>viele Autos und</u> ▢ gab. Jetzt wohnen meine Familie und ich <u>in den</u> ▢. Ich wohne <u>gern</u> hier, weil <u>es ruhig und</u> ▢ <u>ist</u>. Man kann <u>im Winter Ski fahren</u>.

Hanna

lived in a village in the countryside /
very boring / it was too quiet /
now lives in the suburbs of Berlin /
likes it very much / practical /
you can do lots

**SCHREIBEN 4**

NC 4–5

**Schreib einen Text wie in Übung 3.**
Use the notes on the right to help you write a text like Hanna in activity 3. Copy out Hanna's text and replace the <u>underlined</u> sections.

- Vocabulary: talk about transport, the environment and where you live
- Grammar: practise the dative case and different tenses
- Skills: use a text as a model

**SCHREIBEN 1**

**Welche Umweltprobleme gibt es? Füll die Lücken aus.**

*Beispiel:* **a** *das Aussterben von Tieren*

**a** das A _ _ _ _ _ ben von T _ _ _ _ n    **e** die Entw _ _ _ _ _ g
**b** die M _ _ lb _ _ _ e    **f** das _ _ _ _ loch
**c** der _ _ om _ _ _ l    **g** der T _ _ _ bha _ _ _ ffekt
**d** viel _ _ _ kehr    **h** die _ _ ftver _ _ _ _ _ _ _ _ g

**SCHREIBEN 2**

**Welche Verkehrsmittel benutzen sie? Schreib Sätze.**
Write a sentence for each picture. Try to use different tenses (past, present and future) and different subjects (I, he, we, my sister, etc.).

*Beispiel:* **a** *Mein Bruder und ich fahren mit dem Fahrrad zur Schule.*

**LESEN 3**

**Lies den Text und beantworte die Fragen auf Englisch.**

NC 6

**a** Why does Thomas like living in Cologne?    **d** What does Thomas say about Lüneburg? (3)
**b** What activities can you do there?    **e** Why was living in Lüneburg quieter?
**c** What does Thomas not like about the town?    **f** What does he say about Los Angeles?

Ich wohne in der Stadtmitte von Köln. Das finde ich perfekt, weil es hier sehr viel für Jugendliche gibt.

In der Stadt kann man einkaufen und ins Kino gehen. Leider gibt es aber auch viel Kriminalität und zu viele Autos.

Früher haben wir in Lüneburg gewohnt. Das ist eine kleinere Stadt in Norddeutschland. Dort war es ruhiger, weil es nicht so viel Verkehr gab.

In Zukunft werde ich in Los Angeles wohnen, weil es eine interessante Stadt ist.

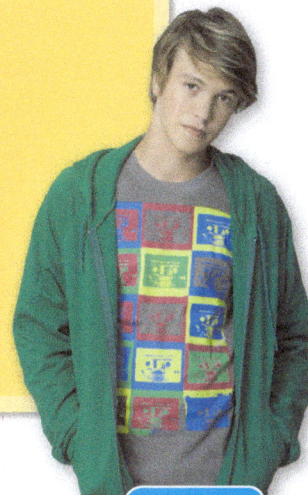

Thomas

**SCHREIBEN 4**

**Wo wohnst du? Schreib einen Text wie Thomas.**

NC 6

**HÖREN 1**

**NC 5**

🎧 **Listen (1–5). Where do they live? Do they like living there? Why? Or why not? (See pages 116–117.)**

*Beispiel:*

|   | Where? | Likes it? | Why? Why not? (1 reason) |
|---|--------|-----------|--------------------------|
| 1 | Big city by the coast | Yes | You can swim, there are lots of beach parties in summer. |

**LESEN 2**

**NC 5**

**Read the article about recycling in Germany and answer the questions in English. (See pages 120–121.)**

*Beispiel:* **a** *Old cars, …*

**a** Name five things that are described as waste.
**b** What was the big problem in the past?
**c** What type of waste is commonly recycled? Give four types.
**d** Why are there three bins per family in Germany?
**e** There is often a fourth bin. What is it for?
**f** What else is done in Germany to help the environment? Give three things.

**SPRECHEN 3**

**NC 6**

**You are talking to your Swiss friend about the environment. Answer his/her questions (a–e).**

**a** Wo wohnst du? Wohnst du gern in …? *(See pages 116–117.)*
**b** Bist du umweltfreundlich? Was machst du für die Umwelt? *(See pages 120–121.)*
**c** Was hast du gestern für die Umwelt gemacht? *(See pages 120–121.)*
**d** Was sind die größten Umweltprobleme? *(See pages 122–123.)*
**e** Was wird man in deiner Schule für die Umwelt machen? *(See pages 124–125.)*

**SCHREIBEN 4**

**NC 4–6**

**Write 1–2 sentences for each picture. Use different tenses and build longer sentences using linking words (*denn, weil, aber* …). (See pages 120–125.)**

*Beispiel:* **a** *Wir haben zu Hause drei Mülleimer, weil …*

### Recycling in Deutschland

Die Liste ist lang: alte Autos, Fernseher, Computer und Handys, alte Zeitungen, altmodische Hosen und T-Shirts. Das ist alles Müll.

Früher hat man den Müll nicht getrennt. Das war ein großes Problem für die Umwelt.

In Deutschland ist Recycling sehr wichtig. Man kann Papier, Plastik, Glas und Dosen recyceln. Jede Familie hat drei Mülleimer: einen für Papier, einen für Biomüll und einen für Restmüll. Oft gibt es auch noch einen Mülleimer für Plastik und Metall.

Und was macht man sonst in Deutschland für die Umwelt? Viele Deutsche sind sehr umweltfreundlich: man nimmt beim Einkaufen keine Plastiktüten, spart Strom und nutzt oft alternative Energien, zum Beispiel Sonnenenergie oder Windenergie.

Man muss …   Man kann …   Früher habe/bin ich …
In Zukunft werde ich …   Am wichtigsten …
Das größte Problem …   … ist schlimmer als …

| Meine Gegend | My area |
|---|---|
| Ich wohne … | I live … |
| in einem Dorf | in a village |
| in einer Stadt/Großstadt | in a town/city |
| in einer Industriestadt | in an industrial town |
| in einer Kleinstadt | in a small town |
| am Stadtrand | in the suburbs |
| an der Küste | by the coast |
| auf dem Land | in the country |
| in den Bergen | in the mountains |
| Ich wohne (nicht) gern hier, weil … | I (don't) like living here because … |
| es viel Kriminalität gibt. | there's a lot of crime. |
| es zu viele Autos gibt. | there are too many cars. |
| es nichts für Jugendliche gibt. | there's nothing for young people. |
| man viel machen kann. | you can do lots, there's lots to do. |
| es … ist. | it's … |
| langweilig | boring |
| laut | noisy |
| praktisch | practical |
| ruhig | quiet |
| sauber | clean |
| schmutzig | dirty |
| schön | nice, beautiful |
| sicher | safe |

| Bus und Bahn | By bus and rail |
|---|---|
| Ich fahre mit … | I go/travel by … |
| dem Auto/Bus/Zug. | car/bus/train. |
| dem Fahrrad/Motorrad. | bike/motorbike. |
| der U-Bahn/Straßenbahn. | underground/tram. |
| Ich fliege mit dem Flugzeug. | I fly by plane. |
| Ich gehe zu Fuß. | I walk/go on foot. |
| zum Flughafen | to the airport |
| zur Schule/Arbeit | to school/work |
| zum Kino | to the cinema |
| nach Frankreich | to France |
| in den Urlaub | on holiday |

| Umweltschutz | Protecting the environment |
|---|---|
| Ich spare Strom. | I save electricity. |
| Ich nehme keine Plastiktüten, sondern Stofftaschen. | I don't take plastic bags, I take cloth bags. |
| Meine Familie nutzt … | My family uses … |
| alternative Energien. | alternative energy. |
| Sonnen-/Windenergie. | solar/wind energy. |

| | |
|---|---|
| Ich dusche/Ich bade nicht. | I shower/I don't have a bath. |
| Wir haben drei Mülleimer. | We have three bins. |
| Wir trennen unseren Müll. | We separate our litter. |
| Ich recycle Papier/Dosen. | I recycle paper/cans. |
| Ich bringe Glasflaschen zum Container. | I take glass bottles to the bottle bank. |

| | |
|---|---|
| Ich habe … | I … |
| gebadet/geduscht. | bathed/showered. |
| … gebracht/genommen. | brought/took … |
| … genutzt/gespart. | used/saved … |
| … getrennt/recycelt. | separated/recycled … |
| Ich bin … gegangen/gefahren. | I went/travelled … |

| | |
|---|---|
| Ich werde … | I will … |
| baden/duschen. | bathe/shower. |
| … bringen/nehmen. | bring/take … |
| … nutzen/sparen. | use/save … |
| … trennen/recyceln. | separate/recycle … |
| … gehen/fahren. | go/travel … |

| Fünf vor zwölf | Five to twelve |
|---|---|
| der Atommüll | nuclear waste |
| das Aussterben von Tieren | extinction of animals |
| die Entwaldung | deforestation |
| der Klimawandel | climate change |
| die Luftverschmutzung | air pollution |
| die Müllberge | rubbish mountains |
| das Ozonloch | hole in the ozone layer |
| der Treibhauseffekt | greenhouse effect |
| viel Verkehr | a lot of traffic |

| | |
|---|---|
| Man muss … | We must … |
| mehr zu Fuß gehen. | walk more. |
| mehr recyceln. | recycle more. |
| die Natur schützen. | protect nature. |

## I can …

- describe where I live and give my opinion of it
- talk about ways to travel
- talk about ways to be environmentally friendly
- talk about environmental problems and solutions
- use the linking word *weil*
- use the dative case
- use the comparative and the superlative
- use strategies for improving my written work
- pronounce the long and short *u* sounds

# 4B.1 Ich habe einen Nebenjob

- Vocabulary: talk about part-time jobs; say what you're saving for
- Grammar: use *für* + accusative
- Skills: ask and answer questions

## HÖREN 1

🎧 „Hast du einen Nebenjob?" Hör zu (a–h) und finde die passenden Bilder.

*Beispiel:* **a** *4*

**a** Ich trage Zeitungen aus.
**b** Ich mache Babysitting.
**c** Ich führe Hunde aus.
**d** Ich arbeite in einem Geschäft.
**e** Ich helfe im Garten.
**f** Ich wasche Autos.
**g** Ich gebe Nachhilfeunterricht.
**h** Ich helfe zu Hause.

## SPRECHEN 2

👥 **A** wählt ein Bild für **B**. **B** antwortet. **A** ↔ **B**.

*Beispiel:* **A** *Bild 2!* **B** *Ich helfe im Garten.*

## HÖREN 3

NC 4

🎧 Hör zu und beantworte die Fragen für Sira, Leo, Anne und David.

|  | Hast du einen Nebenjob? | Wie viel verdienst du? | Wie gefällt dir der Job? |
|---|---|---|---|
| Sira | *Ich helfe im Garten* | 10 Euro | *nicht so gut, oft anstrengend* |

## HÖREN 4

NC 4

🎧 Hör noch einmal zu. Wer sagt a–h? Sira, Leo, Anne oder David?

*Beispiel:* **a** *David*

Mein Job …
**a** ist nicht interessant.  **b** macht Spaß.  **c** ist anstrengend.  **d** ist furchtbar.
**e** ist super.  **f** gefällt mir sehr gut.  **g** macht fit.  **h** ist nicht so gut.

## SPRECHEN 5

NC 4

👥 **A** stellt die Fragen aus Übung 3. **B** ist Sira, Leo, Anne oder David (Übung 3–4). **A** ↔ **B**.

*Beispiel:* **A** *Hast du einen Nebenjob, Sira?*
**B** *Ja, ich helfe im Garten.*
**A** *Und wie viel verdienst du?*
**B** *Ich bekomme …*

**HÖREN 6** NC 3

„Warum hast du einen Nebenjob?" Hör zu und lies.

Ich bekomme kein Taschengeld. Ich arbeite, um Kleidung zu kaufen. Und ich spare fünf Euro pro Woche. Ich spare für ein Handy!

**Grammatik →** p.159

**für**
The preposition *für* (for) is always followed by the accusative case:
**m.** Ich spare für **einen** Computer.
**f.** Ich spare für **eine** Jeans.
**n.** Ich spare für **ein** Fahrrad.

**HÖREN 7** NC 3

Was kaufen Anne, Leo und David? Und wofür sparen sie? Hör zu und finde die passenden Bilder.

*Beispiel: Anne kauft **a** und …; sie spart für …*

a b c d e f

**SPRECHEN 8** NC 4

Macht eine Klassenumfrage und schreibt die Resultate auf.

*Beispiel: Jack hilft zu Hause. Er bekommt vier Pfund. Der Job …*

- Was ist dein Nebenjob?
- Wie viel verdienst du?
- Wie findest du den Job?
- Was kaufst du von deinem Geld?
- Wofür sparst du?

Ich bekomme kein Taschengeld. Ich arbeite, um … zu kaufen. Ich spare für …
einen Computer/MP4-Player
ein Handy/Fahrrad
Kleidung/Make-up

**LESEN 9** NC 5

Lies Janas Nachricht und beantworte die Fragen auf Deutsch.

*Beispiel:* **a** *Sie arbeitet in einer Pizzeria.*

a Was ist Janas Nebenjob?
b Wann arbeitet sie?
c Wo hat sie davor gearbeitet?
d Wie viel verdient sie?
e Warum mag sie den Job?
f Was mag sie nicht so gern?
g Was macht sie mit dem Geld?

Ich arbeite samstags und mittwochs in einer Pizzeria. Ich bekomme acht Euro pro Stunde. Davor habe ich in einem Geschäft gearbeitet.

Der Job gefällt mir, weil die Kollegen alle nett sind. Aber die Arbeit ist ziemlich schwer und ich muss in der Küche abwaschen. Das finde ich nicht so gut.

Ich arbeite, um Make-up und Zeitschriften zu kaufen. Und ich spare für einen Fernseher! Und du?

**SCHREIBEN 10** NC 4–5

Schreib einen Antwortbrief an Jana.

*Beispiel: Ich habe auch einen Nebenjob. Ich …*

**Challenge** You are saving up for your holidays, so you have lots of part-time jobs! Describe what jobs you've done, what you're going to do and/or what you're doing now. Say what exactly you're saving up for.

NC 6–7

# 4B.2 Meine Schule

- Vocabulary: learn about the school system in Germany; compare German and British schools
- Grammar: use different tenses
- Skills: work out the meaning of unknown words

## HÖREN 1 🎧 Hör zu und lies.

**a** *Louise*
Ich gehe auf die Realschule. Nach der 10. Klasse ist die Schule zu Ende. Ich mache also mit sechzehn Jahren meinen Realschulabschluss. Das ist wie ein englischer GCSE-Abschluss.

**b** *Torben*
Ich besuche ein Gymnasium. Ich bin in der 10. Klasse – im ersten Jahr der Oberstufe. Nach der 12. Klasse werde ich mein Abitur machen. Danach werde ich an der Universität studieren.

**c** *Sandra*
Ich gehe auf die Hauptschule. Wir haben viele praktische Fächer. Nach der 9. Klasse werde ich mit fünfzehn Jahren eine Lehre machen. Ich werde drei Jahre lang einen Beruf lernen.

**d** *David*
Ich besuche eine Gesamtschule. Das ist Hauptschule, Realschule und Gymnasium zusammen – bis zur 10. Klasse. Danach kann man einen Abschluss machen oder aufs Gymnasium gehen.

## LESEN 2 Finde die Paare.

*Beispiel:* **a 6**

a die Realschule
b der Abschluss
c das Gymnasium
d die Oberstufe
e das Abitur
f die Universität
g studieren
h die Hauptschule
i die Lehre
j der Beruf
k die Gesamtschule

1 university
2 job, profession
3 upper school, sixth form
4 A levels
5 to study
6 secondary school (to age 16)
7 grammar school
8 secondary school (to age 15)
9 comprehensive school
10 apprenticeship
11 school-leaving qualification

### ? Think

What strategies can you use to help you do activities 2 and 3? For example:

- Identify words that look like English words.
- Use context to help you understand words in the texts.
- Look for similarities with other German words you know.

**LESEN 3**

NC 5

**Beantworte die Fragen auf Englisch.**

a What kind of school does Louise go to?
b How old will Louise be when she finishes school?
c What kind of school does Torben go to?
d What will he do after the sixth form?
e What is special about the subjects in Sandra's school?
f What will she do afterwards?
g What is special about David's school?
h What options does he have later?

**SPRECHEN 4**

NC 4

**Diskutiert in der Gruppe. Ist das eine Schule in Deutschland oder eine Schule in Großbritannien? Schreibt D oder GB für jeden Satz (a–h).**

a Die Schule beginnt um neun Uhr.
b Kinder gehen mit vier Jahren zur Schule.
c Man kann sitzen bleiben: man kann das Schuljahr noch einmal machen.
d Der Unterricht – also die Schule – ist um eins oder halb zwei zu Ende.
e Wir müssen eine Uniform tragen.
f Kinder gehen mit sechs Jahren zur Schule.
g Die Schule beginnt um acht Uhr.
h Der Unterricht ist um sechzehn Uhr zu Ende.

**HÖREN 5**

**Ist alles richtig? Hör zu.**

**SPRECHEN 6**

**Was ist besser/schlechter – Schule in Deutschland oder Großbritannien? Macht eine Klassenumfrage mit den Sätzen aus Übung 4. Schreibt die Resultate auf.**

Beispiel: **A** Die Schule beginnt um neun Uhr.
**B** Das ist besser!

**SCHREIBEN 7**

NC 4–5

**Vergleiche das deutsche Schulsystem mit dem Schulsystem in Großbritannien. Welches System ist besser? Warum?**

Beispiel: In Deutschland gehen Kinder mit sechs Jahren zur Schule, aber in Großbritannien …

**Grammatik → p.162–6**

**Present:** Die Schule ist … Es gibt … Ich habe/mache/gehe/…
**Imperfect:** Es war … Es gab … Ich hatte …
**Perfect:** Ich habe … gemacht. Ich bin … gegangen.
**Future:** Ich werde … machen/gehen.

**Challenge**

Describe your ideal school (*meine Traumschule*). Use as many different tenses as possible!

Beispiel: *Gestern hatten wir in meiner Traumschule nur eine Stunde Unterricht – um 13 Uhr. Heute beginnt meine Traumschule um … Morgen …*

NC 5–7

# 4B.3 Und nächstes Jahr?

- Vocabulary: talk about what you've done this year at school and what you're going to do next year
- Grammar: use the perfect, the present and the future tense
- Skills: use knowledge of language patterns

## LESEN 1 Finde die Paare.

*Beispiel:* **a** *Französisch*

**a** **b** **c** **d** **e**

| Chinesisch | Deutsch |
|---|---|
| Englisch | Erdkunde |
| Französisch | Geschichte |
| Kunst | Informatik |
| Musik | Mathe |
| Religion | Spanisch |
| Sport | |
| Naturwissenschaften | |

(Biologie, Chemie, Physik)

**f** **g** **h** **i** **j**

**k** **l** **m** **n**

> … ist mein Lieblingsfach.
> Ich bekomme gute Noten in …
> Ich habe … als Leistungskurs gewählt.
> Ich lerne seit zwei Jahren …

## HÖREN 2 Hör zu und finde die passenden Fächer (a–n) für Sarah.

*Beispiel:* am Montag: **c**, …

## HÖREN 3 Hör noch einmal zu und beantworte die Fragen auf Englisch.

**NC 5**

**a** How many subjects does Sarah have on Monday?
**b** What does she say about English and geography?
**c** What does she say about maths?
**d** What does she say about French? (2)
**e** What does she say about IT?
**f** What does she say about Chinese?

## SPRECHEN 4 A sagt die Fächer für eure Klasse. Welcher Tag ist das? B sagt den Tag – schnell! A ↔ B.

*Beispiel:*  *A   Wir haben Englisch, zwei Stunden Sport,…*
            *B   Das ist Donnerstag!*

## HÖREN 5 Welche Fächer haben sie dieses Jahr? Und nächstes Jahr? Hör zu und beantworte die Fragen für David, Katja, Phillip, Ines, Tim und Annika.

**NC 6**

*Beispiel:*

| | Dieses Jahr? | Nächstes Jahr? |
|---|---|---|
| David | *Chinesisch* | *Spanisch* |

> Ich heiße David. Ich habe dieses Jahr Chinesisch gelernt, aber das war zu schwierig. Ich werde nächstes Jahr Spanisch lernen. Spanisch ist einfacher!

**SPRECHEN 6**

NC 5–6

👥 **Macht Dialoge. Benutzt die Informationen aus Übung 5.
A ↔ B.**

*Beispiel:* **A** *Was hast du dieses Jahr gemacht, David?*
 **B** *Ich habe Chinesisch gelernt.*
 **A** *Was wirst du nächstes Jahr machen?*

**HÖREN 7**

NC 6

🎧 **Hör zu und lies. Sind die Sätze a–f richtig (R), falsch (F) oder nicht im Text (NiT)?**

*Beispiel:* **a** *R*

**a** Markus ist Deutscher, aber er wohnt jetzt in England.
**b** Er geht auf die Oberstufe eines Gymnasiums.
**c** Er hat fünf Pflichtfächer gewählt.
**d** Seine Lehrer sind sehr nett.
**e** Es gibt in seiner Schule keine Wahlfächer.
**f** In zwei Jahren macht er seinen Abschluss.

Markus (15) kommt aus Berlin und wohnt seit einem Jahr in Brighton. Er ist in Year 9 einer Gesamtschule.

„Ich habe dieses Jahr meine Fächer für Year 10 gewählt. Hier in England gibt es keine Leistungskurse, sondern Pflichtfächer. Ich habe Erdkunde gewählt, weil ich immer gute Noten in Erdkunde habe. Ich habe auch Französisch gewählt, weil das mein Lieblingsfach ist, und ich habe Mathe, Geschichte und Informatik gewählt.
Man muss dazu auch Wahlfächer wählen. Ich habe Sport gewählt, weil ich sportlich bin, Spanisch, weil wir oft in Spanien Urlaub machen, Kunst, weil das einfach ist – und Musik, Biologie und Religion.
Nach Year 11 werde ich dann in diesen Fächern meinen GCSE-Abschluss machen."

**? Think**

How many tenses can you find in Markus's text? When do you use them?

**⚙ Grammatik → p.162–6**

**The perfect, the present and the future tense**

| | |
|---|---|
| Present: | Ich **lerne** … |
| | Ich **gehe** … |
| Perfect: | Ich **habe** … **gelernt**. |
| | Ich **bin** … **gegangen**. |
| Future: | Ich **werde** … **lernen**. |
| | Ich **werde** … **gehen**. |

**SCHREIBEN 8**

NC 5

**„Letzte Woche in der Schule." Schreib sechs Sätze im Perfekt.**

*Beispiel: Ich habe gute Noten bekommen.*

**SCHREIBEN 9**

**„Nächste Woche in der Schule." Schreib deine Sätze aus Übung 8 im Futur.**

**SCHREIBEN 10**

NC 5–6

**Welche Fächer hast du dieses Jahr gewählt? Welche Fächer wirst du für deinen GCSE-Abschluss wählen? Schreib einen Artikel für eine Schulwebseite.**

*Beispiel: Dieses Jahr habe ich Französisch gelernt. Nächstes Jahr werde ich …, weil …*

**◎ Challenge**

Imagine you are moving to Germany next year. Describe what kind of school you will go to and what subjects you will study, and why.

NC 5–6

- Vocabulary: talk about different jobs; say what job you would like to do in the future
- Grammar: use *ich möchte … werden*
- Skills: work out the different masculine and feminine forms of jobs

**HÖREN 1** 🎧 **„Was ist dein Vater/deine Mutter von Beruf?" Hör zu (1–8) und finde die passenden Bilder.**

*Beispiel:* **1 c**

Mein Vater/Meine Mutter ist …
1. Polizist / Polizistin
2. Krankenpfleger / Krankenpflegerin
3. Sekretär / Sekretärin
4. Briefträger / Briefträgerin
5. Geschäftsmann / Geschäftsfrau
6. Informatiker / Informatikerin
7. Arzt / Ärztin
8. Lkw-Fahrer / Lkw-Fahrerin

**SPRECHEN 2** 👥 **Ratespiel: A wählt einen Beruf und buchstabiert ihn. B antwortet – schnell! A ↔ B.**

*Beispiel:* **A** *Meine Mutter ist I -…*
**B** *Informatikerin!*

**? Think**

- Look at the masculine and feminine forms of jobs. Find three ways to make the feminine form.
- Compare these sentences:
  Mein Vater ist Polizist. *My father is a policeman.*
  What is different about the German sentence?

**LESEN 3** **NC 3** **Welcher Beruf ist das? Lies a–d und finde die passenden Berufe (1–4).**

a Ich helfe kranken Hunden, Katzen, …
b Ich mache Kleider, Röcke, Hemden, Blusen.
c Ich mache die Hausarbeit, koche für meine Kinder …
d Du möchtest etwas kaufen? Komm in mein Geschäft!

**SCHREIBEN 4** **Schreib das passende Maskulinum oder Femininum für 1–4 auf.**

*Beispiel:* **1** *Verkäuferin*

**1** Verkäufer

**2** Hausfrau

**3** Tierarzt

**4** Mode-designerin

**HÖREN 5** 🎧 **Ist alles richtig in Übung 3–4? Hör zu.**

**HÖREN 6**
NC 5

🎧 „Ich möchte … werden." Hör zu und beantworte die Fragen für Daniel, Anne, Johann, Bianca und Torben.

| | Was möchtest du werden? | Warum? | Wie wird die Arbeit sein? |
|---|---|---|---|
| Daniel | Arzt (Kinderarzt) | ich mag Kinder | anstrengend, aber … – das ist … |

**SPRECHEN 7**
NC 5

👥 **Macht Dialoge. Benutzt die Informationen aus Übung 6. A ←→ B.**

Beispiel: **A** Daniel, was möchtest du werden?
**B** Ich möchte Kinderarzt werden.
**A** Warum?
**B** Ich möchte Kinderarzt werden, weil …

◉ **Challenge**

Which jobs from page 138 would (and wouldn't) you like to do in the future? Why? Use the questions from activity 6 as a guide. Try to use as many tenses as possible!

NC 5–6

⚙ **Grammatik →** p.166

**Ich möchte … werden**

Use *Ich möchte* if you'd like to have or buy something:

Ich **möchte** eine Currywurst.

But if you want to say what you'd like to **become**, use *Ich möchte + werden* at the end of the sentence:

Ich **möchte** Ärztin **werden**.

▶ **Die Video-Aufgabe**

**VIDEO 8**

**Sieh dir das Video an und finde die passenden Antworten.**

Beispiel: **a 1**

**a** Das Mädchen macht Babysitting, um
   **1** einen Computer zu kaufen.
   **2** später Lehrerin zu werden.

**b** Der Junge
   **1** wird später studieren.
   **2** ist Kellner.

**c** Eine Architektin muss
   **1** Häuser kaufen.
   **2** auf die Universität gehen.

**d** Ein Arzt macht seinen Job
   **1** im Krankenhaus.
   **2** zu Hause.

**e** Der Tontechniker arbeitet
   **1** mit Kindern.
   **2** mit Medien.

**f** Eine Grafikdesignerin muss
   **1** viel vor dem Computer sitzen.
   **2** viele Zeitschriften lesen.

**VIDEO 9**

👥 **What are Sira's and Leo's ideal jobs?**

- Vocabulary: describe your school day; learn about the Swiss school system
- Grammar: use different tenses; use correct word order
- Skills: use knowledge of language patterns

**LESEN 1** **Lies Lenas Blog. Dann füll den Stundenplan aus.**

*Beispiel:*

|  | 8:00 | 8:45 | 9:30 | 10:00 | 11:00 | 13:30 |
|---|---|---|---|---|---|---|
| Heute: | *Geschichte* | | | | | |
| Am Montag: | | | | | | |

Es war heute nicht schlecht in der Schule! Letztes Jahr war ich auf einer Realschule, aber dieses Jahr bin ich auf ein Gymnasium gekommen und die Schüler sind alle total nett.

Heute ist Samstag und wir hatten nur bis Mittag Schule. Um acht Uhr hatten wir Geschichte. Das war wieder total langweilig. Um Viertel vor neun hatten wir Informatik. Das hat Spaß gemacht, weil wir an unserer Klassenwebseite gearbeitet haben. In der kleinen Pause – also um halb zehn – hat meine Klasse den Schulhof aufgeräumt.

Um zehn Uhr hatten wir dann Spanisch. Spanisch ist super und unsere Lehrerin ist sehr nett. Und um elf Uhr hatten wir Deutsch – zwei Unterrichtsstunden lang. Nach der Schule – um halb eins – hatte ich Theater-AG. Ich möchte später Schauspielerin werden.

Am Montag werden wir einen Klassenausflug machen – super! Wir werden mit dem Bus nach Hamburg fahren und dort eine Bootsfahrt auf der Elbe machen. Ich freue mich schon sehr!

**LESEN 2** **Sind die Sätze richtig (R), falsch (F) oder nicht im Text (NiT)?**

**NC 6** *Beispiel:* **a** F

- **a** Letztes Jahr war Lena auf einer Gesamtschule.
- **b** Der Unterricht war heute am Mittag zu Ende.
- **c** Lenas Klasse hat eine eigene Webseite.
- **d** Lena hat in der kleinen Pause Milch getrunken.
- **e** Sie hat jeden Tag Spanisch.
- **f** Sie möchte später Lehrerin werden.
- **g** Morgen wird sie nach Hamburg fahren.

**SCHREIBEN 3** **Du bist dran! Schreib einen Blog so wie Lena.**

**NC 6** *Beispiel: Es war heute … in der Schule. Um … Uhr hatte ich … Nach der Schule habe ich … gemacht. Morgen …*

> ## Grammatik → p.167
>
> **Word order**
> In German sentences, the verb is always the second idea:
>
> Wir **hatten** Deutsch. →
> Heute **hatten** wir Deutsch.
>
> Ich **habe** Tennis gespielt. →
> Gestern **habe** ich Tennis gespielt.

**HÖREN 4**

**NC 5**

🎧 **Hör zu und finde die passenden Sätze.**

*Beispiel:* **a 2**

**a** Für Kinder beginnt die Schule in der Schweiz mit
  **1** fünf Jahren.
  **2** sechs Jahren.
  **3** sieben Jahren.

**b** Die Schüler lernen
  **1** Englisch.
  **2** Latein.
  **3** zwei Landessprachen.

**c** Sie lernen auch
  **1** Schweizer Hochdeutsch.
  **2** Schweizerdeutsch.
  **3** eine andere Sprache.

**d** In der Sekundarschule lernen sie
  **1** viele neue Fächer.
  **2** drei neue Fächer.
  **3** eine neue Fremdsprache.

**e** Leo hat auf dem Gymnasium dreizehn Stunden
  **1** Sprachunterricht.
  **2** Naturwissenschaften.
  **3** Kunst und Musik.

**f** Sira und Leo finden die vielen
  **1** Fächer anstrengend.
  **2** Unterrichtsstunden interessant.
  **3** Fremdsprachen gut.

**SPRECHEN 5**

**NC 4**

👥 **„Schule in England": macht einen Podcast für Leos Schulwebseite.**

- Ab wann (Alter)? (*… beginnt mit … Jahren*)
- Welche Schule/Welcher Schultyp? (*Das ist ein/eine …*)
- Welche Fächer? (*Wir/Die Schüler lernen …*)
- Was ist anders als in der Schweiz? (*Uhrzeiten, Essen, Fächer, Uniform, sitzen bleiben*)

**Challenge**

- Why do you think learning foreign languages is important? Discuss with your partner. Use some of these expressions:

  Es ist wichtig, weil …
  Es ist wichtig, um … zu …
  Ich finde es nützlich, weil … (*I think it's useful because …*)
  Meiner Meinung nach … (*In my opinion …*)
  Ja, das stimmt. (*Yes, that's true.*)
  Nein, das stimmt nicht. (*No, that's not true.*)

- Make a list in German of all the reasons you thought of.

  **NC 4–7**

## Present, past and future, *für* + accusative, *möchte* + *werden*

### Present tense, perfect tense and future tense

- The present tense (*das Präsens*) is used to describe an action that is taking place now, or that takes place regularly or every day:

  Ich **mache** Hausaufgaben. Wir **gehen** um ein Uhr nach Hause.

- The perfect tense (*das Perfekt*) is used if you want to talk about an action in the past:

  Ich **habe** Spanisch **gelernt**. Wir **sind** nach Hamburg **gefahren**.

- The future tense (*das Futur*) is used to talk about what someone will do or is going to do:

  Ich **werde** Chinesisch **lernen**. Ich **werde** mein Abitur **machen**.

**1** Read the message and find four sentences each in the perfect tense, the present and the future.

Hast du am Wochenende Tennis gespielt? Ich habe für den Mathe-Test gelernt. Ich hoffe, ich bekomme eine gute Note! Ich werde aber auch heute Abend Tennis spielen – mit Anja.

Ich habe zwei neue Nebenjobs. Am Sonntag habe ich im Videoladen gearbeitet. Morgen werde ich Autos waschen. Ich spare für ein Handy.

Am Mittwoch fängt die Schule wieder an. Ich werde dieses Jahr Spanisch lernen. Ich habe in der 8. Klasse Chinesisch gelernt – zu schwierig! Und ich werde Deutsch als Leistungskurs wählen.

**2** Now rewrite the message: turn the perfect tense sentences into the present tense, the present tense into the future tense, and the future tense into the perfect tense.

*Beispiel: Spielst du am Wochenende Tennis?*

**3** Fill in the gaps with the correct articles.

*Beispiel:* **a** *einen*

Ich spare für …

a _____ MP4-Player.
b _____ Handy.
c _____ Computerspiel.
d _____ Pullover.
e _____ Fernseher.
f _____ Jeans.

### *für* + accusative

The preposition *für* (for) is always followed by the accusative case:

**m.** Ich spare für **einen** Fußball.

**f.** Ich spare für **eine** Gitarre.

**n.** Ich spare für **ein** Fahrrad.

**4** „Was möchten sie werden?" Write sentences for the pictures.

*Beispiel:* **a** *Thomas möchte Briefträger werden.*

**a** Thomas

**b** Anne

**c** Markus

**d** Hanna

**e** Uwe

**f** Vera

---

**möchte + werden**

- If you want to say what you would like (to have or to buy), use *Ich möchte …*:

  Ich **möchte** ein Handy.

  Ich **möchte** diesen Computer.

- But if you want to talk about what you'd like to **become**, use *Ich möchte + werden* at the end of the sentence:

  Ich **möchte** Informatiker **werden**.

  Jana **möchte** Ärztin **werden**.

---

## Using filler words

To sound more authentic when speaking German, you can use 'filler words' like the ones on the right. Words like this are also useful for giving you more time to think when you're working out what to say!

| | |
|---|---|
| also | *so* |
| bestimmt | *certainly* |
| eben | *just, exactly* |
| eigentlich | *actually* |
| ja, gut | *yes, fine* |
| mal (erzähl <u>mal</u>) | *do (<u>do</u> tell)* |
| na ja | *well* |
| nämlich | *you see, namely* |
| nun | *well* |
| schon, aber … | *quite so, but …* |
| sicher | *certainly* |
| so | *so* |
| tja | *(yes) well, oh well* |
| warum denn? | *how come?* |
| wirklich | *really* |

**5** 🎧 Listen to the conversation. Which words from the list does Jana use? Which ones does Tom use?

*Beispiel:* Jana: also, …
         Tom: …

**6** 👥 Make up a conversation with your partner about school, favourite subjects and future plans. Try to use as many filler words as you can!

## Pronunciation of *ö*

**7** 🎧 Listen and repeat.

# 4B.7 Extra Star

- Vocabulary: talk about jobs, school and future plans
- Grammar: use the present, the perfect and the future tense; use the masculine and feminine forms of jobs
- Skills: use knowledge of language patterns

## SCHREIBEN 1

**Schreib die Berufe a–h im Maskulinum und Femininum auf.**
Write down the missing masculine and feminine forms.

*Beispiel:* **a** *Polizistin*

| | Maskulinum | Femininum |
|---|---|---|
| a | Polizist | |
| b | | Krankenpflegerin |
| c | Sekretär | |
| d | | Hausfrau |
| e | | Informatikerin |
| f | Lkw-Fahrer | |
| g | | Tierärztin |
| h | Verkäufer | |

## SCHREIBEN 2

**Schreib die Sätze richtig auf.**
Rewrite these sentences using the correct word order.

*Beispiel:* **a** *Dieses Jahr habe ich Spanisch gelernt.*

**a** habe ich Jahr gelernt dieses Spanisch.
**b** Jahr werde mein Abitur nächstes machen ich.
**c** Hauptschule ich eine gehe auf.
**d** Leistungskurs als wählen ich Biologie werde.
**e** Noten ich gute habe.
**f** ein ich gemacht Jahr Praktikum dieses habe.

## LESEN 3
**NC 5**

**Sind die Sätze im Präsens (Pr), Perfekt (Pe) oder Futur (F)?**
Are the sentences (activity 2) in the present, perfect or future tense?

*Beispiel:* **a** *Pe*

## LESEN 4
**NC 6**

**Lies den Text und beantworte die Fragen auf Englisch.**
Read the text and answer the questions in English.

**a** What job does Cora want to do?
**b** What jobs do her parents do?
**c** What did she do last summer? What was her opinion of it?
**d** What did she do this year?
**e** What does she say about her grades?
**f** What will she do next year?
**g** What does she say about her main subjects?

Ich heiße Cora und ich möchte später Fotomodell werden. Meine Eltern arbeiten auch in der Modebranche. Meine Mutter ist Modedesignerin und mein Vater ist Modefotograf. Ich habe letzten Sommer ein Praktikum bei meinem Vater gemacht – das war anstrengend, aber auch sehr interessant!

Ich habe dieses Jahr meinen Realschulabschluss gemacht. Ich habe sehr gute Noten bekommen und werde deshalb nächstes Jahr auf die Oberstufe des Gymnasiums kommen. Ich werde Englisch und Kunst als Leistungskurse wählen – ein Fotomodell muss gut Englisch sprechen können!

- Vocabulary: talk about jobs, school and future plans
- Grammar: use the present, the perfect and the future tense; use the masculine and feminine forms of jobs
- Skills: use knowledge of language patterns

**SCHREIBEN 1**

**Schreib die passenden Berufe auf.**

Beispiel: **a** Polizist

**a** **b** **c** **d** **e** **f**

**SCHREIBEN 2**

NC 5

**Schreib die Sätze im Perfekt (a–c) und Futur (d–f) zu Ende.**

Beispiel: **a** Dieses Jahr habe ich gute Noten bekommen.

Dieses Jahr habe ich …          Nächstes Jahr …

**a** **b** **c** **d** **e** **f**

**SCHREIBEN 3**

**Schreib die Sätze a–f aus Übung 2 im Präsens auf.**

Beispiel: **a** Dieses Jahr bekomme ich gute Noten.

**LESEN 4**

NC 6

**Lies den Text und beantworte die Fragen auf Englisch.**

- **a** What jobs do Sven's parents do?
- **b** What does he say about his last school? (3)
- **c** What does he say about his new school? (2)
- **d** What does he say about his grades and subjects this year? (2)
- **e** What will he do next year?
- **f** What will he do after that? Why? (3)

Ich heiße Sven. Meine Mutter ist Sekretärin in einem Büro und mein Vater ist Briefträger.

Also, ich gehe gern zur Schule. Aber letztes Jahr bin ich aufs Gymnasium gegangen. Das war zu schwierig und ich hatte in allen Fächern schlechte Noten. Jetzt gehe ich auf die Realschule und es gefällt mir viel besser. Dieses Jahr habe ich gute Noten bekommen! Ich habe auch Spanisch gelernt.

Nächstes Jahr werde ich meinen Realschulabschluss machen. Danach werde ich eine Lehre in einem Geschäft machen, denn ich möchte Verkäufer werden. Ich möchte in einem Computergeschäft arbeiten, weil ich mich sehr für Informatik interessiere.

**HÖREN 1** · NC 6

🎧 **Listen and answer the questions in English.**
**(See pages 134–139.)**

*Beispiel:* **a** *She goes to a grammar school and …*

**a** What does Maike say about her school?
**b** She mentions two main subjects. What does she say about the first one?
**c** And what does she say about the second one? (3)
**d** What will she do after school? Why?
**e** Where does she want to work later? Why?

**SPRECHEN 2** · NC 6

**Give your own answers to these questions about your school and your future plans. (See pages 134–139.)**

- Wie ist deine Schule?
- Wie sind die Lehrer?
- Wie sind die anderen Schüler?
- Was hast du dieses Jahr gelernt/gemacht?
- Wie gefallen dir deine Fächer?
- Was wirst du nächstes Jahr lernen/machen?

**SCHREIBEN 3** · NC 5

**Write your own answers in German to these questions.**
**(See pages 132–139.)**

- Was für einen Nebenjob möchtest du haben?
- Warum?
- Auf was für eine Schule gehst du?
- Was wirst du nach der Schule (dem Schulabschluss) machen?
- Was für einen Beruf möchtest du haben?
- Warum?

**LESEN 4** · NC 6

**Read the text and answer the questions in English.**
**(See pages 134–139.)**

**a** What did Tobias do last year?
**b** What does he say about his subjects last year?
**c** Where does he go to school now?
**d** What year is he in?
**e** What does he say about his subjects?
**f** What will he do next year and why? (3)
**g** What does he want to do after his A levels? (2)

Ich heiße Tobias und ich war letztes Jahr auf einer Schule in Birmingham in England, weil mein Vater dort gearbeitet hat. Er ist Informatiker. Ich war in Year 9 und ich habe fünf Pflichtfächer und sechs Wahlfächer gehabt. Das war ziemlich schwierig!

Dieses Jahr gehe ich auf ein Gymnasium in Köln. Ich bin in der 10. Klasse – im ersten Jahr der Oberstufe. Ich habe in einigen Fächern schlechte Noten – Mathematik ist zu schwierig und Geschichte ist total langweilig. Ich werde nächstes Jahr zwei Leistungskurse wählen. Ich werde Englisch und Sport wählen, weil ich später Sportmoderator werden möchte.

Nach dem Abitur möchte ich ein Praktikum bei einem Radio- oder Fernsehsender machen – am liebsten in England!

## Ich habe einen Nebenjob — *I have a part-time job*

| | |
|---|---|
| Ich trage Zeitungen aus. | *I deliver newspapers.* |
| Ich mache Babysitting. | *I do babysitting.* |
| Ich führe Hunde aus. | *I walk dogs.* |
| Ich arbeite in einem Geschäft. | *I work in a shop.* |
| Ich helfe im Garten. | *I do gardening.* |
| Ich wasche Autos. | *I wash cars.* |
| Ich gebe Nachhilfeunterricht. | *I give extra tuition.* |
| Ich helfe zu Hause. | *I help at home.* |
| Ich bekomme kein Taschengeld. | *I don't get any pocket money.* |
| Ich bekomme 8 Euro pro Stunde. | *I get 8 euros an hour.* |
| Ich arbeite, um … zu kaufen. | *I work to buy …* |
| Ich spare für … | *I'm saving up for …* |
|   einen Computer. | *a computer.* |
|   ein Fahrrad. | *a bike.* |
|   ein Handy. | *a mobile phone.* |
|   Kleidung/Make-up. | *clothes/make-up.* |
|   einen MP4-Player. | *an MP4 player.* |

## Meine Schule — *My school*

| | |
|---|---|
| die Gesamtschule | *comprehensive school* |
| das Gymnasium | *grammar school* |
| die Hauptschule | *secondary school (to age 15)* |
| die Realschule | *secondary school (to age 16)* |
| Ich besuche eine/die Gesamtschule. | *I go to a comprehensive school.* |
| Ich gehe auf ein/das Gymnasium. | *I go to a grammar school.* |
| Ich bin in der 10. Klasse. | *I'm in Year 11.* |
| Ich werde … | *I will …* |
|   mein Abitur machen. | *do my A levels.* |
|   eine Lehre machen. | *do an apprenticeship.* |
|   auf die Oberstufe kommen. | *go into the sixth form.* |
|   meinen Realschulabschluss machen. | *do my GCSEs.* |
|   an der Universität studieren. | *study at university.* |

## Und nächstes Jahr? — *And next year?*

| | |
|---|---|
| Biologie | *biology* |
| Chemie | *chemistry* |
| Chinesisch | *Chinese* |
| Deutsch | *German* |
| Englisch | *English* |
| Erdkunde | *geography* |
| Französisch | *French* |
| Geschichte | *history* |
| Informatik | *IT* |
| Kunst | *art* |

| | |
|---|---|
| Mathe | *maths* |
| Musik | *music* |
| Naturwissenschaften | *science* |
| Physik | *physics* |
| Religion | *religious education* |
| Spanisch | *Spanish* |
| Sport | *PE* |
| … ist mein Lieblingsfach. | *… is my favourite subject.* |
| Ich bekomme gute Noten. | *I get good grades.* |
| Ich habe … als Leistungskurs gewählt. | *I chose … as main/specialist subjects.* |
| Ich lerne seit zwei Jahren … | *I've been learning … for two years.* |

## Berufe — *Professions*

| | |
|---|---|
| Ich möchte … werden. | *I'd like to be a …* |
| Arzt, Ärztin | *doctor* |
| Briefträger/in | *postman/woman* |
| Geschäftsmann, Geschäftsfrau | *businessman/woman* |
| Hausmann, Hausfrau | *house husband, housewife* |
| Informatiker/in | *IT specialist* |
| Kellner/in | *waiter, waitress* |
| Krankenpfleger/in | *nurse* |
| Lkw-Fahrer/in | *truck driver* |
| Modedesigner/in | *fashion designer* |
| Polizist/in | *policeman/woman* |
| Sekretär/in | *secretary* |
| Tierarzt, Tierärztin | *vet* |
| Verkäufer/in | *shop assistant* |

### ⊙ I can …

- talk about part-time jobs, spending and saving
- talk about school life in Germany and the UK
- talk about what I've done this year at school and what I'm going to do next year
- talk about different jobs and say what job I would like to do in the future
- use *für* + accusative
- use a range of tenses
- use masculine and feminine forms of jobs
- use *ich möchte … werden*
- use strategies to sound more authentic when I speak German
- pronounce the *ö* sound

## Die internationale Schweiz

Ich heiße Leo und ich bin Schweizer – das heißt: ich komme aus der Schweiz. Ich wohne in Affoltern – das ist ein kleines Dorf südlich von Zürich.

Die Schweiz ist ein kleines Land mit sieben Millionen Einwohnern. Aber man kann in wenigen Stunden von der Schweiz aus vier verschiedene Länder besuchen – und vier verschiedene Sprachen sprechen! Warum? In der Schweiz gibt es vier Sprachen: Deutsch – das heißt: Schweizerdeutsch – sprechen rund 64 Prozent der Schweizer, Französisch 20 Prozent, Italienisch sechs Prozent. Dann gibt es noch Rätoromanisch, aber das sprechen nur 0,5 Prozent.

Die meisten deutschsprachigen Schweizer sprechen mindestens drei Sprachen: Schweizerdeutsch – oder „Schwyzerdütsch" – ist anders als „deutsches Deutsch" oder „Hochdeutsch". Wir sagen zum Beispiel nicht: „Hallo!" und „Auf Wiedersehen". Wir sagen: „Grüezi" und „Uf Wiederluege". Deshalb müssen wir in der Schule schon mit sechs Jahren Hochdeutsch lernen. Das ist also unsere zweite Sprache! Und wir lernen mit acht Jahren Französisch – unsere dritte Sprache! Das ist super – und sehr nützlich, finde ich.

---

**LESEN 1**

**Finde a–g in Leos Text.**

*Beispiel:* **a** *Einwohnern*

| | |
|---|---|
| **a** inhabitants | **e** German-speaking |
| **b** in a few hours | **f** at least |
| **c** different countries | **g** useful |
| **d** languages | |

### ? Think

What else do you know about Switzerland? Find photos and information on the internet and make a fact file.

Mention:
- number of inhabitants
- cities
- languages spoken
- things to see
- climate

---

**LESEN 2**

**NC 5**

**Richtig oder falsch? Schreib die falschen Sätze richtig auf.**

*Beispiel:* **a** *Falsch – Leo lives in Affoltern …*

**a** Leo lives in Zurich.
**b** Four languages are spoken in Switzerland.
**c** Most Swiss speak German.
**d** Italian is the second most common language.
**e** Most German-speaking Swiss speak at least three languages.
**f** Swiss German is the same as 'German' German.

# MEIN TAG: MARKUS LANZ

Markus Lanz (25) ist Snowboard-Champion und hat viele Medaillen gewonnen. Der nette und sympathische Deutsche mag Schnee – und das Leben auf dem Land.

▲ Markus, wie war dein Tag gestern? Was hast du alles gemacht?

▲ Also, ich bin vorgestern von einem Snowboard-Turnier in Amerika nach Hause geflogen.

▲ Und zu Hause – wo ist das? Wo wohnst du?

▲ Ich wohne in der Schweiz auf dem Land. Ich habe dort ein Bauernhaus. Also, ich bin am Montagmorgen um sieben Uhr aufgestanden. Ich habe in meinem Fitnesszimmer eine Stunde Bodybuilding gemacht. Danach habe ich mit meinem Fanclub telefoniert und ich habe an meiner offiziellen Webseite gearbeitet. Der Kontakt zu meinen Fans ist sehr wichtig!

▲ Und was hast du am Nachmittag gemacht?

▲ Am Nachmittag bin ich in die Berge gefahren – ich wandere und klettere gern. Aber das Wetter war sehr schlecht und ich bin in die Stadt gefahren. Ich mag Musik – die Beatles sind meine Lieblingsband – und ich sammele Schallplatten – also „altmodische CDs". Ich bin in meinen Lieblings-Secondhandladen gegangen und habe dort fünf Schallplatten gekauft.

## ? Think

Use these strategies to help you work out unknown language:

- Look for cognates – words that look like English words.
  What do you think these words mean?
  - Medaille  • offiziell  • der Kontakt
- Many German words are made up of shorter words, so if you know part of the word you can sometimes work out the rest.
  What do you think these words mean?
  - vorgestern  • das Bauernhaus
- Think about the context – what do the other words in the sentence mean? Try to use context to work out what these words mean:
  - Turnier  • Schallplatten
- Beware of false friends – words that look like English but have a different meaning in German! Look at this sentence:
  - der nette und <u>sympathische</u> Deutsche
  What do you think *sympathische* might mean in English – **a** or **b**?
  **a** sympathetic   **b** pleasant

### LESEN 1 — Finde a–c im Text.

**a** I go hiking
**b** I go climbing
**c** I collect

### LESEN 2 — Beantworte die Fragen auf Englisch.

NC 5

**a** When did Markus come back and from where?
**b** What did he do before breakfast?
**c** What did he do after that?
**d** Why did he drive into town in the afternoon?
**e** What did he do there? Why?

# Fasching

Fasching ist in Köln ein Fest mit vielen Namen, zum Beispiel „Fastnacht" oder „Karneval". Im Januar und Februar feiern die Menschen in der Region Köln viele Partys. Man kann auf diesen Partys essen, trinken, tanzen und sehr viel Spaß haben.

Man verkleidet sich und es gibt viele Veranstaltungen, wo man alte traditionelle Geschichten oder Witze hören kann.

Der Donnerstag vor Aschermittwoch heißt „Weiberfastnacht". In Köln ist dieser Tag ein inoffizieller Feiertag und vor allem für Frauen.

Am Freitag und Samstag danach feiern die Schulen Fasching mit lustigen Umzügen auf den Straßen.

Montag ist der Höhepunkt der Faschingsumzüge. Die Parade ist zwischen sechs und acht Kilometer lang, es gibt Tausende von Menschen und man tanzt und singt fröhlich. Die Musik und die Kostüme sind sehr traditionell.

Auf den Bürgersteigen sehen Millionen von Menschen diesen Umzug. Sie feiern auch – lachen, singen, tanzen und flirten. Außerdem essen sie viele Süßigkeiten – lecker!

Alle Geschäfte sind geschlossen.

Eine Stadt steht Kopf.

## LESEN 1 · Lies den Text. Finde a–i im Text.

*Beispiel:* **a** *Fasching, Fastnacht, Karneval*

a carnival
b there are lots of events
c traditional stories or jokes
d Ash Wednesday
e schools celebrate Carnival with funny parades
f Monday is the climax of the parades
g costumes
h on the pavements
i a city turned upside down

## LESEN 2 · Richtig (R) oder falsch (F)?

NC 5

*Beispiel:* **a** *F*

a Carnival in Cologne is celebrated in October.
b During the Carnival season you can have a lot of fun.
c People dress up.
d The parade is two kilometres long.
e Thousands of people watch the parade.
f You can go shopping during the parades.

## LESEN 3 · Schreib die falschen Sätze (Übung 2) richtig auf.

*Beispiel:* **a** *F – Carnival is celebrated in January and February.*

# EMMA6

EMMA6 – das ist eine deutsche Band aus der Kleinstadt Heinsberg. Die Brüder Peter und Henrik Trevisan und ihr bester Freund Dominik Republik machen schon seit 2006 zusammen Musik.

Und was für eine Musik ist das? Die Band macht Popmusik mit deutschen Texten und hat schon auf vielen Konzerten und Open-Air-Festivals gespielt. 2011 haben sie ihr erstes Album gemacht. Es heißt „Soundtrack für dieses Jahr".

Peter singt und spielt Gitarre in der Band, sein Bruder Henrik spielt Schlagzeug und Dominik ist Bassist und spielt auch Moog-Synthesizer. Die Lieder des Trios erzählen Geschichten – von traurig bis komisch!

2010 und 2011 waren die Jungs sogar als Vorgruppe von „Wir sind Helden" (das ist eine berühmte deutsche Band) mit auf Tour. Ihre erste Single heißt „Paradiso".

## LESEN 1  NC 5
**Lies den Text und wähle die richtigen Antworten.**

a EMMA6 ist
1 eine Mädchenband.
2 ein Trio.

b Sie singen
1 auf Deutsch.
2 auf Englisch.

c Sie haben
1 noch keine Konzerte gemacht.
2 schon viele Konzerte gemacht.

d Peter ist
1 Gitarrist und Sänger.
2 Schlagzeuger und Bassist.

e Die Liedertexte sind
1 manchmal lustig.
2 immer traurig.

f Die Gruppe hat mit „Wir sind Helden"
1 eine CD gemacht.
2 live gespielt.

## LESEN 2  NC 5
**Beantworte die Fragen auf Englisch.**

a Where do the members of EMMA6 come from?
b What relationship do the band members have?
c How long have they been playing together?
d What did they do in 2011?
e What instruments do Henrik and Dominik play?
f How often have the band been touring with 'Wir sind Helden'?

## SOS Freizeitstress

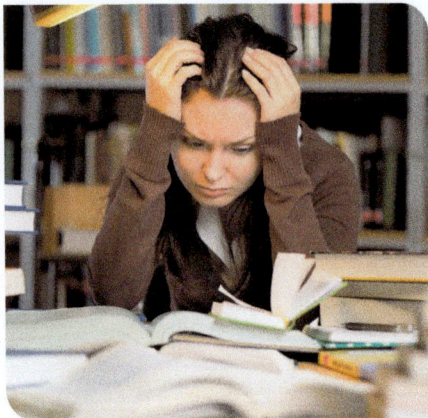

**Erst die Schule und dann die Hobbys: Montag Schwimmen, Dienstag Theater und Tennis, Mittwoch Chor, Donnerstag Gitarre, Freitag Chinesisch. Warum kann die Woche nicht länger sein? Denkst du das auch manchmal? Du bist nicht allein! Mehr als die Hälfte aller Kinder und Jugendlichen haben einen zu vollen Terminkalender und sie haben keine Zeit mehr zum Spielen oder faul sein.**

„Radio-Zoom-Magazin" hat Tipps für dieses Problem:

- Sprich mit deinen Eltern, wenn du glaubst: „Ich mache zu viel." So könnt ihr zusammen eine Lösung finden.

- Sieh dir zusammen mit deinen Eltern deinen Terminkalender an und prüf alle Aktivitäten kritisch. Welche Aktivitäten sind wichtig und welche sind unwichtig? Welches Hobby machst du vielleicht auch nur, weil deine Eltern es gut finden?

- Wenn du alle unwichtigen Aktivitäten aus deinem Terminkalender streichst, dann siehst du: jetzt habe ich „richtige" Freizeit! Und wofür? Das ist doch klar: was möchtest du machen? Zeichnen, mit dem Hund spielen – oder nur faul auf dem Sofa liegen …

- Du kannst jetzt zusammen mit deinen Eltern einmal pro Woche deine Termine für die nächste Woche planen, zum Beispiel immer am Sonntagabend um 18 Uhr. Was kannst du machen und was kannst – oder willst – du nicht machen? So kannst du super in die Woche starten – ohne Freizeitstress!

---

**LESEN 1**

### Finde a–g im Text.

*Beispiel:* **a** *Chinesisch*

**a** Chinese
**b** you're not alone
**c** a diary that is too full
**d** you believe/think
**e** you can find a solution together
**f** examine all activities critically
**g** to cut from your diary

**LESEN 2**

NC 5

### Lies die Sätze. Sind sie richtig (R), falsch (F) oder nicht im Text (NiT)?

*Beispiel:* **a** *R*

**a** Viele Jugendliche haben zu viele Hobbys.
**b** Tennis ist ihr Lieblingshobby.
**c** Fünf Prozent der Jugendlichen haben Freizeitstress.
**d** Deine Eltern können bei diesem Problem helfen.
**e** Du kannst auch Hilfe in der Schule bekommen.
**f** Deine Eltern sollen deine Aktivitäten wählen.
**g** Weniger Aktivitäten heißt mehr Freizeit.
**h** Du musst die Aktivitäten immer am Sonntag planen.

# Spezialitäten des Landes

**a** In Deutschland gibt es verschiedene Gerichte, die typisch für das Land sind. In München, in Süddeutschland, isst man Brezeln mit guter deutscher Butter oder ein saftiges Stück Fleisch, zum Beispiel Schweinshaxe mit Sauerkraut.

**b** Zum Kaffee essen die Deutschen gern Schwarzwälder Kirschtorte aus dem Schwarzwald, oder Apfelstrudel.

**c** Prasselkuchen ist eine typisch ostdeutsche Spezialität aus Blätterteig und Aprikosen.

**d** Zum Mittag sollte man in Österreich paniertes Kalbfleisch mit Pommes oder Kroketten essen. Das Gericht heißt Wiener Schnitzel und ist sehr beliebt – besonders bei Touristen.

**e** Auch die Schweiz hat viel zu bieten. Natürlich kennt jeder die traditionell hergestellte Süßigkeit des Landes ... Na, was ist es? Möchtest du einen Tipp? Nestlé oder Lindt sind die größten Fabrikanten ... Ja, richtig! Schokolade.

**LESEN 1**
**Lies den Text und finde die passenden Bilder.**
Read the text and choose a picture to go with each paragraph.

**LESEN 2** NC 5
**Wie heißt das Essen? Finde diese Spezialitäten im Text.**

**a** A type of sweet that is often brown.
**b** Veal in breadcrumbs.
**c** Puff pastry with apricots.
**d** Pork leg with white cabbage.
**e** This food is named after the German Black Forest.

**? Think**
What strategies do you know for coping with unknown language? Try them out on these texts.

**SCHREIBEN 3**
**Finde fünf weitere deutsche Spezialitäten im Internet.**
Name them and list their ingredients in German. Would you like to try them? Why?

## Du bist Du

Kein Mensch in der Welt hat Augen so wie deine.
Manche sind braun und groß und rund dazu,
doch deine sind einzig, es sind eben deine.
Dich gibt's nur einmal, du bist eben du.

Nicht eine Stimme klingt genau wie deine,
ob sie nun lacht, ob redet oder singt,
denn deine Stimme hast nur du alleine,
sonst gibt es keine, die so klingt.

Du bist etwas Besonderes, denn dich gibt's nur einmal.
Keiner ist genauso wie du eben bist,
hast eigene Gefühle und hast dein Geheimnis
und dein eigenes Glück, das tief in dir ist.

Und keiner kann lächeln, so wie du jetzt lächelst.
Kein Mensch der Welt macht's ganz genau wie du.
Dein Lächeln hast du ganz für dich alleine.
Dich gibt's nur einmal. Du bist eben du.

Du bist was ganz Besonderes, dich gibt's
nur einmal!

---

**LESEN 1** **Lies den Text. Was für ein Text ist das?**
What sort of text is this? What makes you think this? In what style is it written?

**LESEN 2** **Finde a–i im Text und mach Paare mit 1–9.**

*Beispiel:* **a 4**

**a** kein Mensch in der Welt
**b** manche
**c** einzig
**d** nicht eine Stimme klingt
**e** etwas Besonderes
**f** Geheimnis
**g** Glück
**h** tief
**i** lächeln

**1** happiness
**2** secret
**3** to smile
**4** no one on earth
**5** something special
**6** some
**7** deep
**8** not a single voice sounds
**9** unique

**LESEN 3** **Lies den Text noch einmal. Was passt?**

**a** No one
  **1** has the same eyes as you.
  **2** knows the colour of your eyes.

**b** You
  **1** can sing very well.
  **2** have a unique voice.

**c** You also have
  **1** to share your hopes and dreams.
  **2** your own feelings and secrets.

**d** Your happiness
  **1** is deep inside of you.
  **2** depends on other people.

**e** Nobody
  **1** has your smile.
  **2** can smile as nicely as you.

**f** You are
  **1** like everybody else.
  **2** truly unique.

# Woher kommt unsere Energie?

Erdöl, Erdgas und Kohle sind in Deutschland die wichtigsten Energiequellen. Man nutzt auch Uran ... Ja, richtig: Atomenergie.

Das Problem? Es gibt zu wenig Erdöl, Erdgas und Kohle. Und wenn man Erdöl, Erdgas und Kohle verbrennt, produziert man Treibhausgase. Der Treibhauseffekt wird immer schlimmer, die Erde wird wärmer ... Dann kommt der Klimawandel.

Alternative Energien sind besser. Sie heißen auch erneuerbare Energien, weil sie immer wieder „neu" sind. Erneuerbare Energien schützen das Klima, weil sie keine Treibhausgase produzieren.

Die erneuerbaren Energiequellen sind Wind, Wasser, Sonne und Erdwärme. In Zukunft will Deutschland sie immer mehr nutzen. Der Plan ist: bis 2050 wird fünfzig Prozent der Energie in Deutschland aus erneuerbaren Quellen kommen.

---

**LESEN 1**

**Finde die unterstrichenen Vokabeln im Wörterbuch.**

*Beispiel: Erdöl – mineral oil*

**LESEN 2**

NC 7

**Lies den Text und beantworte die Fragen auf Englisch.**

a What sources of energy are used in Germany?
b What are the two main problems with using only these sources of energy?
c Give two advantages of renewable energy sources.
d What are the four sources of renewable energy used in Germany?
e What is Germany's aim for 2050?

**LESEN 3**

**Finde die Paare (1–5 und a–e). Schreib die Sätze ab.**

*Beispiel: 1 b Die Erde wird immer wärmer, weil es zu viele Treibhausgase gibt.*

1 Die Erde wird immer wärmer,
2 Man verbrennt Erdöl, Erdgas und Kohle,
3 Deutschland
4 Erneuerbare Energien sind
5 In Zukunft wird Deutschland

a 50% des Stroms aus Wasser-, Wind- und Sonnenenergie produzieren.
b weil es zu viele Treibhausgase gibt.
c umweltfreundlich.
d um Energie zu produzieren.
e nutzt auch Atomenergie.

# Ein ungewöhnliches Praktikum!

**1**

### Redakteur beim Kinderfernsehen

- Bist du ein Fan von Kinderprogrammen?
- Hast du mit der „Sesamstraße" das ABC gelernt?
- War der Kinderkanal dein Lieblingssender?

Dann mach ein Praktikum beim Kinderfernsehen!

### Was machst du?

Ein normaler Tag im TV-Studio: Du schreibst Dialoge und Reportagen und hilfst bei den Produktionen und sogar beim Filmen mit. Die Arbeit ist extrem abwechslungsreich – manchmal musst du dich nach Feierabend sogar als Affe verkleiden und in einem lustigen Film mitspielen …

### Wie musst du sein?

Du musst gut in einem Team arbeiten können – und darfst keine Probleme mit Stress haben!

**2**

Haarspray auf dem Kuchen, Klebstoff unter der Wurst, Make-up für das Hähnchen? Wie gut sehen die Lebensmittel aus? Das ist bei diesem Praktikum am wichtigsten:

### Food-Stylist

Food-Stylisten arbeiten mit vielen Tricks!

Im Praktikum lernst du alle diese Tricks kennen, denn du hilfst dem Fotografen bei den Fotoshootings. Jeden Tag siehst du das tollste Essen – das du nicht essen kannst, weil es nicht echt ist. Es ist aus Plastik. (Nur so kann der Fotograf fünf oder sechs Stunden lang „leckere" Fotos für Zeitschriften oder Magazine machen.)

**3**

Im Weihnachtsmann-Land für den Weihnachtsmann arbeiten – ein Traumpraktikum nicht nur für Kinder!

### Nordpol-Post: Weihnachtsmann-Helfer/in

### Was machst du?

Viel Arbeit mit der Presse, viel Kontakt zu den Besuchern (z.B. Fotos von dir und den Kindern), sehr sehr viele Briefe ordnen und Antworten auf Englisch schreiben, Souvenirs verkaufen. Du arbeitest in Rovaniemi in Lappland am Polarkreis (Finnland). Dort ist es sehr kalt und es schneit jeden Tag.

### Wie musst du sein?

Nett, fröhlich, fleißig, sehr gut in Englisch.

**LESEN 1**

**Lies die Anzeigen und finde die passenden Bilder.**

**LESEN 2**

NC 7

**Beantworte die Fragen auf Englisch.**

a What does daily work at the TV studio involve?
b Why is the job extremely varied?
c What sort of person is needed for work at the TV studio?
d What three tricks are mentioned for photographing food?
e What is the most important thing at a food photo shoot?
f Why does the photographer use fake food?
g What are the tasks of Santa's helper?
h Where is the job situated?
i What qualities do you need for work as Santa's helper?

# Grammatik

## Introduction

In order to speak or write correctly in a language, we need to know the grammar basics behind the construction of sentences. The ability to identify patterns and to understand and apply grammar rules in German allows you to use the language to say what you want to say.

In this section you will find a summary of the main grammar points covered by this book with some activities to check that you have understood and can use the language accurately.

## Glossary of terms

**noun** *das Nomen* = a person, animal, place or thing

**Maja** und ihre **Katze** spielen im **Garten**. *Maja and her cat are playing in the garden.*

**article** *der Artikel* = the word in front of a noun such as 'the' or 'a'

**der** Hund, **eine** Tasche *the dog, a bag*

**singular** *der Singular* = one of something

**Der Hund** isst **eine Wurst**. *The dog is eating a sausage.*

**plural** *der Plural* = more than one of something

**Die Kinder** gehen in die Schule. *The children are going to school.*

**pronoun** *das Pronomen* = a word used instead of a noun or a name

**Er** isst eine Wurst. *He (It, The dog) is eating a sausage.*
**Sie** gehen in die Schule. *They are going to school.*

**subject** *das Subjekt* = a person or thing 'doing' the action or verb

**Tom** geht ins Kino. *Tom is going to the cinema.*
**Ich** mag Mathe. *I like maths.*

**object** *das Objekt* = a person or thing affected by the action or verb

Jana kauft **eine CD**. *Jana is buying a CD.*
Ich trage **einen Pullover**. *I'm wearing a jumper.*

**nominative case** *der Nominativ* = the subject of the sentence

**Der Hund** heißt Bello. *The dog is called Bello.*
**Eine Banane** kostet 50 Cent. *A banana costs 50 cents.*

**accusative case** *der Akkusativ* = used for the object of a sentence

Ich habe **einen Bruder**. *I have a brother.*
Jan kauft **eine Tasche**. *Jan is buying a bag.*

**dative case** *der Dativ* = used after some prepositions

Ich wohne in **einem Reihenhaus**. *I live in a terraced house.*
Sie fahren mit **dem Zug**. *They are going by train.*

**adjective** *das Adjektiv* = a word which describes a noun

Meine Schwester ist **nett**. *My sister is nice.*
Berlin ist eine **schöne** Stadt. *Berlin is a beautiful city.*

**preposition** *die Präposition* = describes position: where something is

Wir gehen **in** die Disco. *We are going to the disco.*
Meine Tasche ist **auf** dem Bett. *My bag is on the bed.*

# Grammatik

## 1 Nouns and articles
*Nomen und Artikel*

### 1.1 Masculine, feminine or neuter?

All German nouns are either masculine, feminine or neuter. Nouns always start with a capital letter and their articles have different endings:

|          | masculine | feminine | neuter |
|----------|-----------|----------|--------|
| **the**  | der       | die      | das    |
| **a/an** | ein       | eine     | ein    |

⚠️ Every time you learn a new noun, make sure you learn its gender (masculine, feminine or neuter) too.

| Don't learn: | *Hund*      | ✗ |
|--------------|-------------|---|
| Learn:       | *der Hund*  | ✓ |

### 1.2 Singular or plural?

In English, you usually add -*s* to a noun to make it plural when you are talking about more than one thing (one cat → two cats). In German, there are several different ways of forming the plural, but the plural word for 'the' is always *die*:

| der Bleistift (*pencil*)    | → | **die** Bleistift**e**  |
|-----------------------------|---|-------------------------|
| die Schwester (*sister*)    | → | **die** Schwester**n**  |
| der Opa (*grandfather*)     | → | **die** Opa**s**        |
| der Bruder (*brother*)      | → | **die** Br**ü**der      |

⚠️ Each time you learn a new noun, try to learn its plural too.

### 1.3 Compound nouns

Some German nouns are formed by putting two or more shorter nouns together. They are called compound nouns. A compound noun always takes the same gender as the final noun of the compound:

| der Müll + der Eimer  | → | der Mülleimer    |
|-----------------------|---|------------------|
| der Wind + die Energie| → | die Windenergie  |
| der Ozon + das Loch   | → | das Ozonloch     |

---

**A** Make as many compound nouns as you can, using the following nouns. Check them in a dictionary.

*Beispiel: der Schulhof, …*

| der Bus      | die Haltestelle | das Auto | das Plastik |
|--------------|-----------------|----------|-------------|
| der Computer | die Schule      | das Boot | das Spiel   |
| der Film     | die Tüte        | das Haus | das Tier    |
| der Fußball  | die Tür         | das Kino |             |
| der Hof      |                 |          |             |

## 2 Cases
*Fälle*

### 2.1 Subject and object

The subject of a sentence is the person or thing 'doing' the verb. The object of a sentence is the thing or person affected by the verb. We say that the subject and the object are in different cases.

| subject   | verb  | object      |
|-----------|-------|-------------|
| Der Hund  | isst  | eine Wurst. |
| Sven      | kauft | ein Buch.   |

### 2.2 The nominative and accusative case

The endings for *der/die/das* and *ein/eine/ein* never change when they come before the subject of a sentence. We say that the subject is in the nominative case:

|         | masculine | feminine | neuter | plural |
|---------|-----------|----------|--------|--------|
| **the** | der       | die      | das    | die    |
| **a**   | ein       | eine     | ein    | –      |

The endings for *der* and *ein* change slightly when they come before the object of a sentence – but only for masculine nouns. We say that the object of the sentence is in the accusative case:

| subject    | verb           | object                             |
|------------|----------------|------------------------------------|
| Er         | hat<br>liebt   | **einen** Computer.<br>**den** Hund. |
| Sie        | kauft<br>liest | eine CD.<br>die Zeitung.           |
| Uwe<br>Ich | trägt<br>habe  | ein T-Shirt.<br>das Buch.          |

## 2.3 The dative case

The endings for *der/die/das* and *ein/eine/ein* change after certain prepositions (words like *aus, mit, nach, von* and *zu*). We say that the nouns that come after these prepositions are in the dative case:

nach **dem Mittagessen**   *after lunch*
mit **der Straßenbahn**   *by tram*

Remember that *zu* is usually combined with *dem* and *der* to give *zum* (*zu + dem*) and *zur* (*zu + der*):

Wir gehen **zum Park**.   *We're going to the park.*
Ich gehe **zur Schule**.   *I'm going to school.*

## 2.4 *mein, dein, sein, ihr* and *kein*

The words for 'my' (*mein*), 'your' (*dein*), 'his' (*sein*), 'her' (*ihr*) and 'no/none' (*kein*) also change their endings when used before a masculine object in the accusative case:

Tanja hat **meinen** MP3-Player. *Tanja has my MP3 player.*
Ich mag **deinen** Pullover. *I like your jumper.*
Sie liest **seinen** Brief. *She's reading his letter.*
Hast du **ihren** Bruder gesehen? *Have you seen her brother?*
Ich habe **keinen** Computer. *I don't have a computer.*

## 2.5 Summary

Here are all the case endings used in *Zoom Deutsch 2*:

| der/die/das | | | | |
| --- | --- | --- | --- | --- |
| | masculine | feminine | neuter | plural |
| nominative | der | die | das | die |
| accusative | den | die | das | die |
| dative | dem | der | dem | den |

| ein/eine/ein | | | | |
| --- | --- | --- | --- | --- |
| | masculine | feminine | neuter | plural |
| nominative | ein | eine | ein | – |
| accusative | einen | eine | ein | – |
| dative | einem | einer | einem | – |

| mein, dein, sein, ihr, kein<br>These all have the same endings: | | | | |
| --- | --- | --- | --- | --- |
| | masculine | feminine | neuter | plural |
| nominative | mein | meine | mein | meine |
| accusative | meinen | meine | mein | meine |
| dative | meinem | meiner | meinem | meinen |

**B** You are planning a holiday. You need tourist information and some new clothes to take with you! Write sentences saying what you need: *Ich brauche einen/eine/ein …*

der Fahrplan

die Liste von Campingplätzen

das Outfit

die Broschüre über die Stadt

# 3 Prepositions
## *Präpositionen*

Prepositions are words like 'in' and 'on' which tell you where someone or something is. They always change the endings of the articles *der/die/das* and *ein/eine/ein*:

**m.** der Schreibtisch ➞ Das Buch ist **im** Schreibtisch.
        (in + dem)
**f.** die Lampe ➞ Die CD ist **neben** der Lampe.
**n.** das Regal ➞ Der Fußball ist **auf** dem Regal.

Here is a list of all the prepositions used in *Zoom Deutsch 1* and *2*:

| | | | |
| --- | --- | --- | --- |
| an | *on, at* | neben | *next to* |
| auf | *on, on to* | seit | *since* |
| aus | *from, out of* | über | *above, over* |
| bei | *at the home of, with* | unter | *under* |
| für | *for* | von | *from* |
| hinter | *behind* | vor | *in front of* |
| in | *in, into* | zu | *to* |
| mit | *with, by (+ transport)* | zwischen | *between* |
| nach | *after* | | |

**C** **Look at this family. How is everybody travelling?**

*Beispiel: Der Vater fährt mit dem Auto.*

der Vater   die Mutter   der Sohn   die Tochter
der Opa   die Oma

## 3.1 Accusative or dative case?

Prepositions take either the accusative or the dative case:

- *für* always takes the accusative case
- *aus, bei, mit, nach, seit, von* and *zu* always take the dative case
- *an, auf, hinter, in, neben, über, unter, vor* and *zwischen* take either the dative or the accusative case

When followed by the accusative case, the preposition indicates movement or a direction (for example where someone or something is going or moving to):

Tom fährt **in** die Stadt. *Tom drives into town.*
Ich gehe **hinter** den Tisch. *I go behind the table.*

But when followed by the dative, the preposition tells you where someone or something is already:

Tom wohnt **in** der Stadt. *Tom lives in the city.*
Der Test ist **auf** dem Tisch. *The test is on the table.*

Remember to use these shortened forms after *in*:

- masculine and neuter dative: **im** (in + dem)
  **im** Schrank, **im** Hotel
- neuter accusative: **ins** (in + das)   **ins** Hotel

**D** **Accusative or dative? Fill in the correct article for each sentence. Shorten the article where possible (*in dem → im, in das → ins*).**

*Beispiel:* **a** *die*

a   Wir gehen in _____ Disco.
b   Sie tanzt in _____ Disco.
c   Die Post ist neben _____ Supermarkt.
d   Wir sind in _____ Freibad geschwommen.
e   Gestern bin ich in _____ Kino gegangen.

## 4 Adjectives
### Adjektive

Adjectives are the words we use to describe nouns. When an adjective follows a noun, you can use the form in which it appears in the dictionary, with no additional ending:

Das T-Shirt ist **schön**.
Meine Mutter ist **nett**.

But when the adjective is placed directly before a noun, it adds an extra ending according to the gender of the noun and the case used:

| | Nominative case (subject) | Accusative case (object) |
|---|---|---|
| | Das ist/sind … | Ich kaufe … |
| m. | ein toll**er** Computer | einen toll**en** Computer |
| | der toll**e** Computer | den toll**en** Computer |
| f. | eine toll**e** CD | eine toll**e** CD |
| | die toll**e** CD | die toll**e** CD |
| n. | ein toll**es** Buch | ein toll**es** Buch |
| | das toll**e** Buch | das toll**e** Buch |
| pl. | toll**e** Spiele | toll**e** Spiele |
| | die toll**en** Spiele | die toll**en** Spiele |

## 4.1 Demonstrative adjectives

The demonstrative adjective *dieser/diese/dieses* means 'this' in English. Like *der/die/das*, it agrees with the noun it relates to:

| | masculine | feminine | neuter | plural |
|---|---|---|---|---|
| nom. | dieser Brief | diese Tasche | dieses Mädchen | diese Briefe |
| acc. | diesen Brief | diese Tasche | dieses Mädchen | diese Briefe |
| dat. | diesem Brief | dieser Tasche | diesem Mädchen | diesen Brie |

der Stuhl (*the chair*)

Nominative: Dieser Stuhl ist bequem.
*This chair is comfortable.*

Accusative: Ich habe diesen Stuhl bei Harrods gekauft.
*I bought this chair at Harrods.*

Dative: Ich sitze auf diesem Stuhl.
*I'm sitting on this chair.*

## 4.2 The comparative

When you want to say something is smaller, bigger, nicer, etc., you use the comparative form. As in English, you add *-er* to the adjective to form the comparative in German:

klein → klein**er**
schön → schön**er**
billig → billig**er**

For some short adjectives you also have to add an umlaut to the first vowel:

alt → **ält**er
groß → gr**öß**er

And some comparatives are irregular:

gut → **besser**

To say 'than' use *als*:

Die Bluse ist schicker **als** das T-Shirt. *The blouse is smarter than the T-shirt.*

## 4.3 The superlative

To say something is the best (of all), the worst (of all), the biggest/smallest (of all), etc., you use the superlative form. Put *am* before the adjective and (for regular adjectives) add *-sten* to the end:

klein → **am** klein**sten**
schön → **am** schön**sten**
billig → **am** billig**sten**

If the adjective ends in *t, d, s, sch* or *z*, you usually add *-esten*:

laut → **am** laut**esten**
but: groß → **am** größ**ten**

Some superlatives are irregular:

gut → **am besten**

---

**E** **Give the comparative and superlative form of the adjective in brackets.**

*Beispiel:* **a** *Der Verkehr ist schlimmer/am schlimmsten.*

**a** Der Verkehr ist (schlimm).
**b** Die Luftverschmutzung ist (furchtbar).
**c** Die Müllberge sind (schlecht).
**d** Alternative Energien sind (wichtig).
**e** Recycling ist (toll).

# 5 Possessive adjectives
## *Possessivpronomen*

Possessive adjectives show who or what something belongs to ('my dog', 'your brother'):

Das ist **meine** Mutter. *That is my mother.*
Ist das **dein** Pullover? *Is that your jumper?*
**Seine** Katze heißt Mitzi. *His cat is called Mitzi.*
**Ihr** Vater ist sehr streng. *Her father is very strict.*

They come before the noun they describe and they take the same endings as *ein/eine/ein*:

|  | masculine | feminine | neuter | plural |
|---|---|---|---|---|
| **my** | mein Computer | meine Tasche | mein Buch | meine Schuhe |
| **your** | dein Computer | deine Tasche | dein Buch | deine Schuhe |
| **his** | sein Computer | seine Tasche | sein Buch | seine Schuhe |
| **her** | ihr Computer | ihre Tasche | ihr Buch | ihre Schuhe |

# 6 Pronouns
## *Pronomen*

Pronouns are used instead of a noun or a name:

**Ich** heiße Lola. *I am called Lola.*
**Er** ist sehr frech. *He is very naughty.*
**Sie** wohnt in Berlin. *She lives in Berlin.*

Here is a list of all the subject pronouns used in *Zoom Deutsch 2*:

| ich | *I* | wir | *we* |
|---|---|---|---|
| du | *you* | ihr | *you (informal, plural)* |
| er/sie/es | *he/she/it* | sie | *they* |
| man | *one* | Sie | *you (formal)* |

# Grammatik

**F** **Replace the noun in brackets with the correct pronoun.**

*Beispiel:* **a** *wir*

**a** Am Wochenende werden (meine Freunde und ich) ins Kino gehen.

**b** In den Ferien fliegt (mein Bruder) nach Deutschland.

**c** (Meine Schule) wird eine Recycling-Aktion starten.

**d** (Das Motorrad) war sehr teuer.

**e** (Deine Freunde) sind ziemlich nett.

## 6.1 *sie, Sie, du* and *man*

- *sie* (with a small 's') can mean 'she' or 'they':

  Wo wohnt **sie**? *Where does she live?*
  Wo wohnen **sie**? *Where do they live?*

- *Sie* (with a capital 'S') is the polite form of 'you' used when talking to adults, strangers and in formal situations:

  Haben **Sie** Apfelsaft? *Do you have apple juice?*

- *du* is the informal form of 'you' used when talking to family, friends, children or animals:

  Wie alt bist **du**? *How old are you?*
  Hast **du** einen Hund? *Do you have a dog?*

- *man* is often used in German and can mean 'one', 'you', 'they' or 'we':

  Wie kommt **man** zum Schwimmbad? *How does **one**/ How do **you** get to the pool?*
  **Man** spricht Deutsch in der Schweiz. ***They** speak German in Switzerland.*
  **Man** kann ins Kino gehen. ***You** can go to the cinema.*

## 6.2 Object pronouns

The words 'it' and 'them' in these sentences are called object pronouns:

  I like the skirt – I'll buy **it**.
  The trainers are expensive – I won't buy **them**.

In the following sentences, notice how in German the word for 'it' changes (*ihn/sie/es*), depending on the gender of the noun it replaces. Remember that the object of the sentence is in the accusative case (see Section 2.2):

  Ich mag den Rock. Ich kaufe **ihn**. *I like the skirt. I'll buy it.*
  Die Bluse ist schick. Ich trage **sie**.
  *The blouse is smart. I'll wear it.*
  Ich mag das Hemd. Ich nehme **es**. *I like the shirt. I'll take it.*

The word for 'them' is *sie*:

  Die Shorts sind cool. Ich kaufe **sie**.
  *The shorts are cool. I'll buy them.*

# 7 Verbs

## *Verben*

Verbs are words which describe an action. If you can put 'to' in front of a word or '-ing' at the end, it is probably a verb:

| **go** | to go ✓ | going ✓ | = a verb |
| **listen** | to listen ✓ | listening ✓ | = a verb |
| **desk** | to desk ✗ | desking ✗ | = not a verb |
| **happy** | to happy ✗ | happying ✗ | = not a verb |

## 7.1 The infinitive

A verb takes many different forms:

  I **have** a cat.
  Tom **has** a dog.
  They **haven't** any pets.

Not all verb forms are listed in a dictionary. For example, you won't find 'has' or 'haven't'. You will have to look up the infinitive 'to have'.

In German, infinitives are easy to recognise as they always end in *-en* or *-n*:

  spiel**en** *to play*
  wohn**en** *to live*
  sammel**n** *to collect*

## 7.2 The present tense

A verb in the present tense describes an action which is taking place now or takes place regularly.

There are two present tenses in English:

  I am playing tennis. (now)
  I play tennis. (every day)

There is only one present tense in German:

  Ich spiele Tennis. (jetzt – *now*)
  Ich spiele Tennis. (jeden Tag – *every day*)

To describe an action, you need a subject (the person or thing doing the action) and a verb. The ending of the verb changes according to who or what the subject of the sentence is:

  **Ich** lese**.** *I read.*
  **Sie** lies**t.** *She reads.*
  **Wir** geh**en.** *We go.*
  **Er** geh**t.** *He goes.*

## 7.3 Regular verb endings

Most German verbs follow the same pattern. They have regular endings which are always added to the verb stem. The verb stem is the infinitive without its -(e)n ending (e.g. *spielen → spiel, schwimmen → schwimm*):

| | |
|---|---|
| **spielen** | *to play* |
| ich spiel**e** | *I play* |
| du spiel**st** | *you play* |
| er/sie/es/man spiel**t** | *he/she/it/one plays* |
| wir spiel**en** | *we play* |
| ihr spiel**t** | *you play (plural)* |
| sie spiel**en** | *they play* |
| Sie spiel**en** | *you play (formal)* |

## 7.4 Irregular verb endings

Some common verbs do not follow this regular pattern. They are irregular, and they change their endings, as well as their stem, in the *du* and the *er/sie/es* forms.

⚠️ You'll need to learn them by heart.

Here are some examples of common irregular verbs:

| fahren *to go* | lesen *to read* | essen *to eat* |
|---|---|---|
| **a → ä** | **e → ie** | **e → i** |
| ich f**a**hre | ich l**e**se | ich **e**sse |
| du f**ä**hrst | du l**ie**st | du **i**sst |
| er/sie/es f**ä**hrt | er/sie/es l**ie**st | er/sie/es **i**sst |

| tragen *to wear* | sehen *to see* | nehmen *to take* |
|---|---|---|
| **a → ä** | **e → ie** | **e → i** |
| ich tr**a**ge | ich s**e**he | ich n**e**hme |
| du tr**ä**gst | du s**ie**hst | du n**i**mmst |
| er/sie/es tr**ä**gt | er/sie/es s**ie**ht | er/sie/es n**i**mmt |

## 7.5 *haben* and *sein*

The verbs *haben* (to have) and *sein* (to be) don't follow the pattern of any other verbs, so you need to learn them:

| haben | sein |
|---|---|
| ich **habe** | ich **bin** |
| du **hast** | du **bist** |
| er/sie/es **hat** | er/sie/es **ist** |
| wir **haben** | wir **sind** |
| ihr **habt** | ihr **seid** |
| sie **haben** | sie **sind** |
| Sie **haben** | Sie **sind** |

**G** **Fill in the correct form of *haben* or *sein*.**

*Beispiel:* **a** *ist*

**a** Mein Vater _____ Polizist.
**b** Ich _____ Verkäuferin.
**c** Sira _____ rote lockige Haare.
**d** _____ du sportlich?
**e** Meine Eltern _____ ziemlich streng.
**f** _____ du ein Handy?

## 7.6 Separable verbs

Separable verbs consist of two parts: a **prefix** (a small word like *auf*, *ab*, etc.) and a **verb**:

**auf**stehen (*to stand up*)
**auf** = prefix     **stehen** = verb

When you use a separable verb, the verb part of it follows the usual rules for German verb endings. The separable prefix usually (but not always) separates from the verb.

German separable verbs are similar to English verbs like 'tidy up' or 'get up'. In English, you can say either 'Tidy up your room' or 'Tidy your room up'; but in German, the prefix is almost always at the end:

Räum dein Zimmer **auf**!

Commonly used separable prefixes include: *ab-*, *an-*, *auf-*, *aus-* and *ein-*.

| aufstehen *to stand up* | einkaufen *to shop* |
|---|---|
| ich steh**e auf** | ich kauf**e ein** |
| du steh**st auf** | du kauf**st ein** |
| er/sie/es steh**t auf** | er/sie/es kauf**t ein** |
| wir steh**en auf** | wir kauf**en ein** |
| ihr steh**t auf** | ihr kauf**t ein** |
| sie/Sie steh**en auf** | sie/Sie kauf**en ein** |

## 7.7 Reflexive verbs

Some German verbs need an extra pronoun (called a **reflexive pronoun**) to complete the sentence. These verbs are called reflexive verbs. They express actions that you do to yourself, such as washing yourself:

Not reflexive:  Ich wasche **das Auto**. *I'm washing the car.*
Reflexive:      Ich wasche **mich**. *I'm washing myself.*

# Grammatik

There are more reflexive verbs in German than there are in English. So when you learn a German verb, try to also remember if it is reflexive or not.

The verb itself follows the same rules for endings as other verbs (see Section 7.3 and 7.4). The reflexive pronoun (*mich* – myself, *dich* – yourself, *sich* – himself/herself, ...) changes depending on the subject:

| sich waschen *to wash oneself, to get washed* | sich duschen *to (have a) shower* |
|---|---|
| ich wasch**e mich** | ich dusch**e mich** |
| du wäsch**st dich** | du dusch**st dich** |
| er/sie/es wäsch**t sich** | er/sie/es dusch**t sich** |
| wir wasch**en uns** | wir dusch**en uns** |
| ihr wasch**t euch** | ihr dusch**t euch** |
| sie/Sie wasch**en sich** | sie/Sie dusch**en sich** |

**H** **Fill in the correct reflexive pronouns.**

*Beispiel:* **a** *mich*

> dich   mich   sich   uns   sich   mich

a   Ich wasche _____.
b   Meine Schwester setzt _____.
c   Duschst du _____ jeden Tag?
d   Wir treffen _____ mit Freunden.
e   Ich ziehe _____ an.
f   Max wäscht _____ jeden Morgen.

Some verbs are **reflexive** and **separable**:

| sich anziehen *to get dressed* | |
|---|---|
| ich ziehe **mich an** | wir zieh**en uns an** |
| du zieh**st dich an** | ihr zieh**t euch an** |
| er/sie/es zieh**t sich an** | sie/Sie zieh**en sich an** |

## 7.8 Modal verbs

Modal verbs (*können, wollen, sollen, dürfen* and *müssen*) are used to say what you 'can', 'want to', 'should', 'are allowed to' and 'must' do. When you use a modal verb in a sentence, the main verb goes to the end in its infinitive form:

> Wir **können** ein Picknick **machen**. *We can have a picnic.*
> Ich **will** ins Kino **gehen**. *I want to go to the cinema.*
> Man **soll** viel Obst **essen**. *One should eat lots of fruit.*
> **Darfst** du auf die Party **gehen**? *Are you allowed to go to the party?*
> Er **muss** zu Hause **helfen**. *He must help at home.*

| können | wollen | sollen |
|---|---|---|
| ich **kann** | ich **will** | ich **soll** |
| du **kannst** | du **willst** | du **sollst** |
| er/sie/es/man **kann** | er/sie/es/man **will** | er/sie/es/man **soll** |
| wir **können** | wir **wollen** | wir **sollen** |
| ihr **könnt** | ihr **wollt** | ihr **sollt** |
| sie/Sie **können** | sie/Sie **wollen** | sie/Sie **sollen** |

| dürfen | müssen |
|---|---|
| ich **darf** | ich **muss** |
| du **darfst** | du **musst** |
| er/sie/es/man **darf** | er/sie/es/man **muss** |
| wir **dürfen** | wir **müssen** |
| ihr **dürft** | ihr **müsst** |
| sie/Sie **dürfen** | sie/Sie **müssen** |

**I** **Replace the modal verb in brackets with the correct verb form.**

*Beispiel:* **a** *muss*

a   Ich (müssen) für die Party viel organisieren.
b   Wir (können) eine Strandparty machen.
c   Claas (dürfen) nicht auf die Party gehen.
d   Auf einer Party (sollen) man viel Spaß haben.
e   Ich (wollen) tanzen!

## 7.9 The perfect tense with *haben*

If you want to talk about an action in the past, you use the perfect tense (*das Perfekt*).

The perfect tense is normally formed with:

- the present tense of *haben* (see 7.5)
- the past participle of the main verb

To form the past participle:

- take the infinitive: *spielen*
- remove the -en ending: *spiel~~en~~*
- add *ge-* and -*t*: **ge**spiel**t**

Some verbs that form their perfect tense with *haben* omit the *ge-* from the beginning of the past participle, but they still add -*t* at the end:

| besuchen (*to visit*) | → | besuch**t** |
|---|---|---|
| besichtigen (*to visit*) | → | besichtig**t** |
| recyceln (*to recycle*) | → | recycel**t** |
| telefonieren (*to telephone*) | → | telefonier**t** |

The past participle goes to the end of the sentence:

> Ich kaufe Souvenirs. → Ich **habe** Souvenirs **gekauft**.
> Wir wohnen in einem Wohnwagen. → Wir **haben** in einem Wohnwagen **gewohnt**.
> Er besucht seine Oma. → Er **hat** seine Oma **besucht**.

## 7.10 The perfect tense with *sein*

A small number of verbs form their perfect tense with *sein* instead of *haben*. They are usually verbs of motion (to go, to travel) and their past participles are formed with *ge-* and *-en* (instead of *ge-* and *-t*):

Ich fahre nach Spanien. → Ich **bin** nach Spanien **gefahren**.
Wir fliegen nach Schottland. → Wir **sind** nach Schottland **geflogen**.

## 7.11 The perfect tense of separable verbs

To form the perfect tense of separable verbs (*abwaschen*, *fernsehen*, *aufräumen*), put the prefix (*ab*, *fern*, *auf*) in front of the past participle:

Wir waschen ab. → Wir haben **ab**gewaschen.
Er sieht fern. → Er hat **fern**gesehen.
Ich räume mein Zimmer auf. → Ich habe mein Zimmer **auf**geräumt.

## 7.12 Irregular past participles

Here are some common verbs that form their past participles with *ge-* and *-en*. The ones marked with * use *sein* instead of *haben* in the perfect tense.

| infinitive | | past participle |
|---|---|---|
| abwaschen | *to do the washing-up* | abgewaschen |
| anziehen (sich) | *to get dressed* | angezogen |
| aufstehen* | *to get up, to stand up* | aufgestanden |
| ausziehen (sich) | *to get undressed* | ausgezogen |
| backen | *to bake* | gebacken |
| beginnen | *to begin* | begonnen |
| bekommen | *to get* | bekommen |
| brechen | *to break* | gebrochen |
| essen | *to eat* | gegessen |
| fahren* | *to go/travel* | gefahren |
| fernsehen | *to watch TV* | ferngesehen |
| fliegen* | *to fly* | geflogen |
| geben | *to give* | gegeben |
| gehen* | *to go* | gegangen |
| gewinnen | *to win* | gewonnen |
| helfen | *to help* | geholfen |
| kommen* | *to come* | gekommen |
| lesen | *to read* | gelesen |

| nehmen | *to take* | genommen |
|---|---|---|
| schlafen | *to sleep* | geschlafen |
| schreiben | *to write* | geschrieben |
| schwimmen* | *to swim* | geschwommen |
| sehen | *to see* | gesehen |
| singen | *to sing* | gesungen |
| tragen | *to wear* | getragen |
| treffen | *to meet* | getroffen |
| trinken | *to drink* | getrunken |

**J** **Rewrite these present tense sentences in the perfect tense.**

*Beispiel:* **a** *Wir haben ein Eis gegessen.*

a Wir essen ein Eis.
b Ich fahre mit dem Fahrrad.
c Er liest ein Sportmagazin.
d Gehst du zu Fuß?
e Ich sehe viel fern.
f Ich stehe um sieben Uhr auf.

## 7.13 The imperfect tense

In German, the perfect tense is used for describing events in the past, particularly when <u>talking</u> about what you have done and referring to the <u>recent</u> past.

The imperfect is used for descriptions in the past (as in French). It is also used for writing about events in the past in a more formal way, for example in novels and newspapers.

Some of the most commonly used forms are:

es war       *it was*
ich hatte    *I had*
es gab       *there was/were*
ich wollte   *I wanted*

| | **sein** *to be* | **haben** *to have* |
|---|---|---|
| ich | war (*was*) | hatte (*had*) |
| du | warst (*were*) | hattest (*had*) |
| er/sie/es | war (*was*) | hatte (*had*) |
| wir | waren (*were*) | hatten (*had*) |
| ihr | wart (*were*) | hattet (*had*) |
| sie/Sie | waren (*were*) | hatten (*had*) |

# Grammatik

**K** Fill in the correct form of *haben* or *sein* in the imperfect tense.

*Beispiel:* **a** *war*

a Die Party ▭ klasse.
b Wir ▭ viel Spaß.
c Meine Freunde ▭ auch auf der Party.
d Paul ▭ das beste Outfit.
e Die Gäste ▭ sehr cool.

## 7.14 Talking about the future

You can use the future tense to talk about things in the future. It is formed with the present tense of the verb *werden* and the infinitive of the main verb, which is sent to the end of the sentence:

Ich **werde** nach Italien **fahren**. *I will go to Italy.*
Wir **werden** Souvenirs **kaufen**. *We will buy souvenirs.*

The present tense of *werden* is as follows:

| werden | |
|---|---|
| ich **werde** | wir **werden** |
| du **wirst** | ihr **werdet** |
| er/sie/es **wird** | sie/Sie **werden** |

**L** Rewrite the sentences in the future tense.

*Beispiel:* **a** *Wir werden eine Party machen.*

a Wir machen eine Party.
b Ich fahre im Sommer nach Frankreich.
c Paul spart mit seinem neuen Computer viel Strom.
d Wind, Wasser und Sonne sind die neuen Energiequellen.
e Meine Schwester liest am Wochenende einen Krimi.

## 7.15 *möchten*

The verb *möchten* means 'would like':

Ich **möchte** ein Eis. *I **would like** an ice cream.*

It also means 'would like to' when it is followed by a verb in the infinitive:

Paul und ich **möchten** ins Kino **gehen**. *Paul and I **would like to go** to the cinema.*
Ich **möchte** in die Schweiz **fliegen**. *I **would like to fly** to Switzerland.*

| möchten *would like (to)* | |
|---|---|
| ich möchte | wir möchten |
| du möchtest | ihr möchtet |
| er/sie/es/man möchte | sie/Sie möchten |

**M** Rewrite the following sentences using *möchten*.

*Beispiel:* **a** *Ich möchte Medizin studieren.*

a Ich studiere Medizin.
b Er macht sein Abitur.
c Sie macht eine Lehre als Krankenpflegerin.
d Wir machen unseren GCSE-Abschluss.
e Ich habe einen Nebenjob.

## 7.16 The imperative (giving instructions)

The imperative form of the verb is used to give instructions or advice.

If you are talking to a friend, use the *du* form of the verb without the word *du*, and remove the *-st* ending:

Du trinkst mehr Wasser. → **Trink** mehr Wasser!
*You drink more water. → Drink more water!*

Du isst. → **Iss**!
*You eat. → Eat!*

If you are talking to an adult, use the *Sie* form but put the verb first:

Sie trinken mehr Wasser. → **Trinken Sie** mehr Wasser!
*You drink more water. → Drink more water!*

Sie essen. → **Essen Sie**!
*You eat. → Eat!*

**N** Write two sentences for each of a–d: one giving advice to a friend and the other to an adult.

*Beispiel:* **a** *Iss keine Schokolade! Essen Sie …*

a essen / keine Schokolade
b trinken / keinen Alkohol
c machen / mehr Sport
d gehen / zu Fuß

# 8 Negatives
## *Negationen*

### 8.1 *nicht*

The negative *nicht* means 'not' and often comes directly after the verb:

Ich bin **nicht** groß. *I'm not tall.*
Jan geht **nicht** ins Kino. *Jan is not going to the cinema.*
Katja isst **nicht** gern Fisch. *Katja does not like eating fish.*

### 8.2 *kein/keine/kein*

Use *kein/keine/kein* to say 'no', 'not a(ny)'. It is always followed by a noun and follows the pattern of *ein/eine/ein* (see the Summary table in Section 2.5):

Ich habe **keinen** Füller. *I do not have a fountain pen.*
Rudi trinkt **keine** Milch. *Rudi doesn't drink milk.*
Ich esse **kein** Fleisch. *I do not eat meat.*
Ich habe **keine** Haustiere. *I do not have any pets.*

# 9 Gern, lieber, am liebsten

To say what you like or don't like doing, use *gern* or *nicht gern* with a verb. The words *gern* and *nicht gern* follow the verb:

Ich spiele **gern** Gitarre. *I like playing guitar.*
Ich spiele **nicht gern** Tennis. *I don't like playing tennis.*

To say what you prefer doing, use *lieber*:

Ich gehe **lieber** ins Kino. *I prefer going to the cinema.*

To say what you like doing most of all, use *am liebsten*:

Ich fahre **am liebsten** Rad. *Most of all I like cycling.*

# 10 Word order
## *Wortstellung*

### 10.1 Subject–verb

Sentences usually start with the subject (the person or thing doing the action). The verb is always the second piece of information:

| 1 | 2 | 3 |
|---|---|---|
| Ich | **gehe** | ins Kino. *I'm going to the cinema.* |
| Mein Bruder | **spielt** | Fußball. *My brother plays football.* |

### 10.2 Time–manner–place

When a sentence contains several pieces of information, the order of the different parts is time–manner–place:

| | time | manner | place |
|---|---|---|---|
| Ich fahre | am Nachmittag | mit dem Bus | nach Hamburg. |

### 10.3 Time–verb–subject

If you want to stress the time element, you put this piece of information at the beginning of the sentence. However, you then need to swap over the subject and the verb so that the verb is still the second piece of information:

| 1 | 2 | 3 | | 1 | 2 | 3 | 4 |
|---|---|---|---|---|---|---|---|
| Ich | **habe** | Mathe. | → | Am Dienstag | **habe** | ich | Mathe. |

### 10.4 The linking words *weil* and *wenn*

Words such as *und*, *aber*, *oder*, *denn* and *sondern* are called linking words. They are used for joining phrases and sentences together and for building longer sentences. These words do not change the word order of the sentence.

But other linking words like *wenn* (when) and *weil* (because) change the word order of the sentence. They send the verb to the end.

> **O** **Rewrite these sentences using correct word order.**
>
> *Beispiel:* **a** *Das Leben in einer Großstadt ist toll, weil es viel für Jugendliche gibt.*
>
> **a** Das Leben in einer Großstadt ist toll, weil / gibt / es / viel für Jugendliche / .
> **b** Meine Mutter will auf dem Land wohnen, weil / mag / sie / die Natur / .
> **c** Ich fahre gern Ski, wenn / schneit / es / .
> **d** Meine Schwester liebt Realityshows, weil / sind / sie / spannend / .
> **e** Ich schwimme im Freibad, wenn / sonnig und warm / ist / es / .

### 10.5 *um … zu …*

You use *um … zu …* (in order to) to say why you do something. There are two ways of using it:

- Put *um* at the beginning of the clause (after the comma) and put *zu* at the end followed by an infinitive:

  Wir machen oft Sport, **um** fit **zu bleiben**. *We often do sport in order to keep fit.*

- Or you can start the sentence with *um … zu …* If you do this, the verb must be the first item in the next clause:

  **Um** fit **zu bleiben**, **essen** wir Obst. *In order to keep fit, we eat fruit.*

  We call this a verb sandwich (verb–comma–verb).

## 11 Asking questions

*Fragen*

You can ask a question …

- by putting the verb at the start of the sentence:
  Du hast einen Bruder. → **Hast** du einen Bruder?
  Bremen ist schön. → **Ist** Bremen schön?

- by using a question word at the start of the sentence:
  **Wie** heißt du? *What is your name?*
  **Wo** wohnst du? *Where do you live?*

Here is a list of all the question words in *Zoom Deutsch 1* and *2*:

| | |
|---|---|
| **wann** | Wann haben wir Deutsch? *When do we have German?* |
| **warum** | Warum gefällt dir dieser Film? *Why do you like this film?* |
| **was** | Was isst du? *What are you eating?* |
| **welcher/-e/-es** | Welches T-Shirt kaufst du? *Which T-shirt are you buying?* |
| **wer** | Wer ist das? *Who is that?* |
| **wie** | Wie alt bist du? *How old are you?* |
| **wie viel** | Wie viel kostet das? *How much does that cost?* |
| **wo** | Wo ist der Bahnhof? *Where is the station?* |
| **wofür** | Wofür sparst du? *What are you saving up for?* |
| **woher** | Woher kommst du? *Where do you come from?* |
| **wohin** | Wohin fährst du? *Where are you travelling/ going to?* |

## Hilfreiche Ausdrücke

### Numbers — Zahlen

| | | | | |
|---|---|---|---|---|
| 1 | eins | | 30 | dreißig |
| 2 | zwei | | 31 | einunddreißig |
| 3 | drei | | 40 | vierzig |
| 4 | vier | | 50 | fünfzig |
| 5 | fünf | | 60 | sechzig |
| 6 | sechs | | 70 | siebzig |
| 7 | sieben | | 80 | achtzig |
| 8 | acht | | 90 | neunzig |
| 9 | neun | | 100 | hundert |
| 10 | zehn | | 200 | zweihundert |
| 11 | elf | | 300 | dreihundert |
| 12 | zwölf | | 400 | vierhundert |
| 13 | dreizehn | | 500 | fünfhundert |
| 14 | vierzehn | | 600 | sechshundert |
| 15 | fünfzehn | | 700 | siebenhundert |
| 16 | sechzehn | | 800 | achthundert |
| 17 | siebzehn | | 900 | neunhundert |
| 18 | achtzehn | | 1000 | tausend |
| 19 | neunzehn | | | |
| 20 | zwanzig | | | |
| 21 | einundzwanzig | | | |
| 22 | zweiundzwanzig | | | |
| 23 | dreiundzwanzig | | | |
| 24 | vierundzwanzig | | | |
| 25 | fünfundzwanzig | | | |
| 26 | sechsundzwanzig | | | |
| 27 | siebenundzwanzig | | | |
| 28 | achtundzwanzig | | | |
| 29 | neunundzwanzig | | | |

### Greetings — Begrüßungen

| | |
|---|---|
| Hello | *Hallo!* |
| Good day | *Guten Tag!* |
| Good morning | *Guten Morgen!* |
| Good evening | *Guten Abend!* |
| Good night | *Gute Nacht!* |
| Goodbye | *Tschüs! (informal)* |
| | *Auf Wiedersehen!* |

### Monate

*Januar Februar März April Mai Juni Juli August September Oktober November Dezember*

### Days — Wochentage

| | | | |
|---|---|---|---|
| Monday | *Montag* | Friday | *Freitag* |
| Tuesday | *Dienstag* | Saturday | *Samstag* |
| Wednesday | *Mittwoch* | Sunday | *Sonntag* |
| Thursday | *Donnerstag* | | |

### Dates — Daten

on the … — *am …*

| | | | |
|---|---|---|---|
| 1st | *1. ersten* | 9th | *9. neunten* |
| 2nd | *2. zweiten* | 10th | *10. zehnten* |
| 3rd | *3. dritten* | 11th | *11. elften* |
| 4th | *4. vierten* | 20th | *20. zwanzigsten* |
| 5th | *5. fünften* | 21st | *21. einundzwanzigsten* |
| 6th | *6. sechsten* | 22nd | *22. zweiundzwanzigsten* |
| 7th | *7. siebten* | 30th | *30. dreißigsten* |
| 8th | *8. achten* | | |

# Vokabular

## A

der **Abend (-e)** *n* evening
das **Abendessen (-)** n
   evening meal
  **abends** in the
   evening
der **Abenteuerfilm (-e)** *n*
   adventure film
  **aber** but
  **abfahren** *v* to leave,
   depart
das **Abitur** *n* A levels
der **Abschluss** *n*
   school-leaving
   qualification
  **abwaschen** *v* to do
   the washing-up
der **Actionfilm (-e)** *n*
   action film
der **Affe (-n)** *n* monkey
  **aktuell** *adj* present,
   current
  **allein** *adj* alone
die **Allergie (-n)** *n* allergy
  **allerneueste** *adj*
   latest, most up-to-
   date
  **alles** everything
der **Alltag** *n* daily routine
  **also** therefore, so
  **alt** *adj* old
  **alternativ** *adj*
   alternative
  **altmodisch** *adj* old-
   fashioned
die **Ampel (-n)** *n* traffic
   lights
sich **amüsieren** *v* to enjoy
   oneself
  **an** on, at
  **anderer/andere/
   anderes** other
  **anfangen** *v* to begin
  **ankommen** *v* to arrive
  **anstrengend** *adj*
   tiring, strenuous
die **Antwort (-en)** *n*
   answer
  **antworten** *v* to
   answer
die **Anzeige (-n)** *n* advert
sich **anziehen** *v* to get
   dressed

der **Apfel (Äpfel)** *n* apple
die **Aprikose (-n)** *n*
   apricot
die **Arbeit (-en)** *n* work
  **arbeiten** *v* to work
der **Arm (-e)** *n* arm
  **arrogant** *adj* arrogant
der **Arzt (Ärzte)** *n* doctor
   (*male*)
die **Ärztin (-nen)** *n* doctor
   (*female*)
  **Aschermittwoch** Ash
   Wednesday
die **Atomenergie** *n*
   nuclear energy
der **Atommüll** *n* nuclear
   waste
  **auch** also
  **auf** on, on to
der **Aufkleber (-)** *n* sticker
  **aufpassen auf** *v* to
   look after
  **aufräumen** *v* to tidy
   up
  **aufstehen** *v* to get up,
   stand up
  **aufwachen** *v* to wake
   up
das **Auge (-n)** *n* eye
  **aus** from, out of
der **Ausflug (-üge)** *n* trip
  **ausführen** *v* to take
   out for a walk (*e.g.*
   *dogs*)
  **ausfüllen** *v* to fill in
die **Ausrede (-n)** *n* excuse
  **aussehen** *v* to look
   like
  **außerdem** also
das **Aussterben von
   Tieren** *n* extinction
   of animals
  **austragen** *v* to deliver
   (*newspapers*)
  **auswählen** *v* to
   choose
sich **ausziehen** *v* to get
   undressed
das **Auto (-s)** *n* car
der **Autor (-en)** *n* author
   (*male*)
die **Autorin (-nen)** *n*
   author (*female*)

## B

  **Babysitting machen**
   *v* to do babysitting
  **backen** *v* to bake
die **Bäckerei (-en)** *n*
   baker's shop
  **baden** *v* to have a
   bath

das **Badezimmer (-)** *n*
   bathroom
der **Bahnhof (-öfe)** *n*
   railway station
  **bald** soon
die **Banane (-n)** *n* banana
die **Band (-s)** *n* band (*of
   musicians*), group
der **Bassist (-en)** *n* bass
   player (*male*)
die **Bassistin (-nen)** *n*
   bass player (*female*)
der **Bauch (-äuche)** *n*
   stomach
  **Bauchschmerzen** *n pl*
   stomach ache
  **bauen** *v* to build
das **Bauernhaus (-äuser)**
   *n* farmhouse
der **Baum (-äume)** *n* tree
  **beantworten** *v* to
   answer
  **beginnen** *v* to begin
  **bei** at the home of,
   with
  **bei mir/dir** at my/
   your house
das **Bein (-e)** *n* leg
zum **Beispiel** for example
  **bekannt** *adj* well-
   known
  **bekommen** *v* to get
  **benutzen** *v* to use
  **bequem** *adj*
   comfortable,
   convenient
der **Berg (-e)** *n* mountain
der **Bericht (-e)** *n* report
der **Beruf (-e)** *n*
   profession, job
  **berühmt** *adj* famous
  **beschreiben** *v* to
   describe
  **besichtigen** *v* to visit,
   look around (*a
   tourist attraction*)
  **besser** better
am **besten** best (of all)
  **bestimmt** definitely
  **besuchen** *v* to visit; to
   go to (*a school*)
das **Bett (-en)** *n* bed
das **Bild (-er)** *n* picture
  **billig** *adj* cheap
  **Biologie** *n* biology
der **Biomüll** *n* organic
   waste
die **Birne (-n)** *n* pear
  **bis** until
  **bitte** please
der **Blätterteig** *n* puff
   pastry
  **blau** *adj* blue

  **bleiben** *v* to stay
  **blöd** *adj* silly, stupid
der **Blog (-s)** *n* blog
  **blond** *adj* blonde
die **Blume (-n)** *n* flower
die **Bohne (-n)** *n* bean
das **Boot (-e)** *n* boat
die **Bootsfahrt (-en)** *n*
   boat trip
die **Bratwurst (-ürste)** *n*
   fried sausage
  **brauchen** *v* to need
  **braun** *adj* brown
  **brechen** *v* to break
die **Brezel (-n)** *n* pretzel
der **Brief (-e)** *n* letter
der **Brieffreund (-e)** *n*
   penfriend (*male*)
die **Brieffreundin
   (-nen)** *n* penfriend
   (*female*)
der **Briefträger (-)** *n*
   postman
die **Briefträgerin (-nen)** *n*
   postwoman
die **Brille (-n)** *n* glasses,
   spectacles
  **bringen** *v* to bring
die **Broschüre (-n)** *n*
   brochure
das **Brot (-e)** *n* bread
die **Brücke (-n)** *n* bridge
der **Bruder (-üder)** *n*
   brother
das **Buch (-ücher)** *n* book
der **Buchstabe (-n)**
   *n* letter (*of the
   alphabet*)
der **Bürgersteig (-e)** *n*
   pavement
das **Büro (-s)** *n* office
der **Bus (-usse)** *n* bus
die **Bushaltestelle (-n)** *n*
   bus stop
das **Butterbrot (-e)** *n*
   sandwich, slice of
   bread and butter

## C

das **Café (-s)** *n* café
der **Campingplatz (-ätze)**
   *n* campsite
die **Castingshow (-s)** *n*
   talent show
die **CD (-s)** *n* CD
die **Chatseite (-n)** *n* chat
   room (*online*)
  **chatten** *v* to chat
  **Chemie** *n* chemistry
  **Chinesisch** *n* Chinese
   (*language*)
die **Chips** *n pl* crisps

# Vokabular

der **Chor (-öre)** *n* choir
die **Cola (-s)** *n* cola
der **Computer (-)** *n* computer
das **Computerspiel (-e)** *n* computer game
der **Container (-)** *n* recycling bank, skip
der **Cousin (-s)** *n* cousin (*male*)
die **Cousine (-n)** *n* cousin (*female*)

## D

**da** there
**damit** with it/them
**danach** then, afterwards
vielen **Dank** thank you (very much)
**danke** thank you
**dann** then
**das** the, that
**dauern** *v* to last
**davor** before
**decken** *v* to set (*a table*)
**dein** your
**dekorieren** *v* to decorate
**denken** *v* to think
**denn** because
**der** the
**deshalb** therefore, so
**Deutsch** *n* German (*language*)
**Deutschland** *n* Germany
**deutschsprachig** *adj* German-speaking
der **Dialog (-e)** *n* dialogue
**dick** *adj* fat, thick
**die** the
**dieser/diese/dieses** this, these
**direkt** direct, directly
die **Disco (-s)** *n* disco
der **Dokumentarfilm (-e)** *n* documentary
die **Dokumentarserie (-n)** *n* documentary series
**doof** *adj* silly, stupid
das **Dorf (-örfer)** *n* village
**dort** there
die **Dose (-n)** *n* can, tin
**dran: ich bin/du bist dran** it's my/your turn
**draußen** outside
die **Druckerpatrone (-n)** *n* printer cartridge

**du** you
**dürfen** *v* to be allowed to
sich **duschen** *v* to have a shower
die **DVD (-s)** *n* DVD

## E

**echt** *adj* real, genuine
die **Ecke (-n)** *n* corner
das **Ei (-er)** *n* egg
**ein** a, an
**einfach** simple, easy; one-way (*ticket*)
**einkaufen** *v* to shop, do the shopping
der **Einkaufsbummel (-)** *n* shopping trip
**einladen** *v* to invite
die **Einladung (-en)** *n* invitation
**einmal** once
der **Einwohner (-)** *n* inhabitant
das **Eis (-)** *n* ice cream
**elektronisch** *adj* electronic
die **Eltern** *n pl* parents
die **E-Mail (-s)** *n* email
die **Energie (-n)** *n* energy
die **Energiequelle (-n)** *n* energy source
**energiesparend** *adj* energy-saving
**Englisch** *n* English (*language*)
**enthalten** *v* to contain
sich **entspannen** *v* to relax
die **Entwaldung** *n* deforestation
**er** he, it
die **Erde (-n)** *n* the earth
das **Erdgas** *n* natural gas
**Erdkunde** *n* geography
das **Erdöl** *n* mineral oil
die **Erdwärme** *n* geothermal energy
**erfolgreich** *adj* successful
**erneuerbar** *adj* renewable
**erster/erste/erstes** first
der **Erwachsene** *n* adult
**es** it
**essen** *v* to eat
das **Essen (-)** *n* food
die **Essensreste** *n pl* food leftovers

**etwas** something
der **Euro (-s)** *n* euro

## F

das **Fach (-ächer)** *n* subject (*at school*)
**fahren** *v* to travel, go, drive
die **Fahrkarte (-n)** *n* ticket
der **Fahrplan (-äne)** *n* timetable
das **Fahrrad (-äder)** *n* bicycle
der **Fahrradkeller (-)** *n* bike cellar
die **Fahrt (-en)** *n* journey
**falsch** *adj* false, incorrect
die **Familie (-n)** *n* family
**fantastisch** *adj* fantastic
der **Fantasyfilm (-e)** *n* fantasy film
der **Fasching** *n* carnival
das **Fastfood** *n* fast food
die **Fastnacht** *n* carnival
**faul** *adj* lazy
**faulenzen** *v* to laze around
**was fehlt dir?** what's wrong with you?
**feiern** *v* to celebrate
der **Feiertag (-e)** *n* public holiday
die **Ferien** *n pl* holidays
**fernsehen** *v* to watch TV
im **Fernsehen** on TV
der **Fernseher (-)** *n* TV set
das **Fest (-e)** *n* festival
das **Feuerwerksfest (-e)** *n* fireworks festival
das **Fieber** *n* fever, high temperature
der **Film (-e)** *n* film
die **Filmkritik (-en)** *n* film review
**finden** *v* to find
der **Finger (-)** *n* finger
der **Fisch (-e)** *n* fish
das **Fleisch** *n* meat
**fleißig** *adj* hard-working
**fliegen** *v* to fly
der **Flughafen (-äfen)** *n* airport
das **Flugzeug (-e)** *n* aeroplane
der **Fluss (-üsse)** *n* river
das **Formel-1-Rennen** *n* Formula One racing
das **Foto (-s)** *n* photo

**fotografieren** *v* to take photos
die **Frage (-n)** *n* question
der **Fragebogen (-)** *n* questionnaire
**fragen** *v* to ask
**Frankreich** *n* France
**Französisch** *n* French (*language*)
die **Frau (-en)** *n* woman
**frech** *adj* naughty, cheeky
das **Freibad (-äder)** *n* open-air pool
die **Freizeit** *n* leisure time
sich **freuen (auf)** *v* to look forward (to)
der **Freund (-e)** *n* friend (*male*)
die **Freundin (-nen)** *n* friend (*female*)
**freundlich** *adj* friendly
**frieren** *v* to freeze
**frisch** *adj* fresh
**fröhlich** *adj* cheerful
**früh** *adj* early
im **Frühling** in spring
das **Frühstück** *n* breakfast
**frühstücken** *v* to have breakfast
die **Frühstücksflocken** *n pl* breakfast cereal
das **Funkenmariechen (-)** *n* red-coat girl (*at the Cologne carnival*)
**für** for
**furchtbar** *adj* awful
der **Fuß (-üße)** *n* foot
zu **Fuß** on foot, walking
der **Fußball (-älle)** *n* football
das **Futter** *n* animal food
**füttern** *v* to feed (*an animal*)

## G

die **Gans (-änse)** *n* goose
**ganz** *adj* whole
**gar nicht** not at all
**gar nichts** nothing at all
der **Garten (-ärten)** *n* garden
der **Gast (-äste)** *n* guest
das **Gebäude (-)** *n* building
**geben** *v* to give
der **Geburtstag (-e)** *n* birthday

**gefällt es dir?** do you like it?

**es gefällt mir** I like it

die **Gegend (-en)** n region, area

**gehen** v to go

die **Geige (-n)** n violin

das **Geld** n money

**gemein** adj mean, nasty

das **Gemüse** n sing vegetables

**geöffnet** adj open

**geradeaus** straight ahead

das **Gericht (-e)** n dish (meal)

**gern: ich lese gern** I like reading

die **Gesamtschule (-n)** n comprehensive school

das **Geschäft (-e)** n shop

der **Geschäftsmann (-änner)** n businessman

die **Geschäftsfrau (-en)** n businesswoman

das **Geschenk (-e)** n present

die **Geschichte (-n)** n story, history

**geschlossen** adj closed

die **Geschwister** n pl brothers and sisters

**gestern** yesterday

**gesund** adj healthy

das **Getränk (-e)** n drink

das **Getreideprodukt (-e)** n cereal product

**gewinnen** v to win

es **gewittert** it's stormy, there's thunder and lightning

es **gibt** there is/are

die **Gitarre (-n)** n guitar

die **Glasflasche (-n)** n glass bottle

**glatt** adj straight, smooth

**glauben** v to believe, think

das **Grad** n degree (temperature)

**grau** adj grey

**grillen** v to have a barbecue

die **Grippe** n flu

**groß** adj big, tall

**Großbritannien** n Great Britain

die **Großstadt (-ädte)** n city

**grün** adj green

die **Gruppe (-n)** n group

die **Gurke (-n)** n cucumber

**gut** adj good

das **Gymnasium (-sien)** n grammar school

die **Gymnastik** n gymnastics

## H

das **Haar (-e)** n hair

**haben** v to have

der **Hafen (-äfen)** n harbour, port

das **Hähnchen (-)** n chicken

**halb** half

das **Hallenbad (-äder)** n indoor swimming pool

**Halsschmerzen** n pl sore throat

die **Haltestelle (-n)** n stop (bus/tram stop, etc.)

**Hammer: der totale Hammer** totally cool, awesome

die **Hand (-ände)** n hand

das **Handy (-s)** n mobile phone

**hart** adj hard

der **Hase (-n)** n hare

**hassen** v to hate

**hässlich** adj ugly

der **Hauptbahnhof (-öfe)** n main railway station

die **Hauptschule (-n)** n secondary school (to age 15)

das **Haus (-äuser)** n house

die **Hausaufgaben** n pl homework

nach **Hause** home (going to one's home)

zu **Hause** at home

die **Hausfrau (-en)** n housewife

der **Hausmann (-änner)** n house husband

der **Heiligabend** n Christmas Eve

**heiß** adj hot

**heißen** v to be called

**hektisch** adj hectic

**helfen** v to help

das **Hemd (-en)** n shirt

im **Herbst** in autumn

**herunterladen** v to download

**hervorragend** outstandingly, excellently

**heute** today

**hier** here

die **Hilfe (-n)** n help

**hinter** behind

**hin und wieder** now and then

**hin und zurück** return (ticket)

**historisch** adj historic

das **Hobby (-s)** n hobby

der **Hof (-öfe)** n yard, playground

**hören** v to hear

das **Hörspiel (-e)** n radio play

die **Hose** n sing trousers

das **Hotel (-s)** n hotel

der **Hund (-e)** n dog

## I

**ich** I

**ihr** you (pl), her

**Ihr** your (formal)

**immer** always

**in** in, into

**indisch** adj Indian

die **Industrie (-n)** n industry

die **Industriestadt (-ädte)** n industrial town

**Informatik** n IT

der **Informatiker (-)** n IT specialist (male)

die **Informatikerin (-nen)** n IT specialist (female)

**Inliner fahren** v to go rollerblading

**interessant** adj interesting

sich **interessieren (für)** v to be interested (in)

im **Internet** on the internet

das **Interview (-s)** n interview

## J

die **Jacke (-n)** n jacket

das **Jahr (-e)** n year

die **Jeans** n sing jeans

**jeder/jede/jedes** every

**jetzt** now

**joggen** v to go jogging

der **Joghurt** n yoghurt

das **Jugendbuch (-ücher)** n book for young people

die **Jugendherberge (-n)** n youth hostel

der **Jugendliche** n young person, teenager

das **Jugendzentrum (-zentren)** n youth club

**jung** adj young

der **Junge (-n)** n boy

## K

der **Kaffee (-s)** n coffee

das **Kalbfleisch** n veal

**kalt** adj cold

der **Kanal (-äle)** n channel (TV)

der **Kapuzenpullover (-)** n hooded jumper

die **Karaoke-Anlage (-n)** n karaoke machine

das **Karaoke-Spiel (-e)** n karaoke game

der **Karfreitag** n Good Friday

der **Karneval** n carnival

die **Karotte (-n)** n carrot

die **Karte (-n)** n card

die **Kartoffel (-n)** n potato

der **Käse (-)** n cheese

der **Kassettenrekorder (-)** n cassette recorder

die **Katze (-n)** n cat

**kaufen** v to buy

**kein** no, not any, not a

der **Keks (-e)** n biscuit

der **Kellner (-)** n waiter

die **Kellnerin (-nen)** n waitress

das **Kind (-er)** n child

das **Kino (-s)** n cinema

die **Kirche (-n)** n church

**klasse** adj great

die **Klasse (-n)** n class

**klassisch** adj classical

der **Klebstoff** n glue

die **Kleidung** n sing clothes

**klein** adj small

**klettern** v to climb

der **Klimawandel** n climate change

das **Knie (-)** n knee

**knubbelig** adj knobbly

# Vokabular

**kochen** *v* to cook, make
die **Kohle (-n)** *n* coal
**Köln** Cologne
**komisch** *adj* strange, funny
**kommen** *v* to come
die **Komödie (-n)** *n* comedy
**kompliziert** *adj* complicated
**können** *v* to be able to, can
das **Konzert (-e)** *n* concert
der **Kopf (-öpfe)** *n* head
**Kopfschmerzen** *n pl* headache
der **Körper (-)** *n* body
**kosten** *v* to cost
die **Kostümparty (-s)** *n* fancy-dress party
das **Krafttraining** *n* weight training
**krank** *adj* ill
das **Krankenhaus (-äuser)** *n* hospital
der **Krankenpfleger (-)** *n* nurse (*male*)
die **Krankenpflegerin (-nen)** *n* nurse (*female*)
die **Kreuzung (-en)** *n* crossroads
der **Krimi (-s)** *n* crime novel
die **Kriminalität** *n* crime
die **Küche (-n)** *n* kitchen
der **Kuchen (-)** *n* cake
die **Kuh (-ühe)** *n* cow
das **Küken (-)** *n* chick
**Kunst** *n* art
**kurz** *adj* short
die **Küste (-n)** *n* coast

**L**

**lächeln** *v* to smile
**lachen** *v* to laugh
der **Laden (-äden)** *n* shop
die **Lampe (-n)** *n* lamp
das **Land (-änder)** *n* country, countryside
**lang** *adj* long
**langsam** *adj* slow
**langweilig** *adj* boring
**lassen** *v* to leave
**laufen** *v* to run
**launisch** *adj* moody
**laut** *adj* loud, noisy
**lauwarm** *adj* lukewarm
das **Leben** *n* life

**lecker** *adj* delicious
die **Lehre (-n)** *n* apprenticeship
der **Lehrer (-)** *n* teacher (*male*)
die **Lehrerin (-nen)** *n* teacher (*female*)
die **Leichtathletik** *n* athletics
**leid: es tut mir leid** I'm sorry
**leider** unfortunately
**leise** *adj* quiet
der **Leistungskurs (-e)** *n* main/specialist subject (*at school*)
**lernen** *v* to learn
**lesen** *v* to read
**letzter/letzte/letztes** last
die **Leute** *n pl* people
das **Licht** *n* light
**lieb** *adj* sweet, lovely
**lieben** *v* to love
das **Lieblingsfach (-ächer)** *n* favourite subject
der **Liebesfilm (-e)** *n* love story (*film*)
das **Lieblingshobby (-s)** *n* favourite hobby
die **Lieblingssendung (-en)** *n* favourite TV programme
das **Lied (-er)** *n* song
**liegen** *v* to lie, be situated
**links** (on/to the) left
die **Liste (-n)** *n* list
der **Lkw-Fahrer (-)** *n* truck driver (*male*)
die **Lkw-Fahrerin (-nen)** *n* truck driver (*female*)
**lockig** *adj* curly
**lösen** *v* to solve
die **Lösung (-en)** *n* solution
die **Lücke (-n)** *n* gap
die **Luft** *n* air
die **Luftverschmutzung** *n* air pollution
**lustig** *adj* funny

**M**

**machen** *v* to make, do
das **Mädchen (-)** *n* girl
**ich mag** I like
die **Magie** *n* magic
das **Make-up** *n* make-up
**man** one, you, they, we
**manchmal** sometimes

der **Mann (-änner)** *n* man
**Mathe** *n* maths
die **Mauer (-n)** *n* wall
die **Medaille (-n)** *n* medal
das **Meer (-e)** *n* sea
**mehr** more
**mein** my
**meinen** *v* to think
die **Meinung (-en)** *n* opinion
**meist: der/die/das meiste …, die meisten** … most
**meistens** mostly
die **Meisterschaft (-en)** *n* championship
die **Melone (-n)** *n* melon
die **Menschen** *n pl* people
die **Migräne (-n)** *n* migraine
die **Milch** *n* milk
die **Milchprodukte** *n pl* dairy products
**mindestens** at least
das **Mineralwasser** *n* mineral water
**mit** with, by (*transport*)
das **Mittagessen (-)** *n* lunch
**mittags** at midday
**mittelgroß** *adj* medium-sized
die **Mitternacht** *n* midnight
**ich möchte** I would like
der **Modedesigner (-)** *n* fashion designer (*male*)
die **Modedesignerin (-nen)** *n* fashion designer (*female*)
das **Modegeschäft (-e)** *n* fashion shop
der **Moderator (-en)** *n* presenter (*male*)
die **Moderatorin (-nen)** *n* presenter (*female*)
**mögen** *v* to like
der **Monat (-e)** *n* month
der **Morgen (-)** *n* morning
**morgens** in the morning
das **Motorrad (-äder)** *n* motorbike
der **MP3-Player (-s)** *n* MP3 player
der **Müll** *n* rubbish
der **Müllberg (-e)** *n* rubbish mountain
der **Mülleimer (-)** *n* rubbish bin
**München** Munich

der **Mund (-ünder)** *n* mouth
das **Museum (Museen)** *n* museum
das **Musical (-s)** *n* musical
die **Musik** *n* music
**musikalisch** *adj* musical
der **Musiker (-)** *n* musician (*male*)
die **Musikerin (-nen)** *n* musician (*female*)
das **Musikgeschäft (-e)** *n* music shop
die **Musiksendung (-en)** *n* music programme
der **Musikstil (-e)** *n* style of music
**muskulös** *adj* muscular
**müssen** *v* to have to, must
die **Mutter (-ütter)** *n* mother

**N**

**nach** after, to
der **Nachhilfeunterricht** *n* extra tuition
der **Nachmittag (-e)** *n* afternoon
**nachmittags** in the afternoon
die **Nachricht (-en)** *n* message
die **Nachrichten** *n pl* the news
**nächster/nächste/nächstes** next, nearest
die **Nacht (-ächte)** *n* night
die **Nase (-n)** *n* nose
die **Natur** *n* nature
**natürlich** of course
**Naturwissenschaften** *n pl* science
**neben** next to
der **Nebenjob (-s)** *n* part-time job
**neblig** *adj* foggy
**nehmen** *v* to take
**nervig** *adj* irritating
**nett** *adj* nice
**neu** *adj* new
das **Neujahr** *n* New Year's Day
**nicht** not
**nichts** nothing

**nie** never
**der Nikolaustag** St Nicholas' Day
**noch einmal** once again
**im Norden** in the north
**normalerweise** usually
**die Note (-n)** *n* mark, grade
**die Nudeln** *n pl* pasta
**nur** only
**nutzen** *v* to use
**nützlich** *adj* useful

## O

**die Oberstufe** *n* upper school, sixth form
**das Obst** *n* fruit
**oder** or
**offiziell** *adj* official
**oft** often
**ohne** without
**das Ohr (-en)** *n* ear
**Ohrenschmerzen** *n pl* earache
**der Ohrring (-e)** *n* earring
**die Oma (-s)** *n* grandma
**der Onkel (-)** *n* uncle
**der Opa (-s)** *n* grandad
**der Orangensaft (-äfte)** *n* orange juice
**organisieren** *v* to organise
**im Osten** in the east
**der Osterhase (-n)** *n* Easter bunny
**das Ostern** *n* Easter
**Österreich** *n* Austria
**das Outfit (-s)** *n* outfit
**das Ozonloch (-öcher)** *n* hole in the ozone layer

## P

**paniert** *adj* coated with breadcrumbs
**das Papier (-e)** *n* paper
**der Park (-s)** *n* park
**die Party (-s)** *n* party
**passen** *v* to fit, match
**passend** *adj* matching
**peinlich** *adj* embarrassing
**die Pflanze (-n)** *n* plant
**der Pfirsich (-e)** *n* peach
**das Pflichtfach (-ächer)** *n* compulsory subject (*at school*)
**Physik** *n* physics
**das Picknick (-e)** *n* picnic

**der Pilot (-en)** *n* pilot (*male*)
**die Pilotin (-nen)** *n* pilot (*female*)
**die Pizza (-s)** *n* pizza
**planen** *v* to plan
**das Plastik** *n* plastic
**die Plastiktüte (-n)** *n* plastic bag
**der Polizist (-en)** *n* policeman
**die Polizistin (-nen)** *n* policewoman
**die Pommes** *n pl* chips
**die Post** *n* post office
**das Praktikum (-ika)** *n* work experience placement
**praktisch** *adj* practical
**der Preis (-e)** *n* price, prize
**pro** per
**das Problem (-e)** *n* problem
**produzieren** *v* to produce
**prüfen** *v* to examine
**die Prüfung (-en)** *n* exam
**der Pullover (-)** *n* jumper
**putzen** *v* to clean

## Q

**die Quizsendung (-en)** *n* quiz show

## R

**Rad fahren** *v* to cycle
**das Radio (-s)** *n* radio
**der Radiosender (-)** *n* radio station
**das Ratespiel (-e)** *n* guessing game
**das Rätsel (-)** *n* puzzle
**rauchen** *v* to smoke
**die Realityshow (-s)** *n* reality TV show
**die Realschule (-n)** *n* secondary school (*to age 16*)
**rechts** (on/to the) right
**recyceln** *v* to recycle
**reden** *v* to talk
**das Regal (-e)** *n* shelf
**regnen** *v* to rain
**reich** *adj* rich
**die Reihenfolge (-n)** *n* sequence, order
**der Reis** *n* rice
**die Reise (-n)** *n* journey
**reiten** *v* to go horse-riding

**Religion** *n* religious education
**der Rennfahrer (-)** *n* racing driver (*male*)
**Rennrad fahren** *v* to go cycle racing
**die Reportage (-n)** *n* report
**das Restaurant (-s)** *n* restaurant
**richtig** *adj* true, correct
**riesig** *adj* huge
**der Rock (-öcke)** *n* skirt
**Rollschuh fahren** *v* to go roller-skating
**der Roman (-e)** *n* novel
**romantisch** *adj* romantic
**der Rosenmontag** *n* the day before Shrove Tuesday
**rot** *adj* red
**Rückenschmerzen** *n pl* backache
**ruhig** *adj* quiet

## S

**das Sachbuch (-ücher)** *n* non-fiction book
**sagen** *v* to say, tell
**der Salat (-e)** *n* salad, lettuce
**salzig** *adj* salty
**die Sammelkarte (-n)** *n* collectable card
**sammeln** *v* to collect
**der Sänger (-)** *n* singer (*male*)
**die Sängerin (-nen)** *n* singer (*female*)
**der Satz (-ätze)** *n* sentence
**sauber** *adj* clean
**das Sauerkraut** *n* pickled cabbage
**das Saxofon (-e)** *n* saxophone
**die S-Bahn** *n* city and suburban railway
**Schach spielen** *v* to play chess
**der Schal (-s)** *n* scarf
**die Schallplatte (-n)** *n* vinyl record
**der Schauspieler (-)** *n* actor (*male*)
**die Schauspielerin (-nen)** *n* actor (*female*)
**schenken** *v* to give (*as a present*)

**schicken** *v* to send
**die Schiffsfahrt (-en)** *n* boat trip
**das Schlagzeug (-e)** *n* drums
**der Schlagzeuger (-)** *n* drummer (*male*)
**die Schlagzeugerin (-nen)** *n* drummer (*female*)
**schlecht** *adj* bad
**schlimm** *adj* bad
**Schlittschuh fahren** *v* to go ice-skating
**das Schloss (-össer)** *n* castle, palace
**schmecken** *v* to taste
**schmutzig** *adj* dirty
**der Schnee** *n* snow
**schneien** *v* to snow
**schnell** *adj* fast
**die Schokolade (-n)** *n* chocolate
**schon** already
**schön** *adj* beautiful, nice
**der Schrank (-änke)** *n* wardrobe, cupboard
**schreiben** *v* to write
**die Schreibmaschine (-n)** *n* typewriter
**der Schreibtisch (-e)** *n* desk
**schüchtern** *adj* shy
**der Schuh (-e)** *n* shoe
**das Schuldach (-dächer)** *n* school roof
**die Schule (-n)** *n* school
**der Schüler (-)** *n* pupil (*male*)
**die Schülerin (-nen)** *n* pupil (*female*)
**der Schulhof (-höfe)** *n* school yard
**die Schulkantine (-n)** *n* school canteen
**schützen** *v* to protect
**schwarz** *adj* black
**das Schwarzbrot (-e)** *n* rye bread
**die Schwarzwälder Kirschtorte (-n)** *n* Black Forest gateau
**die Schweinshaxe (-n)** *n* leg of pork
**die Schweiz** *n* Switzerland
**schwer** *adj* difficult
**die Schwester (-n)** *n* sister
**schwierig** *adj* difficult
**das Schwimmbad (-äder)** *n* swimming pool

# Vokabular

**schwimmen** *v* to swim

der **Science-Fiction-Film (-e)** *n* science fiction film

der **See (-n)** *n* lake

**segeln** *v* to sail

**sehen** *v* to see

die **Sehenswürdigkeit (-en)** *n* sight, place of interest

**sehr** very

die **Seifenoper (-n)** *n* soap opera

**sein** *v* to be

**sein** his, its

**seit** for, since

der **Sekretär (-e)** *n* secretary (*male*)

die **Sekretärin (-nen)** *n* secretary (*female*)

**selten** rarely, seldom

der **Senf (-e)** *n* mustard

sich **setzen** *v* to sit down

die **Shorts** *n pl* shorts

**sicher** *adj* safe

**sie** she, it, they, them

**Sie** you (*formal*)

**Silvester** New Year's Eve

**singen** *v* to sing

**sitzen bleiben** *v* to repeat a year (*in school*)

**Skateboard fahren** *v* to go skateboarding

**skaten** *v* to go skateboarding

**Ski fahren** *v* to go skiing

**sofort** immediately

**sogar** even

der **Sohn (-öhne)** *n* son

die **Solarzelle (-n)** *n* solar panel

**sollen** *v* to be supposed to

im **Sommer** in summer

**sondern** but

ein **Sonnenbad nehmen** *v* to sunbathe

die **Sonnenenergie** *n* solar energy

**sonnig** *adj* sunny

**Spanisch** *n* Spanish (*language*)

**spannend** *adj* exciting

**sparen** *v* to save

**Spaß haben/machen** *v* to have/be fun

**spät** late

wie **spät ist es?** what time is it?

**spazieren gehen** *v* to go walking

die **Spezialeffekte** *n pl* special effects

das **Spiel (-e)** *n* game

**spielen** *v* to play

die **Spielregel (-n)** *n* rule of the game

**spitze** *adj* great

der **Sport** *n* sport, PE

**sportlich** *adj* sporty

das **Sportmagazin (-e)** *n* sports magazine

die **Sportsendung (-en)** *n* sports programme

die **Sprache (-n)** *n* language

**sprechen** *v* to speak

**springen** *v* to jump

das **Stadion (-dien)** *n* stadium

die **Stadt (-ädte)** *n* town

die **Stadtmitte (-n)** *n* town centre

der **Stadtplan (-äne)** *n* street map

der **Stadtrand** *n* suburbs, edge of town

die **Stadtrundfahrt (-en)** *n* sightseeing tour of a town

**stark** *adj* strong; great, really cool, wicked

**Staub saugen** *v* to vacuum

der **Stiefel (-)** *n* boot

die **Stimme (-n)** *n* voice

das **stimmt (nicht)** that's (not) true

die **Stofftasche (-n)** *n* cloth bag

der **Strand (-ände)** *n* beach

die **Strandparty (-s)** *n* pool/beach party

die **Straße (-n)** *n* street

die **Straßenbahn (-en)** *n* tram

**streichen** *v* to cross out

**streng** *adj* strict

**stressig** *adj* stressful

**stricken** *v* to knit

der **Strom** *n* electricity

**studieren** *v* to study

der **Stuhl (-ühle)** *n* chair

die **Stunde (-n)** *n* hour

**suchen** *v* to look for

im **Süden** in the south

**super** *adj* great

der **Supermarkt (-ärkte)** *n* supermarket

**surfen** *v* to surf

**süß** *adj* sweet

die **Süßigkeiten** *n pl* sweets

**sympathisch** *adj* nice

## T

der **Tag (-e)** *n* day

der **Tag der Deutschen Einheit** *n* Day of German Unity

die **Tageszeitung (-en)** *n* daily newspaper

die **Tante (-n)** *n* aunt

**tanzen** *v* to dance

die **Tasche (-n)** *n* bag

das **Taschengeld** *n* pocket money

**tauschen** *v* to swap, exchange

**teilen** *v* to divide

**teilnehmen** *v* to take part

das **Telefon (-e)** *n* telephone

**telefonieren (mit)** *v* to talk on the phone (with)

der **Terminkalender (-)** *n* diary

der **Test (-s)** *n* test

**teuer** *adj* expensive

**Theater spielen** *v* to be in a drama group, do drama

das **Ticket (-s)** *n* ticket

das **Tier (-e)** *n* animal

der **Tierarzt (-ärzte)** *n* vet (*male*)

die **Tierärztin (-nen)** *n* vet (*female*)

das **Tierheim (-e)** *n* animal shelter

**tierische Fette** *n pl* animal fats

der **Tisch (-e)** *n* table

das **Tischtennis** *n* table tennis

die **Tochter (-öchter)** *n* daughter

**tolerant** *adj* tolerant

**toll** *adj* great

die **Tomate (-n)** *n* tomato

die **Tomatensoße (-n)** *n* tomato sauce

die **Tonne (-n)** *n* bin

der **Tontechniker (-)** *n* sound technician (*male*)

die **Tontechnikerin (-nen)** *n* sound technician (*female*)

**total** totally, completely

**traditionell** *adj* traditional

**tragen** *v* to wear

**trainieren** *v* to train

die **Traube (-n)** *n* grape

der **Traum (-äume)** *n* dream

**traurig** *adj* sad

**treffen** *v* to meet

der **Treibhauseffekt (-e)** *n* greenhouse effect

**trennen** *v* to separate

**trinken** *v* to drink

das **T-Shirt (-s)** *n* T-shirt

**tun** *v* to do

die **Tür (-en)** *n* door

der **Turm (-ürme)** *n* tower

**turnen** *v* to do gymnastics/PE

das **Turnier (-e)** *n* tournament

die **Tüte (-n)** *n* bag

## U

die **U-Bahn (-en)** *n* underground

die **U-Bahn-Station (-en)** *n* underground station

**üben** *v* to practise

**über** about, above, over

**überall** everywhere

**überbewertet** *adj* overrated

die **Übung (-en)** *n* activity, exercise

das **Ufer (-)** *n* riverbank

die **Uhr (-en)** *n* clock, watch, time

die **Uhrzeit (-en)** *n* time

die **Umfrage (-n)** *n* survey

**umsteigen** *v* to change (*trains*)

die **Umwelt** *n* environment

**umweltfeindlich** *adj* harmful to the environment

**umweltfreundlich** *adj* environmentally friendly

der **Umweltschutz** *n* protection of the environment

die **Umweltverschmut-zung** *n* pollution
der **Umzug (-üge)** *n* procession, parade
**unbequem** *adj* uncomfortable, inconvenient
**und** and
**unfreundlich** *adj* unfriendly
**ungeduldig** *adj* impatient
**ungewöhnlich** *adj* unusual
die **Universität (-en)** *n* university
**unpraktisch** *adj* impractical
**unten** below, downstairs
**unter** under
**unterhaltsam** *adj* entertaining
der **Unterricht** *n* lessons
**unterstrichen** *adj* underlined
das **Uran** *n* uranium
der **Urlaub (-e)** *n* holiday

**V**

der **Vater (-äter)** *m* father
die **Veranstaltung (-en)** *n* event
**verbrennen** *v* to burn
**verbringen** *v* to spend (*time*)
**verdienen** *v* to earn
der **Verein (-e)** *n* club
**vergessen** *v* to forget
der **Verkäufer (-)** *n* shop assistant (*male*)
die **Verkäuferin (-nen)** *n* shop assistant (*female*)
der **Verkehr** *n* traffic
die **Verkehrsmittel** *n pl* means of transport
sich **verkleiden** *v* to get dressed up (*in fancy dress*)
**verschieden** *adj* different, various
**verstehen** *v* to understand
sich **verstehen (mit)** *v* to get on (with)
der **Videoclip (-s)** *n* video clip
**viel** much, a lot
**vielleicht** perhaps
das **Viertel (-)** *n* quarter

**voll** full
die **Vollkornprodukte** *n pl* wholemeal products
**von** from
**vor** in front of, before
**vor (zwei Wochen)** (two weeks) ago
**vorbei** past, over
**vorgestern** the day before yesterday
**vorlesen** *v* to read aloud

**W**

der **Wagen (-)** *n* wagon, carnival float
**wählen** *v* to choose
das **Wahlfach (-ächer)** *n* optional subject (*at school*)
der **Wald (-älder)** *n* forest, wood
**wandern** *v* to go walking
**wann** when
**warm** *adj* warm
**warten (auf)** *v* to wait (for)
**warum** why
**was** what
**waschen** *v* to wash
sich **waschen** *v* to get washed
**was für** what kind of
das **Wasser** *n* water
**Wasserski fahren** *v* to go water-skiing
die **Webseite (-n)** *n* web page
**weh tun** *n* to hurt
das **Weihnachten** *n* Christmas
der **Weihnachtsbaum (-äume)** *n* Christmas tree
der **Weihnachtsmann (-änner)** *n* Father Christmas
**weil** because
**weiß** *adj* white
ich **weiß (nicht)** I (don't) know
das **Weißbrot (-e)** *n* white bread
**welcher/welche/welches** which
die **Welt** *n* the world
**wenig** a few, little
**wenn** when, if
**wer** who
**werden** *v* to become
im **Westen** in the west

der **Wettbewerb (-e)** *n* competition
das **Wetter** *n* weather
**wichtig** *adj* important
**wie** how
**wieder** again
**Wien** Vienna
**wie viel(e)** how much/many
**windig** *adj* windy
im **Winter** in winter
**wir** we
**wirklich** really
der **Witz (-e)** *n* joke
**wo** where
die **Woche (-n)** *n* week
das **Wochenende (-n)** *n* weekend
**wofür** for what
**woher** where from
**wohin** where to
**wohnen** *v* to live
die **Wohnung (-en)** *n* flat
das **Wohnzimmer (-)** *n* living room
**wollen** *v* to want
das **Wort (-örter)** *n* word
das **Wörterbuch (-ücher)** *n* dictionary
**wünschen** *v* to want, wish for
die **Wurst (-ürste)** *n* sausage
die **Wüstenrennmaus (-äuse)** *n* gerbil

**Z**

der **Zahn (-ähne)** *n* tooth
**Zahnschmerzen** *n pl* toothache
**zaubern** *v* to do magic tricks
der **Zeh (-en)** *n* toe
der **Zeichentrickfilm (-e)** *n* animation, cartoon
die **Zeichentrickserie (-n)** *n* cartoon series
**zeichnen** *v* to draw
**zeigen (auf)** *v* to point (to)
die **Zeit (-en)** *n* time
die **Zeitschrift (-en)** *n* magazine
die **Zeitung (-en)** *n* newspaper
**ziemlich** rather
das **Zimmer (-)** *n* room
der **Zoo (-s)** *n* zoo
**zu** too, to
der **Zucker** *n* sugar
**zuerst** first
der **Zug (-üge)** *n* train

**zuhören** *v* to listen to
die **Zukunft** *n* future
in **Zukunft** in (the) future
**zurück** back
**zusammen** together
**zweimal** twice
**zwischen** between

# OXFORD
## UNIVERSITY PRESS

Great Clarendon Street, Oxford OX2 6DP

Oxford University Press is a department of the University of Oxford.

It furthers the University's objective of excellence in research, scholarship, and education by publishing worldwide in
Oxford  New York  Auckland  Cape Town  Dar es Salaam  Hong Kong
Karachi  Kuala Lumpur  Madrid  Melbourne  Mexico City  Nairobi
New Delhi  Shanghai  Taipei  Toronto

With offices in
Argentina  Austria  Brazil  Chile  Czech Republic  France  Greece
Guatemala  Hungary  Italy  Japan  South Korea  Poland  Portugal
Singapore  Switzerland  Thailand  Turkey  Ukraine  Vietnam

Oxford is a registered trade mark of Oxford University Press
in the UK and in certain other countries

© Oxford University Press 2012

British Library Cataloguing in Publication Data

Data available

ISBN 978 019 912778 8

20  19  18  17  16  15

Printed and bound by CPI Group (UK) Ltd, Croydon, CR0 4YY

Paper used in the production of this book is a natural, recyclable product made from wood grown in sustainable forests. The manufacturing process conforms to the environmental regulations of the country of origin.

## Acknowledgements

The publishers would like to thank the following for permission to reproduce photographs: **p.7tl**: clearandtransparent/iStock; **p.7tr**: Helga Esteb/Shutterstock; **p.7bl**: Rolf Vennenbernd/epa/Corbis; **p.8**: clearandtransparent/iStock; **p.9**: Gemenacom/Shutterstock; Robert Nicholas/Alamy/Photolibrary; Klaus Ohlenschläger/DPA Picture Alliance; Péter Gudella/Shutterstock; WoodyStock/Alamy/Photolibrary; Catchlight Visual Services/Alamy/Photolibrary; Péter Gudella/Shutterstock; **p.11**: clearandtransparent/iStock; **p.12**: mike.irwin/Shutterstock; **p.18**: Blend Images/Alamy/Photolibrary; **p.18**: Boris Franz/Shutterstock; **p.21**: Kess/Shutterstock; **p.21**: ecco/Shutterstock; **p.22tl**: Pizuttipics/Fotolia; **tr**: Natalie Erhova/Shutterstock; **ml**: Manfred Bail/Photolibrary; **mr**: Madarakis/Shutterstock; **bl**: Hemera/Thinkstock; **br**: Chris Cooper-Smith/Alamy/Photolibrary; **p.25**: Karlova Irina/Shutterstock; **p.29**: Brian Rasic/Rex Features; **p.33**: iStockphoto/Thinkstock; **p.34**: clearandtransparent/iStock; **p.34**: Michael Schiffhorst/iStock; **p.36**: Piccolo/Fotolia; **p.42**: kentoh/Shutterstock; **p.43**: Dmitriy Shironosov/Shutterstock; **p.44**: mart/Shutterstock; **p.44**: gualtiero boffi/Shutterstock; **p.44**: trendywest/Shutterstock; **p.48**: newyear2008/Shutterstock; **p.48**: Ambient Ideas/Shutterstock; **p.49**: Picsfive/Shutterstock; **p.50**: Lucas Jackson/Reuters; **p.50**: Michael Schiffhorst/iStock; **p.54 l-r**: Yuri Arcurs/Shutterstock; Goodluz/Shutterstock; FocusDigital/Alamy/Photolibrary; Sho Shan/Alamy/Photolibrary; **p.55 top row l-r**: iStockphoto/Thinkstock; Hemera/Thinkstock; Horten/Dreamstime; Jessamine/Dreamstime; iStockphoto/Thinkstock; Lucian Milasan/Dreamstime; **p.55 bottom row l-r**: Zentilia/Shutterstock; Hemera Technologies/PhotoObjects.net/Getty Images/Thinkstock; Horten/Dreamstime; Jiri Hera/Shutterstock; Pizuttipics/Fotolia; Interfoto/Alamy/Photolibrary; **p.56 l-r**: Brian Rasic/Rex Features; David Fisher/Rex Features; Gary Wolstenholme/Redferns/Getty Images; Everett Collection/Rex Features; Jim Smeal/BEI/Rex Features; Watkins/Rex Features; **p.58 l-r**: Interfoto/Alamy; C.Weinstein/Everett/Rex Features; Moviestore collection Ltd/Alamy; nasirkhan/Shutterstock; **p.59**: Walt Disney Productions/The Kobal Collection/The Picture Desk; Ensuper/Shutterstock; **p.61**: iStockphoto/Thinkstock; **p.63**: Universal/Everett/Rex Features; **p.65**: Paramount/Everett/Rex Features; **p.66**: Skunk Taxi/Shutterstock; **p.68 top row l-r**: Dennis MacDonald/Alamy/Photolibrary; Jim Lane/Alamy/Photolibrary; iStockphoto/Thinkstock; **p.68 bottom row l-r**: iStockphoto/Thinkstock; Bob Daemmrich/Alamy/Photolibrary; Charles Krupa/AP Photo; **p.69**: iStockphoto/Thinkstock; **p.71**: Digital Vision/Thinkstock; **p.72 l-r**: Jupiterimages/Pixland/Thinkstock; Glen Jones/Shutterstock; Jupiterimages/Brand X Pictures/Thinkstock; incamerastock/Alamy; Alexander Rochau/Fotolia; **bl**: Hemera/Thinkstock; **br**: Hemera/Thinkstock; **p.73**: iStockphoto/Thinkstock; Günter Schiffmann/DPA Picture Alliance; Picture Alliance/ZB;

Brad Collett/Shutterstock; Pavel K/Shutterstock; Marko I/Shutterstock; **p.74**: VikaSuh/Shutterstock; **p.76 l-r**: Richard Peterson/Shutterstock; iStockphoto/Thinkstock; Tania Mara Pimentel Gomes; Annamarinenko/Dreamstime; Mirabelle Pictures/Shutterstock; Arco Images GmbH/Alamy/Photolibrary; **p.77**: Jeanne Hatch/Shutterstock; **p.81**: Cultura RF/DPA Picture Alliance; **p.82**: Altafulla/Shutterstock; **p.82**: Monkey Business Images/Shutterstock; **p.82**: Skunk Taxi/Shutterstock; **p.84**: Sonny Meddle/Rex Features; **p.85**: Paramount/Everett/Rex Features; **p.91**: Eric Milos/Shutterstock; **p.91**: M.i.S.-Sportpressefoto/DPA Picture Alliance; **p.96**: Paramount/Everett/Rex Features; **p.97**: Corbis RF Best/Alamy; **p.97**: Sabri Deniz Kizil/Shutterstock; **p.98**: europhotos/Shutterstock; **p.100**: with kind permission from 'Die Jugendherbergen, Deutsches Jugendherbergswerk, Hauptverband für Jugendwandern und Jugendherbergen e.V.'; **p.101**: with kind permission from 'Die Jugendherbergen, Deutsches Jugendherbergswerk, Hauptverband für Jugendwandern und Jugendherbergen e.V.'; **p.102 l-r**: Stenosis; Philipp Laferi; Oliver Pickett; Arco Images GmbH/DPA Picture Alliance; Gs1311/Fotolia; DPA Picture Alliance; **p.103t**: ZB/DPA Picture Alliance; **p.103m**: Imagebroker/Alamy/Photolibrary; **p.103b**: Alice Wiegand; **p.103 l-r**: Stadt Duesseldorf; picture-alliance/Horst Ossinger; Dieterich W/Photolibrary; IgoUgo.com; **p.109 l-r**: Mika/DPA Picture Alliance; Yadid Levy/Robert Harding/Rex Features; KolnKongress GmbH; Press/Rex Features; F1online digitale Bildagentur GmbH/Alamy/Photolibrary; **p.111**: koteus/Shutterstock; Toponium/Shutterstock; Ilonika/Shutterstock; **p.112**: with kind permission from 'Die Jugendherbergen, Deutsches Jugendherbergswerk, Hauptverband für Jugendwandern und Jugendherbergen e.V.'; **p.114**: europhotos/Shutterstock; **p.116 top row l-r**: Blickwinkel/Alamy/Photolibrary; F1online digitale Bildagentur GmbH/Alamy/Photolibrary; Kuttig-Travel/Alamy/Photolibrary; Eric Gevaert/Shutterstock; **p.116 middle row l-r**: Tubol Evgeniya/Shutterstock; Yuri Arcurs/Shutterstock; **p.116 bottom row l-r**: Sergey Kamshylin/Shutterstock; Dmitriy Shironosov/Shutterstock; **p.120 top row l-r**: Lux Igitur/Alamy/Photolibrary; Colour/Shutterstock; Stefan Sollfors/Alamy/Photolibrary; **p.120 middle row l-r**: iStockphoto/Thinkstock; Ryan McVay/Digital Vision/Thinkstock; Monkey Business/Fotolia; **p.120 bottom row l-r**: iStockphoto/Thinkstock; EB-Stock/DPA Picture Alliance; koratmember/Shutterstock; Visdia/Dreamstime; **p.122 top row l-r**: Palmaria/Shutterstock; iStockphoto/Thinkstock; NASA, coloured by John Wells/Science Photo Library; Joyfull/Dreamstime; Petr Student/Shutterstock; **p.122 bottom row l-r**: Darren J. Bradley/ShutterstockComstock/Thinkstock; artiomp/Shutterstock; Hung Chung Chih/Shutterstock; **p.125**: Ton Koene/Dpa Picture Alliance; Catchlight Visual Services/Alamy/Photolibrary; **p.127**: Roy Langstaff Photography/Photographers Direct; **p.128**: Palmaria/Shutterstock; John Hemmings/Shutterstock; Tracy Whiteside/Dreamstime; **p.129**: Science/NASA; Goodshoot RF/Thinkstock; **p.130 l-r**: Stefan Sollfors/Alamy/Photolibrary; Comstock/Thinkstock; Joyfull/Dreamstime; Visdia/Dreamstime; Tupungato/Shutterstock; **p.134 top to bottom**: Sherrie Nickol/Photolibrary; Andrew Paterson/Alamy/Photolibrary; Robert Walls/Photolibrary; Joel Sartore/National Geographic Stock; **p.135**: Canoneer/Shutterstock; AISPIX/Shutterstock; **p.137**: Jim Wileman/Alamy/Photolibrary; **p.138 top row l-r**: Andrey Tirakhov/Shutterstock; Imagebroker/Alamy/Photolibrary; Paul Gibson/Alamy/Photolibrary; **p.138 bottom row l-r**: Alexander Raths/Shutterstock; Dmitriy Shironosov/Shutterstock; Comstock/Thinkstock; Mikhail Tchkheidze/Shutterstock; Elena Elisseeva/Shutterstock; **p.140**: iStockphoto/Thinkstock; romvo/Shutterstock; **p.141**: Cwlupica/Alamy/Photolibrary; **p.144**: Form Advertising/Alamy/Photolibrary; **p.146**: RubberBall/Alamy/Photolibrary; Tupungato/Shutterstock; **p.148**: Fedor Selivanov/Shutterstock; Perov Stanislav/Shutterstock; **p.149**: Sportstock/Shutterstock; Solid/Shutterstock; **p.150**: Dpaweb/DPA Picture Alliance; **p.151**: Vladimir Koletic/Shutterstock; Sheftsoff/Shutterstock; **p.152 l-r**: Pressmaster/Fotolia; Bob Pardue - Teen Lifestyle/Alamy/Photolibrary; Bonita R. Cheshier/Shutterstock; **p.153 l-r**: Rynio/Stockfood/OTHK; dirkr/iStock; Birgit Reitz-hofmann/Dreamstime; Mikael Damkier/Shutterstock; Ingrid Balabanova/Shutterstock; **p.154**: Thinkstock Images/Comstock/Getty Images/Thinkstock; G.Light/Shutterstock; Yaro/Shutterstock; YanLev/Shutterstock; **p.155**: visdia/Shutterstock; anweber/Shutterstock; **p.156 l-r**: F1online digitale Bildagentur GmbH/Alamy/Photolibrary; Kim Karpeles/Alamy/Photolibrary; Elzbieta Sekowska/Shutterstock

All other photos by OUP

Illustrations by Peter Bull, Stefan Chabluk, Paul Daviz, Venetia Dean, Robin Edmonds, The Boy FitzHammond, Jo Goodberry, John Hallett, Tim Kahane, Olivier Prime, Anita Romeo, Simon Smith, Rob Steen, Laszlo Veres.

Cover illustration by: Oxford Designers & Illustrators

The authors and publisher would like to thank the following people for their help and advice: Pat Dunn (editor), Angelika Libera (language consultant), Julie Green and Suzanne Prout (course consultants).

Audio recordings produced by Colette Thomson for Footstep Productions Ltd; Andrew Garratt (engineer).

Video shot on location in Cologne, with grateful thanks to Colette Thomson, Footstep Productions Ltd (producer and director), Angelika Libera (scriptwriter), Paul Keating (cameraman), Arne Wohlgemuth (sound), Birgit Hackenberg (location manager), Sira Thierij and Leonhard Buck (actors).

Every effort has been made to contact copyright holders of material reproduced in this book. If notified, the publishers will be pleased to rectify any errors or omissions at the earliest opportunity.